# WALKING
## WITH THE
# Women
### OF THE
# NEW
# TESTAMENT

*Heather Farrell has managed to draw us into her highly personal relationship with the women of the scriptures while still educating us about their whos, whats, and wheres. Her love for these women is evident in the poetic language she uses to describe their scriptural scenes, and the reverence she shows for their plights and accomplishments. And she extends that love to all readers of the scriptures, encouraging us to seek for women, celebrate them, and learn from them as she has. She generously shares her process for gaining insights, motivating each of us to find and love women in the scriptures as diligently as she has.*

—Neylan McBaine, director of the *Mormon Women Project*

*Walking with the Women of the New Testament is filled with the stories I missed in the scriptures. After reading it, I found reading my scriptures felt different: I suddenly started noticing women in stories where I had been sure they weren't. I especially love how the book points out the life experiences these ancient women had in common with me. Their clothes, language, and traditions were different, but we share the experiences of being daughters, sisters, wives, mothers, workers, worriers, and Christians. Reading this book brought these women closer to me.*

—Annette Pimentel, interview producer and writer for the *Mormon Women Project*

# WALKING WITH THE

## Women

### OF THE

# NEW
# TESTAMENT

· Written by ·

HEATHER FARRELL

· Art by ·

MANDY JANE WILLIAMS

**CFI**
AN IMPRINT OF CEDAR FORT, INC.
SPRINGVILLE, UTAH

ISBN 13: 978-1-4621-1421-4

Published by CFI, an imprint of Cedar Fort, Inc.
2373 W. 700 S., Springville, UT 84663
Distributed by Cedar Fort, Inc., www.cedarfort.com

LIBRARY OF CONGRESS CATALOGING-IN-PUBLICATION DATA

Farrell, Heather, author.
Walking with the women of the New Testament / Heather Farrell and Mandy Williams.
    pages cm
Includes bibliographical references and index.
Summary: Highlights many of the women in the New Testament.
ISBN 978-1-4621-1421-4
1. Women in the Bible. 2. Women in Christianity--History. 3. Bible. New Testament--Criticism, interpretation, etc. I. Williams, Mandy, 1985- author. II. Title.

BS2445.F37 2014
225.9'22082--dc23

2014023795

Cover design and interior layout/design by Shawnda T. Craig
Cover design © 2014 Lyle Mortimer
Edited by Jessica B. Ellingson

Printed in China
10 9 8 7 6 5 4 3 2 1

Printed on acid-free paper

*To my daughters, and my granddaughters yet to be: may you always remember who you are.*

*—Heather*

*To the inspiring and courageous women who have proceeded me, and to the ones in my life today.*

*—Mandy*

2023

... and to my precious daughter Caley emma ... always remember you are a daughter of the most high King. Our Savior Jesus Christ ... you Know WHO you ARE

♡

mama

*Three years ago* the idea for this book began formulating in my mind. I knew exactly what I wanted it to be about and exactly whom I would ask to do the artwork. I told my husband about it but remarked that it would be a miracle if I ever got the opportunity to write it. Well, I guess miracles happen, because you have this book in your hands. It is truly incredible to me, and I feel so grateful for all those who have helped me along the way.

I am grateful for Camille Fronk Olsen, whose class on women in the scriptures at BYU opened my eyes and my heart to the treasure trove of women within the pages of the scriptures. I have been grateful for her continued support and encouragement as I have taken what I learned in her class and made it my own.

I am grateful to Cedar Fort for believing in me and giving me the opportunity to make this book a reality, and being incredibly patient with me as I've navigated the world of publishing for the first time.

I am grateful to Annette Pimentell, my husband's aunt, who kindly agreed to read through the first draft of the book and didn't complain once when the book changed to include three times more women (and pages) than previously expected.

I am grateful for Mandy Jane Williams and her willingness to jump into this project with me. Her artwork and her interpretation of these women's stories have taken my breath away more than once. I feel incredibly blessed to have her support in bringing these women to life.

I am grateful to my blog readers—every one of you—for your continued support and encouragement of my work. Thank you for your comments, your e-mails, your prayers, and your love. You have been such a blessing in my life, and I know this book would never have happened without you.

I am grateful to my children for being willing to listen to stories of women from the scriptures for bedtime stories, and for being patient with me while I wrote this book (even though I know you groaned every time I turned on the computer).

Lastly, I am grateful to my husband, Jon, for his faith in me and for his unwavering support of my dreams. Sir, you have truly given me wings to fly, and for that, I will love you forever.

—*Heather*

"*With a grateful heart*, I would like to sincerely thank everyone involved in the art of the this book. I want to thank my amazing husband, Bryan, my children, my parents, my in-laws and all of my family and extended family. Their help has been immeasurable. I want to express my thanks and love to the many, many women, men, and children willing to model for these pictures. I know that it was a big step out of their comfort zone. I found so much joy in seeing the beauty and light in every single one of them. I would also like to thank my book partner, Heather, for extending the invitation to me to help with this project and for the opportunity to get to know her and gain a much bigger knowledge and testimony of the Book of Mormon and Jesus Christ. Finally, I would like to thank my Heavenly Father, who has strengthened me in weakness and insecurity and guided me in taking on a project much bigger than myself. Thank you."

Because of the amount of models that contributed to the art of this book, we had to add the complete list to our website, www.thewomeninthenewtestament.com

—*Mandy*

# Table of Contents

# Table of Contents

# Introduction

*When I was a teenager,* two of my neighbors walked together every morning. Rain or shine, the two women traversed the sidewalks of our town. One morning while I drove past them, I noticed that they seemed to be doing just as much talking as walking. They were obviously good friends, and it occurred to me that much of that friendship probably developed as they walked and shared their stories with each other: their challenges, joys, disappointments, and triumphs. While I have studied the women of the New Testament, I have often thought of these two women.

New Testament women would have been experienced walkers. Since animals were used to carry supplies, feet were the main mode of transportation for everyone. Women walked everywhere they needed to go, carrying water, food, children, and anything else needed to support life. I imagine that many of them, like the two women in my neighborhood, shared their lives with one another as they walked.

Even though we are not able to physically walk with these New Testament women, we can metaphorically walk with them as we study their lives in the scriptures. In this book, you will find the stories of nearly eighty women whom, as you learn their stories and study their lives, you can come to know as friends and sisters. Most important, walking with them will teach you about Jesus. Many of the women in this book knew Jesus Christ. They followed him, literally walking in His footsteps. They can help you come to know Him like they knew Him.

James E. Talmage wrote, "The greatest champion of woman and womanhood is Jesus the Christ."[1]  As I have studied Christ's interactions with women, I have come to see just how true this statement is. In a time period when women's participation in religious life was limited to that of an observer, Christ invited them to be active participants in His church—learning, serving, teaching, and leading. This was a radical idea and one that must have appealed to many women who were hungry for more knowledge and understanding.

Katherine H. Shirt wrote,

> The Gospels record his [Christ's] ability to step outside the perspective of a Jewish male to see women simply as individuals. In a society where women were not allowed to study the scriptures, he taught the Samaritan women at the well and he excused Mary from serving with Martha in order to study things of more value. Women were not permitted to function as legal witnesses, yet he allowed women to be the first witnesses to the resurrection. His parables balanced the shepherd hunting for the lost sheep with the woman hunting for the lost coin.

As Dorothy Sayers wrote, "Perhaps it is no wonder that the women were first at the Cradle and last at the Cross. They had never known a man like this Man—there never has been such another. A prophet and teacher who never nagged at them, never flattered or coaxed or patronized; who never made arch jokes about them . . . who took their questions and arguments seriously; who never mapped out their sphere for them, never urged them to be feminine or jeered at them for being female; who had no axe to grind and no uneasy male dignity to defend."[2]

Jesus broke down barriers between people, especially between men and women, in an incredible way. He challenged the mentality and customs of a fallen world and elevated the status of women to the plane on which God sees them: a view of women that didn't base a woman's worth on her physical appearance, her marital status, her ability to bear children, or what she had done but instead celebrated her intrinsic worth as a daughter of God.

I know that as I have studied the lives of the women in the New Testament, my understanding of myself and my role in God's plan has grown. It began when I was pregnant with my oldest son, who was born just before Christmas. Throughout his pregnancy and birth, I felt a real sisterhood with Mary, the mother of Christ. Not only was I amazed that she walked anywhere while nine months pregnant, but I realized what a great sacrifice she had made for the world. I was touched by her example and I felt her strength give me courage to bring forth my own "firstborn son."

Spurred on by my newfound appreciation for Mary I began to search the internet for stories and information about women in the scriptures. What I found surprised me. There were few good sources of information on women in the Old Testament and New Testament, and none for the women in the Book of Mormon, Doctrine and Covenants, or Pearl of Great Price. I knew from a class I had taken from Camille Fronk Olsen at BYU that there were lots of women in the scriptures. I wondered why no one had taken the time to write about them. I was sad that they seemed to be forgotten. *Someone really should write about them*, I thought. "No, Heather," the Holy Ghost whispered to me. "You should write about them." And so I did. I began a blog called Women in the Scriptures (womeninthescriptures.com) and now, more than six years later, I have written on dozens and dozens of women and haven't even begun to scratch the surface. Someday I hope that I will write about them all, which with over five hundred women in the scriptures might take some time!

I don't have a degree in ancient studies, Hebrew, Greek, or any other subject that would justify my writing a book on the women of the New Testament. My only credentials are that I love the scriptures and I love the women in the scriptures. I have spent thousands of hours searching out their stories and studying their lives. I know them like I do good friends, and often their stories come into my heart at the moment I need them.

I have felt Priscilla walk beside me when my husband and I moved a thousand miles away from our family to go where the Lord called us. I have felt the strength of Junia infuse my soul as I have stood to defend my faith. I have had the woman who gave her last mite hold my hand when God asked me to give more than I thought I could. I have had Mary and Martha weep with me at the loss of my loved ones. I have looked into the eyes of the woman with an issue of blood as she rejoiced with me when I too was healed by touching the power of Christ.

I hope that as you read this book you will also begin to feel of their spirits and learn from their examples. I hope you will see that they were real women with real lives, real feelings, and real problems. Their homes, their language, and their situations may seem foreign to you, but they were women and their lives weren't all that different from yours. In fact, there isn't a single problem that modern women face that New Testament women didn't also wrestle with: heartache, disappointment, marriage, children, divorce, abandonment, health problems, family feuds, birth, death, covenants, politics, priesthood, apostasy, old age, war—they knew about those.

Mostly, I hope that this book will inspire you to open your scriptures and read their stories for yourself, that you will invite them into your life. I promise you that if you take the time to get to know them, they will become your friends. They will walk with you on your own journey and help you navigate the roads of life. Most important, they will help you come to know Jesus of Nazareth—of His love, His compassion, His wisdom, and His mercy—truly the greatest champion and advocate that womanhood has ever had.

# *Learning* to *See Women*

*Whenever I have the opportunity* to speak about women in the scriptures, I make it a point to ask the audience how many women they think are in the scriptures. Their answers always surprise me. "Twenty or thirty," they say, with an occasional daring person venturing a tentative, "One hundred?" It astounds people when they hear that there are over five hundred women (named and unnamed) in the scriptures.[1] In the New Testament alone there are almost one hundred women or groups of women mentioned and over seventy teachings specifically referring to women.[2]

This is a treasure trove of gospel information about women! Yet numerous replies indicate to me that many people think that women have simply been left out of the scriptures. I think the problem is that in our society we often don't see women. Too often we take their influence in our lives and in our society for granted. Similarly in the scriptures, we simply don't see the women. The pages of the scriptures are filled with their stories and their influence, but too often we skip right past them, not even realizing that they are there.

I want to share a few techniques that have helped me open my eyes—my spiritual eyes—to learn to see the women in the scriptures.

## • Open Your Scriptures •

Unfortunately, women and their stories are often left out of Church materials, videos, and images. The ones that are included usually focus on the same few women. So, if you aren't regularly opening your scriptures and studying them for yourself, you will probably never hear about the majority of the women within the pages of the scriptures. Seeing the women in the scriptures requires you to open and read your scriptures!

Don't be intimidated by scripture study. It doesn't take any special qualifications, simply a desire to come closer to God and a questioning and inquisitive mind. Just open up your scriptures, say a prayer to invite the Holy Ghost to help you learn, write down what you learn, and then be consistent about doing it. You will receive answers and insight. As Zina D. H. Young, the third president of the Relief Society, said,

> If someone told you by digging long enough in a certain spot you would find a diamond of unmeasured wealth, do you think you would begrudge time or strength, or means spent to obtain that treasure? . . . If you will dig in the depths of your [scriptures] . . . you will find, with the aid of the Spirit of the Lord, the pearl of great price, the testimony of the truth of this work.[3]

## • Go Slow and Ask Questions •

Oftentimes all we get about a woman in the scriptures is a name or a brief mention of her and nothing else. It can be easy, when all you have is a name, to skip over her and her story. I have found that when I take the time to go slowly through my scriptures, thinking and pondering about all the people in the chapter, I learn much more about what she may have experienced, what her life was like, and what type of woman she was. It also helps to pause when I find a woman in the scriptures and to ask myself questions like these:

1. What do I know about this woman?
2. What is unique about this woman and her story?
3. What do I know about her family, her husband, and her children?
4. Who else in the scriptures would she have known?
5. How does she fit into the overall story of the chapter or the book of scripture I am studying?
6. How would her experiences have been different from the men in the story?
7. How would their experiences have been similar?
8. How was her life impacted by the culture and time period in which she lived?
9. Does she (or does she not) exemplify a Christlike quality?
10. What type of influence would she have had on those around her?
11. What would I ask her if I could meet her or people who knew her?
12. How might her experience be similar to something I can relate to?
13. What can I (or someone else I know) learn from her experiences?

Each woman's story will mean something different to you than it does to someone else. That is the beauty of the scriptures: the stories deal with universal themes and can be read in many different ways. There is real power in being able to find your own answers and discoveries in the scriptures. Going slowly through the scriptures and stopping to ask questions will help you find your own answers and will help you pay more attention to the women. Remember, don't pass over a woman just because she is only mentioned as a daughter, a widow, a wife, or a child—she has a story too.

## • Write Things Down •

One of the best things I ever did to improve my scripture study was to start keeping a "women in the scriptures" journal. I got a simple composition notebook and began reading in the Old Testament. Whenever I came across a woman, I wrote down the reference in my notebook. I also included references to anything having to do with women (like breasts and wombs), and things like wisdom and charity that are referred to as "she." It took me almost two years, but I read through the entire standard works, making notes in my journal. When I started, I thought one notebook was going to be plenty big, but I ended up filling two notebooks! Studying the scriptures this way opened up my eyes and my heart and taught me, in a powerful way, how much God loves women.

I also went through my scriptures and marked all the stories that were about or had references to women. I did this because I once heard President Hinckley challenge the youth to read through the Book of Mormon and put a red check mark next to every reference of Jesus Christ they found. He promised that by doing this, "there will come to you a very real conviction . . . that this is in very deed another witness for the Lord Jesus Christ."[4] I wanted to gain a better testimony of God's love for women and better understand women's roles, and so I did something similar to President Hinckley's challenge. Marking my scriptures this way has been an incredible experience. Not only does it make it easy for me to find their stories, but it also gives me a powerful visual testimony every time I open my scriptures that women are not forgotten by God.

I can promise that as you go through your scriptures—either marking or writing down in a journal all the women (or references to women) that you find—you will be amazed. You will begin to see the women in the scriptures and will gain a deeper understanding of how much God loves His daughters.

You will discover your spiritual heritage, and I promise that it will change the way you see yourself—and women—in God's kingdom.

## • Read Between the Lines •

It is important to remember that, even if they aren't mentioned, there are woman in every story in the scriptures. Every man mentioned in the scriptures had a mother, may have had a wife and daughters, and certainly would have interacted with women in his life. Remembering that women are always in the background of the story can help you piece together what they would have experienced and whom they would have influenced.

Also remember that New Testament scriptures that refer to disciples, sons, or men often include women. As Kathryn H. Shirt wrote:

> One of the features of our literary heritage is that when we refer to men and women together, we use masculine nouns and pronouns. To a certain extent, this convention need not be a problem. As Madeleine L'Engle wrote, "I am female, of the species, man. Genesis is very explicit that it takes both male and female to make the image of God, and that the generic word, man, includes both. . . . When mankind was referred to it never occurred to me that I was not part of it."

On the other hand, while the word *man* can refer generically to a man or to a woman, there are instances where *man* refers only to a male. . . . Our family learned that when we attempted to read the scriptures together substituting "man and woman" for "man" or "son and daughter" for "son." . . .

As we tried to determine when inclusive language was appropriate, we became aware of a significant difference in the religious perspectives of men and women. Where men can freely assume the scriptures are speaking to them personally, women must ponder and weigh the evidence. . . .

As women we have several options. . . . One alternative is to object to the male language and male culture saturating the scriptures and reject the scriptures as irrelevant to our needs as women. Another option is, as obedient daughters of God, to accept the scriptures but be overwhelmed by their predominantly male perspective and underestimate our own spiritual potential. . . . [H]owever, we have yet another approach. We can immerse ourselves in the scriptures and, at the same time, by being open to the influence of his Spirit, relate them to our own lives and circumstances.[5]

As you read the New Testament, remember that Christ's teachings were for both men and women, and that even if women aren't specifically mentioned, they are always there.

## • Rely on the Holy Ghost •

Surprisingly, I have found in my own study of the women in the scriptures that I rarely need to seek information outside the context of the story and what is in the Bible Dictionary and Topical Guide. Every so often, if I want to understand more about the historical or cultural context of a story, I will refer to outside books and websites for guidance, but primarily I rely on the scriptures and the assistance of the Holy Ghost.

It has been amazing to me, as I have invited the Holy Ghost into my scripture study, how He has enlightened my understanding. There are times when I will be reading through a story and I get to a part that just doesn't seem to make sense or seems out of character with what I know of the gospel. Oftentimes when I look down in the footnotes (or look in Joseph Smith's inspired translation of the Bible), I will find that Joseph Smith gave additional insight to that passage to clarify it. This process has taught me that while there is much truth in the Bible, some of it is missing, and that if we want those gaps filled in, we don't have to turn to outside sources. The Holy Ghost can enlighten our understanding and teach us.

## • Find the Bread Crumbs •

Often all we get in the scriptures are incomplete stories about women that leave us with more questions than answers. Finding those answers requires us to search and ponder enough that the Holy Ghost can teach us what those stories mean. That process of seeking is what President Julie B. Beck called searching for "bread crumbs" of wisdom.[6]

Eating only one bread crumb about women in the scriptures will not nourish you; after eating it, you will still feel like you are starving for more information. Yet, if you begin to diligently search the scriptures with your eyes open to the women, you will find crumb after crumb after crumb. Soon you will be feasting on bread crumbs and be filled with an understanding. Even more, if you invite the Holy Ghost to teach, He will help you begin to see the full, glorious picture of God's vision for women in His kingdom. Like the Apostles, who after Christ fed the five thousand, gathered up more baskets of bread than they started with, the Holy Ghost will fill your mind and heart.

I know that this is what has happened to me as I have searched the scriptures with my eyes open to the women within their pages. The Holy Ghost has taught me and I have learned incredible spiritual truths that have settled deep in my heart and changed how I look at the world. I can relate to what Elder Packer said: "Much of what I have come to know falls into the category of things which cannot be taught but can be learned."[7]

Even though I have tried my best in this book, I cannot teach you what I know about the women of the New Testament; but you, through the assistance of the Holy Ghost, can learn it. In Christ's parable, when five virgins realized that they did not have enough oil to last through the night, the other five were unable to give them more. They advised, "Go . . . and buy for yourselves" (Matthew 25:9). Just like these ten virgins, each of us must fill our own lamps with the oil of truth and testimony. It cannot be given to us. We must earn our oil by searching, studying, praying, fasting, and learning for ourselves.

So it is my hope that reading this book will spark a desire within you to open your own scriptures and to learn more about these women—and about God's plan for women—for yourself. I hope that you will take the time to fill your lamp with a testimony of how much God loves women and that you will begin to glimpse who you are in His plan so that when He comes, you will be waiting and prepared to meet Him.

# Christ's Lineage

*"And Jacob begat Joseph the husband of Mary, of whom was born Jesus, who is called Christ."*

*Matthew 1:16*

*While this book tells* only the stories of the women who are unique to the New Testament, it is important to note that there are many Old Testament women mentioned in the New Testament as well.[1] Among the Old Testament women mentioned in the New Testament are the women of Christ's genealogy. Both Luke and Matthew list Christ's genealogy through his mortal father Joseph. Yet James E. Talmage wrote, "A personal genealogy of Joseph was essentially that of Mary also, for they were cousins. Joseph is named as son of Jacob by Matthew, and as son of Heli by Luke; but Jacob and Heli were brothers, and it appears that one of the two was the father of Joseph and the other the father of Mary."[2] It seems that both Matthew and Luke's intent with listing Jesus's family history was to establish the fact that he was born through the royal line of Judah and truly was the "Christ, the son of David, the son of Abraham" (Matthew 1:1).

Matthew's genealogy is especially interesting because in it he mentions four Old Testament women: "Thamar," the Greek version of Tamar (Genesis 38); "Rachab," the Greek version of Rahab (Joshua 2); Ruth (Ruth 1–4); and "her that hath been the wife of Uriah," who would have been Bathsheba (2 Samuel 11). It is strange that Matthew chose to include the names of these four women when he didn't mention any other mothers, including the wives of the patriarchs: Sarah, Rebekah, Rachel, and Leah. I wonder why he included the women he did and not the others.

That is a question I don't have the answer to, but it is interesting that all four of the women's stories—Tamar, Rahab, Ruth and Bathsheba—are examples of times when women had to make hard choices in order to choose the right. Tamar, when faced with a group of men who would not perform their duty toward her, took matters into her own hands and arranged circumstances so that the line of Judah—the lineage which had been promised the Messiah—would not die out. Rahab showed bravery and kindness in welcoming the Israelite spies and, in doing so, saved herself and her whole household from death during the destruction of Jericho. Ruth, despite the desperation of her situation, relied on the Lord to guide her and had the courage to go against the norm in arranging her own marriage instead of having it arranged for her. And Bathsheba, even though entangled in a hard situation, made the most of it and raised one of Israel's most incredible kings: Solomon.

All of these women lived remarkable lives and showed spiritual maturity, intelligence, and courage. I think that Matthew may have included these women's names as a reminder that there had been many miraculous events preserving the line of Judah, a reminder to his readers that with God, nothing was impossible. If God could work miracles through Tamar, Rahab, Ruth, and Bathsheba, He could certainly work one for Mary, the mother of Jesus. Regardless of Matthew's motives, the genealogy shows us that Christ came from a line of remarkable women, who understood the importance of their work in God's plan and sometimes took drastic measures to ensure that His work would move forward.

In the Old Testament, the Prophet Ezekiel likened Jerusalem to an unwanted child whom the Lord rescued. Ezekiel described all the things that would have been done to a baby, had it been wanted. He wrote, "in the day thou wast born thy navel was not cut, neither wast thou washed in water to supple thee; thou wast not salted at all, nor swaddled at all" (Ezekiel 16:4).

It is appropriate, since Jerusalem is often referred to as a "she," that Ezekiel used the analogy of a baby being abandoned by its parents. In Biblical times, sons were often more valued than daughters, and it was common among many New Testament cultures to routinely "expose" or leave unwanted female babies out to die. Yet, as Josephus wrote, the Jews were different because they believed that God wanted them to "bring up all our offspring."[3] This means that Jewish baby girls probably had a better chance at life than baby girls did in other New Testament cultures.

A newborn girl who was given a chance at life probably would have been greeted much as Ezekiel described. As we do today, the baby's umbilical cord would have been cut and the baby washed in water to "supple" or clean it.

Ezekiel then described two unfamiliar newborn practices: salting and swaddling. Salting a newborn probably referred to a custom of sprinkling babies with a few grains of salt in to indicate purity and dedication, similar to the salted offerings made to God in the temple.[4] The salt may have been thought to have health benefits for babies as well.[5]

Swaddling a baby meant to wrap or bind the baby tightly in strips of cloth to help the child's limbs grow strong and straight. The practice may have been similar to our modern day practice of swaddling a baby in blankets to help calm and soothe it. The main difference being that in New Testament times babies usually didn't wear any other clothing or diaper besides the swaddling clothes. Swaddling was also viewed as an important health practice of newborns and was done until they were around three months old. We know that Jesus was wrapped in "swaddling clothes" shortly after His birth and that it was an important sign for the shepherds. The angel who visited told them that they would recognize Jesus because He would be "wrapped in swaddling clothes, lying in a manger" (Luke 2:12).

# Elisabeth

"And it came to pass, that, when Elisabeth heard the salutation of Mary, the babe leaped in her womb; and Elisabeth was filled with the Holy Ghost: And she spake out with a loud voice, and said, Blessed art thou among women, and blessed is the fruit of thy womb. And whence is this to me, that the mother of my Lord should come to me? For, lo, as soon as the voice of thy salutation sounded in mine ears, the babe leaped in my womb for joy. And blessed is she that believed: for there shall be a performance of those things which were told her from the Lord."

*Luke 1:41–45*

*Elisabeth, the wife of Zacharias,* became the mother of John the Baptist, who was born only six months before his cousin, Jesus. Before he was even born, it was prophesied by his father that John would "go before the face of the Lord to prepare his ways" (Luke 1:76). John's ministry among the children of Israel was to help prepare them to hear the words of Christ, whom he said was "one mightier than I . . . the latchet of whose shoes I am not worthy to stoop down and unloose" (Mark 1:7). In the same way that John prepared the way for Christ to accomplish His divine mission, Elisabeth, helped prepare the way for Mary to accomplish her divine mission.

In Luke 1, we read that Elisabeth and Zacharias were righteous and "blameless" before God, and yet they had never been granted children. They were both "stricken in years" when Zacharias, performing his Levitical duties in the temple, was visited by an angel, who told him that Elisabeth would bear a son and that his name would be John. Zacharias doubted, and so the angel struck him dumb. Yet just as the angel Gabriel promised, Elisabeth became pregnant in her old age. She hid her pregnancy from everyone until she was five months along, saying, "Thus hath the Lord dealt with me in the days wherein he looked on me, to take away my reproach among men" (Luke 1:25).

When Elisabeth was in her sixth month of pregnancy, Mary, her young cousin, was visited by the same angel that had spoken with Zacharias and told her that she would bear the Son of God. Mary doubted, asking, "How shall this be, seeing I know not a man?"(Luke 1:34). The angel explained that the Holy Ghost would overshadow her and told her that Elisabeth was six months pregnant as proof that "with God nothing shall be impossible" (verse 37). Not long after this visit with the angel, Mary left her home in Nazareth and traveled to "a city of Juda" (verse 39), which was about sixty-seven miles away, to visit Elisabeth. I imagine that she was anxious to know if what the angel had told her was true and to gain the strength to handle the heavy burden that had been placed upon her young shoulders.

When she got to Elisabeth's house, Mary was greeted with two additional witnesses that what the angel had told her was true. First, Mary could plainly see that Elisabeth, despite her old age, was more than six months pregnant. Second, Elisabeth's baby leapt within her when he heard Mary's voice, and Elisabeth was filled with the Holy Ghost. Elisabeth knew, before Mary even told her, that she was carrying the Savior and the Redeemer of the world within her womb. Elisabeth blessed Mary and prophesied to Mary that "there shall be a performance of those things which were told her from the Lord" (Luke 1:45).

The story of Elisabeth and Mary demonstrates that when God gives us a commandment or inspiration, He always gives us multiple witnesses to proclaim the truthfulness of His word. Mary must have felt quite afraid and alone as she faced her future life. She was betrothed and pregnant and didn't know how her future husband would react, and she knew she faced the possibility of being stoned to death. She also didn't know how her family would react or how she would be able to explain her situation to them. What a blessing for her to have Elisabeth, who, through the power of the Holy Ghost, was able to discern what had happened to her and who was able to give her the emotional and spiritual strength she needed to go forward on the hard path she had accepted from the Lord.

Just like He did for Mary, God sends people into our lives to pave the way for us to accomplish our divine missions on this earth. He sends people to us who will guide us onto the right path, who will validate our feelings and bear testimony to the promptings, dreams, visions, and revelations that we have received from the Lord. I know that for me, my sister-in-law was my Elisabeth, and it was her example and encouragement that guided me and sustained me when I was fearful about becoming a mother. She gave birth to her first child just six months before I gave birth to mine, and she was the one I turned to when my fears overpowered my faith and when I began to doubt myself and the Lord. She, like Elisabeth did for Mary, bore testimony to what I knew the Lord had told me and gave me the courage to go forth in faith.

I have also felt, like Mary and Elisabeth so beautifully demonstrated, the power that comes from friendships between older women and younger women. Sister Bonnie Oscarson said,

> I love the example we have in the first chapter of Luke which describes the sweet relationship between Mary, the mother of Jesus, and her cousin Elisabeth. . . .
>
> This young maiden and her cousin, who was "well stricken in years," shared a common bond in their miraculous pregnancies, and I can only imagine how very important the three months they spent together were to both of them as they were able to talk together, empathize with each other, and support one another in their unique callings. What a wonderful model they

are of feminine nurturing between generations. Those of us who are a little more mature can have a tremendous influence on the younger generations. . . .

> If there are barriers, it is because we ourselves have created them. We must stop concentrating on our differences and look for what we have in common; then we can begin to realize our greatest potential and achieve the greatest good in this world. Sister Marjorie P. Hinckley once said,
>
> "Oh, how we need each other. Those of us who are old need you who are young. And, hopefully, you who are young need some of us who are old. It is a sociological fact that women need women. We need deep and satisfying and loyal friendships with each other."
>
> Sister Hinckley was right; oh, how we need each other![1]

I know that there are people in all of our lives who are sent to "go before the face of the Lord to prepare His ways" and give us the strength we need to accomplish what the Lord has sent us here to do. As we endeavor to do the work that God has given us, let us not forget that He has given us everything we need to be successful and that He sends us people when we need them. There are angels all around us. We never know when we may be someone else's "Elisabeth" and it will be our turn to reach out and give someone the courage, strength, and faith to do the work God has given them.[2]

# Childbirth

Two of the best examples we have of childbirth in the New Testament are the stories of Elisabeth, the mother of John the Baptist, and Mary, the mother of Jesus. Their experiences can help us better understand what childbirth may have been like for most New Testament women.

Elisabeth was nearly six months pregnant when Mary came to visit her from Nazareth. Elisabeth was "stricken in age" and had hid her pregnancy from others for five months. It would have been very hard for a woman of this day to seclude herself from other people, and so it may have been that Elisabeth hid her pregnancy by wearing loose clothing. We don't know why she hid her pregnancy, but it seems to be an important detail because it lets us know that the only way Mary would have known of her condition was her message from the angel Gabriel.

Mary's visit with Elisabeth ended just about the time that her own pregnancy would have begun to be noticeable. We don't know exactly why Mary left Elisabeth, but according to Josephus unmarried Jewish women were not allowed to be present during the birth of a baby. When Elisabeth's delivery time drew near, Mary may have been compelled to leave her and return to Nazareth.

When Elisabeth gave birth she would have most likely had the assistance of midwives and would have been surrounded by women she trusted. In Elisabeth's case, it was her "neighbors and cousins" (Luke 1:58) who rejoiced with her at the birth of her son. While I am sure that women gave birth in a variety of positions, we do know that they used birthing bricks or birth stools for support during birth. In Exodus, it talks about how the midwives Puah and Shiphrah saw the women "upon the stools" (Exodus 1:16), referring to u-shaped stools that wealthy woman sat on to give birth. Poorer women used bricks, or simply the arms of the women around them, to support themselves. In Genesis, Rachel said that her servant Bilhah would "bear upon my knees" (Genesis 30:3), indicating that woman-to-woman support was an important aspect of childbirth.

We often assume that Mary gave birth with only Joseph nearby, but I think that is unlikely. Luke 2 says that "there was no room for them in the inn" (verse 7). *Inn* is a confusing translation of this verse because it brings to mind a public building where Mary and Joseph would have had to pay for their stay and had to room among strangers. The Greek word that is translated as "inn" is *kataluma* and refers to the "upper room" of the house, a space which was often reserved for guests.[3]

# Childbirth Continued

It is likely that Mary and Joseph were staying with Joseph's family in Bethlehem and that, perhaps because there were higher ranking relatives in the house, there was no room left in the guest room for Mary and Joseph. Luke's note that Mary laid baby Jesus in a manger indicates that they were probably staying on the bottom level of the house where animals were kept. We can assume that Mary gave birth surrounded by family and support.

After giving birth, a woman was considered "unclean" (*tuma*) for seven days after the birth of a male baby and two weeks after the birth of a female. During this time she would have been ritually unclean, meaning anything or anyone she touched would also experience *tuma*, and become unclean. The rules she would have followed were similar to the ones followed for menstruation. (See "Menstruation" on page 52.) After her bleeding stopped, she was no longer required to be separate from others. Even so, her purification was not complete and she was unable to enter the temple or to touch holy things until forty days after the birth of a boy and twice that long after the birth of a girl.

The *tuma* a woman experienced after childbirth was not because her body was dirty or because she had sinned in creating life. The birth of a child is one of the supernal examples of God's ability to create new life. When a woman is with a child, she is filled with the power of God. When the child is born, this intense level of holiness departs and there is a greater potential for tuma. This may also explain why a woman is considered to be unclean twice as long for giving birth to girl instead of a boy. All females, from the moment of their birth, bear within them the power to give life—an open manifestation of godliness. By giving life to a girl, a woman has doubled the potential for life and consequently doubled the potential for death.

Once the "days of her purification" (Luke 2:22) had passed for a woman, she was required to go the temple and offer a lamb, or if she was poor two turtledoves, to complete her purification and bring her back to her state of holiness before the Lord.[4] When Mary and Joseph went to the temple shortly after the birth of Jesus, it was so that Mary could make this offering and complete her purification after childbirth.

# The Seven Sorrows and Joys of *Mary*

*Mary was one of the most remarkable women* to ever live. She ranks right up there with Eve as the woman whose choices have had the biggest impact on the world. Elder Bruce R. McConkie wrote,

> Can we speak too highly of her whom the Lord has blessed above all women? There was only one Christ, and there is only one Mary. Each was noble and great in preexistence, and each was foreordained to the ministry he or she performed. We cannot but think that the Father would choose the greatest female spirit to be the mother of His Son, even as he chose the male spirit unto him to be the Savior.[1]

Mary was truly an incredible woman, and her example of virtue, courage, obedience, and love can be a beacon of strength to us in our own lives.

There is a Roman Catholic devotion to Mary called the "Seven Sorrows" that commemorates each of Mary's major sorrows throughout her life.[2] I have taken liberty with this theme and chosen what I think were Mary's seven greatest sorrows, which consequently were also her greatest joys. I think it is appropriate to examine Mary's life through the sorrows and joys she had to

experience because not only does it give us a glimpse of the fortitude and courage of this great woman but also helps us realize what Jesus taught when He promised that our "sorrow shall be turned into joy" (John 16:20). Her life is a reminder that every great trial in our lives also has the potential to bring great blessings and joy.

## First Sorrow and Joy of Mary: Meeting with the Angel Gabriel

Mary was a young woman, probably around thirteen or fourteen, when the angel Gabriel visited her. She was living in Nazareth and was "espoused," or betrothed (see "Marriage" on page 32), to marry a man named Joseph. Nephi's vision of Mary in the Book for Mormon tells us that she was "most beautiful and fair above all other virgins" (1 Nephi 11:15). While it is likely that Mary was physically beautiful, I think the type of beauty that Nephi was talking about came from her being close to God.

Sister Elaine Dalton called this type of beauty "deep beauty" and said that,

> It is the kind of beauty that doesn't wash off. It is spiritual attractiveness. Deep beauty springs from virtue. [. . .] When you are virtuous, chaste, and morally clean, your inner beauty glows in your eyes and in your face. [. . .] We have been taught

that 'the gift of the Holy Ghost . . . quickens all the intellectual faculties, increases, enlarges, expands and purifies all the natural passions and affections. [. . .] It develops beauty of person, form and features.' [. . .] That is the beauty [. . .] that really matters and the only kind of beauty that lasts."[3]

Mary had beauty that came from being virtuous and thus full of spiritual power.

Gabriel came "in unto" Mary, which lets us know that his visitation probably occurred indoors. It seems that Mary was confused by his greeting and wondered "what manner of

> "for thou hast found favour with God."

salutation this should be." Seeing her alarm, Gabriel reassured her, "Fear not, Mary: for thou hast found favour with God" (Luke 1:28–30). He then told her that, if she chose, she would give birth to a son named Jesus, who would "reign over the house of Jacob for ever" (Luke 1:33). Mary wondered aloud how she could bear a child if she had never been intimate with

At one point during Christ's ministry when the Pharisees were especially angry, they slung these words at him: "We be not born of fornication" (John 8:41). Their words indicate that Jesus's unusual birth was common knowledge but that some people assumed He was an illegitimate child. The Pharisees' stinging words about His parenthood were probably not the first ones Christ had heard in His life. I can only imagine that if Christ faced these types of accusations and judgments that Mary must also have faced them, not just during her pregnancy but for the rest of her life. Because Joseph married Mary instead of "put[ting] her away privily" (Matthew 1:19), many people must have assumed that he was the father of her child. He also would have faced judgments from people that were unfounded in truth. His dedication to Mary and Jesus is impressive. God chose a truly remarkable man to father His son.

a man. Gabriel told her that the Holy Ghost would come to her and that she would give birth to the Son of God. He also told her that her cousin Elisabeth (see "Elisabeth" on page 15) had conceived a baby in her old age, indicating that this miracle would give Mary confirmation that what he said was true and that "with God nothing shall be impossible" (Luke 1:35–37).

Mary must have wrestled with how to respond to Gabriel. Becoming the mother of the Son of God meant risking everything she valued: her life, her social standing, and all her plans and hopes for the future. Under Mosaic law, Joseph, her betrothed, would have the right to stone her to death if she become pregnant before marriage. Yet with words that must have made the heavens roar with joy, Mary humbly told Gabriel, "Behold the handmaid of the Lord; be it unto me according to thy word" (Luke 1:38).

Choosing to embrace what was asked of her was Mary's first sorrow but also her first joy. Despite the loss of her reputation and the potential risk to her life, Mary found joy in the promises given her. In her own words, she said, "My soul doth magnify the Lord, and my spirit hath rejoiced in God my Saviour. For he hath regarded the low estate of his handmaiden: for, behold, from henceforth all generations shall call me blessed. For he that is mighty hath done to me great things; and holy is his name" (Luke 1:46–49).[4]

I imagine that over the nine months she carried Jesus, her life was filled with heartache and worry. Yet underneath that sorrow, she must have felt an abiding sense of peace and love, knowing that she was doing what God had asked her. When she finally "brought forth her firstborn son" (Luke 2:7) and saw that His birth was heralded by angels, her joy must have overflowed. In her arms lay the Son of God, a child whose life would make all lives worth living. It is no wonder that she "kept all these things, and pondered them in her heart" (Luke 2:19).

## Second Sorrow and Joy of Mary: The Prophecy of Simeon

*"And Joseph and his mother marvelled at those things which were spoken of him. And Simeon blessed them, and said unto Mary his mother, Behold, this child is set for the fall and rising again of many in Israel; and for a sign which shall be spoken against; (Yea, a sword shall pierce through thy own soul also,) that the thoughts of many hearts may be revealed."*

Luke 2:33–35

After Jesus's birth, Mary observed "the days of her purification" (see "Childbirth" on page 18) and came to Jerusalem with two turtledoves to make a sacrifice. The Mosaic law required that a woman must bring to the temple a "lamb of the first year" (Leviticus 12:6) to complete her purification. If she was unable to afford a lamb, she could bring two turtledoves, or two young pigeons. Temple worship was an important thing to the Jews and this sacrifice would have been anticipated and planned for months beforehand. Mary and Joseph must have been in abject poverty to bring two doves instead of a lamb. Yet in reality, they did bring a lamb—the Lamb of God, whose blood would be spilt for the sins of the world and whose death would break the bonds of death forever.

While at the temple, Mary and Joseph were approached by a man named Simeon, who had been promised that he would not die "before he had seen the Lord's Christ" (Luke 2:26). He had been led by the Spirit to go to the temple that day, and when he held Jesus in his arms, he recognized Him as the promised Christ. While Simeon held baby Jesus, he rejoiced and prophesied many things about Him that caused His parents to marvel. Afterward, Simeon blessed them and told Mary, "(Yea, a sword shall pierce through thy own soul also,) that the thoughts of many hearts may be revealed" (Luke 2:35).

This encounter with Simeon was Mary's second sorrow and joy. Joy because of the beautiful things Simeon prophesied about her son, and joy in knowing that Simeon was giving her an additional witness to what the angel Gabriel had told her about who her son would be. Yet this encounter was also a sorrow because, as Simeon told her, not only would her son suffer, but she too would suffer and have her soul pierced through for the benefit of others—a daunting promise for any young mother to contemplate.

## Third Sorrow and Joy of Mary: The Flight into Egypt

*"The angel of the Lord appeareth to Joseph in a dream, saying, Arise, and take the young child and his mother, and flee into Egypt, and be thou there until I bring thee word: for Herod will*

*seek the young child to destroy him. When he arose, he took the young child and his mother by night, and departed into Egypt."*
*Matthew 2:13–14*

When Jesus was about two years old, Mary and Joseph received a visit from "Wise Men from the east" (Matthew 2:1). These men, guided by a new star, had been led to the house of Mary and Joseph. When they came into the house and saw Jesus with His mother, they fell down in worship and gave Him gifts of gold, frankincense, and myrrh. We often assume that there were three Wise Men because there were three gifts, but the scriptures don't specify how many came. It is safe to speculate that these Wise Men, because they had come so far, did not travel alone but with a great caravan. I can only imagine the commotion and excitement that their arrival would have stirred up in Mary and Joseph's humble neighborhood!

After the departure of the Wise Men, Joseph received another visit from an angel, who told him that Herod, the king of Judea, would "seek the life of the young child to destroy him" (verse 13). Herod was constantly worried about losing his throne to a Jewish uprising. When he heard the Wise Men speak of a "King of the Jews," he was troubled, "and all Jerusalem with him" (verses 2–3). Jerusalem had every right to be worried; Herod was a wicked king. When the Wise Men didn't return to tell him where this King of the Jews was, he "was exceedingly wroth" and sent out a decree that all the children two years

old and younger should be killed (verse 16). For me, this has to be one of the worst scenes in all of the scriptures. When I think of my little children and how much I love them, my heart breaks to think of the suffering these families endured. I can't imagine how horrific it would have been to witness this massive infanticide. No wonder there was "lamentation, and weeping, and great mourning, . . . and [they] would not be comforted, because they [the children] are not" (verse 18).

The angel, knowing what Herod would do to the children, told Joseph that he should take Jesus and Mary and "flee" into Egypt and "be thou there until I bring thee word" (verse 13). This flight into Egypt was Mary's third sorrow and joy. It was a sorrow because going to Egypt meant leaving behind her home and family without knowing how long it would be until she could return. As anyone who has ever made a big move can tell you, starting over in a new place is never easy. Going to Egypt was also a sorrow because she discovered that there were people who wanted to kill her son. Later, learning what had happened after they left, she must have also grieved to know that so many innocent children were killed and so many mothers suffered while she and her son had escaped.

Yet, the flight into Egypt was also a joy because it gave her evidence that God was aware of her and Jesus and that He would preserve their lives. It was a joy because she had Joseph at her side, a righteous man who had received revelation from

God for their family. We might even speculate that this move to Egypt was a joy because it removed Mary and Joseph from the gossip and judgments that must have accompanied their marriage and Jesus's birth. Their exodus to Egypt was a fresh start, a chance to establish and strengthen their marriage, their family, and their faith.

## *Fourth Sorrow and Joy of Mary: The Loss of Jesus in the Temple*

*"And when they had fulfilled the days, as they returned, the child Jesus tarried behind in Jerusalem; and Joseph and his mother knew not of it. . . . And it came to pass, that after three days they found him in the temple, sitting in the midst of the doctors, both hearing them, and asking them questions. And all that heard him were astonished at his understanding and answers."*

*Luke 2:43–47*

It was common for Jews to travel to Jerusalem for Passover. On their return from one such trip, Mary and Joseph had traveled a day toward home with their caravan before they realized that Jesus was not with them. Jesus was twelve years old by this time and Mary and Joseph would have had several other children to take care of. (See "Jesus's Sisters" on page 61.) They assumed that He was traveling with His friends or cousins somewhere among the caravan, but when they "sought him among their kinsfolk and acquaintance," they realized that He was not there (Luke 2:44).

When Mary and Joseph discovered Jesus was missing, they were terrified and retraced their steps back to Jerusalem as fast as they could. Most parents can relate to how horrible it feels to realize you have lost or forgotten your child. I once lost my son at a swimming pool for half an hour and I was beside myself with desperation. I can't even imagine how Mary and Joseph must have felt, especially when it took them three days to find Him.

When they finally found Jesus, He was in the temple with others, "both hearing them, and asking them questions" (verse 46). Today, when Jewish boys turn thirteen—or twelve for girls—they are able to participate fully in all traditions and ceremonies such as prayer, worship services, and scripture reading. It is also the age they are expected to be accountable for their own actions and decisions. Since Christ was about this age and He was found in the temple, it may be that this trip to Jerusalem had been His first experience participating in temple worship. He was separated from His parents for several days, all of which He spent in the temple learning, asking, and teaching. The Mosaic law bore testimony of Christ's mission, so going to the temple must been an incredible experience. It appears that He understood the temple, and what it symbolized, better than many of the adults and priests. The scriptures record that Jesus taught adults and "all that heard him were astonished at his understanding and answers" (verses 46–47). I imagine that temple worship answered many of His questions about Himself and His future responsibilities.

Mary was desperate with panic when she finally found Jesus in the temple. She cried, "Son, why hast thou thus dealt with us? behold, thy father and I have sought thee sorrowing." Jesus seemed not at all remorseful, answering, "How is it that ye sought me? wist ye not that I must be about my Father's business?" (verses 48–49). Jesus was reminding her that He had not been lost at all.  He had been in the temple—in His Father's house.

Jesus's words must have brought Mary both joy and sorrow. She felt joy because she saw that His talents were awakening and that He was beginning to understand His mission. Yet, her joy may also have been tinged with sorrow. I imagine that her feelings may have been similar to those of a modern-day mother watching her twelve-year-old son pass the sacrament for the first time. She is excited and happy that he is growing into a man. Yet at the same time, she might feel sadness and loss, knowing that he is no longer her little child.

Mary could see that her son—just barely a man—was already starting down the path that He had been born to travel, a hard and lonely path that would eventually take Him away from her all together. She was starting to glimpse who her son really was and what awaited Him in His mortal ministry, and that would have been a sorrow and a joy.

## Fifth Sorrow and Joy of Mary: Who Is My Mother?

*"There came then his brethren and his mother, and, standing without, sent unto him, calling him. And the multitude sat about him, and they said unto him, Behold, thy mother and thy brethren without seek for thee. And he answered them, saying, Who is my mother, or my brethren? And he looked round about on them which sat about him, and said, Behold my mother and my brethren! For whosoever shall do the will of God, the same is my brother, and my sister, and mother."*

*Mark 3:31–35*

At the start of Jesus's mortal ministry, Mary and her other sons sought Jesus, only to find Him surrounded by a great crowd. They came to the place where Jesus taught and, standing outside, asked to be able to speak with Him.  When Jesus received the message that His mother and His brothers stood outside waiting, He asked, "Who is my mother, or my brethren?" Looking around at the crowd, He announced: "For whosoever shall do the will of God, the same is my brother, and my sister, and mother" (Mark 3:35).

I'm sure Jesus wasn't dismissing or disregarding His mother and His family. For all we know, after saying this He may have gone out and spoken with His family. I think that what Jesus was trying to teach was that even though Mary and His brothers were Christ's physical family, even they must become part of His spiritual family. Their close relationship to

> ## "Who is my mother, or my brethren?"

Him was not enough to save them, but they—like all of God's children—had to listen, believe, and do the will of God. Even Christ's mother had to become a disciple.

To me, this scene must have been another of Mary's sorrows and joys. When Jesus was first born, I don't think Mary fully understood the magnitude of His mission on the earth. She knew God had an important mission for Him, but she, like Christ's other disciples, had to gain a testimony of Him, line upon line, grace upon grace. The New Testament gives us evidence that Mary did go through the conversion process and that she became one of His most stalwart disciples.

Mary's personal conversion to Christ would have brought her an incredible amount of joy, which only would have been magnified by her love for her son. Yet, I think that this process of discipleship must have also brought her sorrow. While she would always hold a place of love and regard in Jesus's life, Christ's spiritual family would take precedence in His life. Realizing that being a member of His spiritual family was more important than being a member of His physical family must have brought, along with joy, moments of sorrow. Those moments when even she, His mother, had to wait outside the door.

## Sixth Sorrow and Joy of Mary: Christ's Crucifixion

*"When Jesus therefore saw his mother, and the disciple standing by, whom he loved, he saith unto his mother, Woman, behold thy son!"*

*John 19:26*

Several times in the New Testament, Christ called His mother, Mary, "woman." At the start of His ministry, when Mary expressed concern that there was no wine, He responded, "Woman, what have I to do with thee? mine hour is not yet come" (John 2:4). And then at the end of His ministry, when

He was dying on the cross, He looked down at His mother and exclaimed, "Woman, behold thy son!" (John 19:26).

In modern English the use of the word *woman* sounds derogatory and coarse, or as one pastor I read said, "like a motorcycle biker talking to his . . . mama."[5] Yet, Jesus obviously used this word with respect for His mother. In fact, He used the word more as a title than as a pet name or a term of endearment. He called her "woman" much in the same way that we might call someone "lady." To me, the word *lady* indicates a woman of nobility, influence, and power, which is what the word *woman* would have meant to Mary when Christ called her by it.

There was so much meaning tied up in that one little word. Yes, Mary was His mother. Yes, she was His friend. Yes, she was His disciple. But she was a woman. I don't think it was a coincidence that He addressed her by this title at both the start of His ministry and at the end of His ministry. He recognized in her the nobility, power, influence, and glory that is inherent in being a woman. Even in His final moments on the cross, there was no greater title He could use for her.

These words on the cross were Mary's sixth sorrow and joy. I cannot even begin to imagine the emotions that might have overcome Mary while she watched her beloved son suffer and die on the cross. Christ's words to her to "behold her son" were almost a command that she not shrink from watching—in all His blood and pain—the sacrifice of her son, that she stand as a witness to the great and final sacrifice of the Lamb of God. And watch she did. With four close friends beside her, she watched every moment while He suffered, while He pled, and while He gave His last breaths on the cross, crying out, "Father, into thy hands I commend my spirit" (Luke 23:46).

After Christ's death, a Roman soldier came and, instead of breaking His legs to make sure He was dead, "pierced his side, and forthwith came there out blood and water" (John 19:34). It has been said that this blood and water was evidence that Christ's heart had ruptured, that He had literally died of a broken heart.[6] The only other time I can think of that blood and water naturally flow from an orifice is during childbirth, when a woman must shed both water and blood in order to create new life. To me, the blood and water from Christ's side is symbolic of the new life—the spiritual life—that His death gave each of us.

I wonder if, while Mary watched in agony, she remembered the words Simeon had spoken to her in the temple, that "a sword shall pierce through thy own soul also" (Luke 2:35). This may have been a time when the sorrow that Mary experienced may have almost overpowered every other emotion. Yet, like every great sorrow in life, it would not last forever, and for Mary, the joy of the Resurrection was just around the corner.

### Seventh Sorrow and Joy of Mary: Christ's Resurrection and Ascension

*"And when they were come in, they went up into an upper room, where . . . all continued with one accord in prayer and supplication, with the women, and Mary the mother of Jesus, and with his brethren."*

Acts 1:13–14

I don't think Mary or any of Christ's disciples truly understood that Christ would be physically resurrected. They understood that Jesus, like all souls, would someday live again, but I don't think that any of them were expecting to have Christ rise from the grave after only three days. The news of the Resurrection would have been joyous for all of Jesus's followers, but it must have been especially meaningful to Mary. She may have grieved the deepest at His death and may have rejoiced the greatest at His Resurrection.

We also know that after Christ's Resurrection, He stayed among the Jews, "being seen of them forty days" (Acts 1:3). During this time, Christ showed Himself to the Apostles, some disciples, and the women who followed Him. I think we can assume that Mary was also among those who were taught by Christ and who felt the nail prints in His feet and hands. It must have been incredible for her to have her son, whom she thought she'd lost, in her arms again.

Yet, the joy that Mary experienced at the resurrection of her son must have been cut short when she had to say good-bye to Him again when He ascended to His Father. Even though she knew she would see Him again someday, it must have been hard to see Him leave. Yet even this sorrow was filled with joy because while the Apostles watched "steadfastly toward heaven as he went up," two angels came down and told them, "this same Jesus, which is taken up from you into heaven, shall so come in like manner as ye have seen him go into heaven" (verses 10–11). It was a promise that Jesus would one day come again.

After Jesus's Ascension, the last mention we have of Mary in the scriptures is that she, along with the Apostles, her sons, and the other women, met in an upper room where they "continued with one accord in prayer and supplication" (verse 14). Mary's presence here among the Apostles tells us that she stayed a strong and powerful disciple of Jesus after His death, and probably until the day of her death.

Mary was one of the greatest women to ever live on the face of the earth. As I ponder the challenges and joys of her life, I am impressed by what she endured and what she accomplished.

Perhaps as she pondered on the joy and sorrow of Christ's death and Resurrection, she remembered the words that He had taught to His Apostles, speaking about how they would feel at His parting:

> Verily, verily, I say unto you, That ye shall weep and lament, but the world shall rejoice: and ye shall be sorrowful, but your sorrow shall be turned into joy. A woman when she is in travail hath sorrow, because her hour is come: but as soon as she is delivered of the child, she remembereth no more the anguish, for joy that a man is born into the world. And ye now therefore have sorrow: but I will see you again, and your heart shall rejoice, and your joy no man taketh from you. (John 16:20–22)

Mary, perhaps more than anyone else, understood the sorrow that Christ spoke of. In her life she had experienced many sorrows, yet she also experienced incredible joy. God doesn't promise that our mortal experience will be without pain, suffering, and sorrow. In fact, we can be guaranteed we will experience these things. Yet, as Mary can attest, it is in the times of our greatest sorrow that we also discover the "joy no man taketh from you."

# Marriage

Not long after a girl began to menstruate (somewhere around twelve to fourteen years old) she would become betrothed. In Jewish culture, marriage was a two-step process. The first step was the betrothal, which was when the marriage contract was signed in front of witnesses and a young man paid the father a "bride price" for his future wife and gave her a ring or jewelry of value. A betrothal was a covenant arrangement and the couple was considered to be husband and wife even though they did not yet share a home or a bed. A betrothal could last for a year or longer and could only be broken by going through a formal divorce. This is the situation that Mary and Joseph were in when Mary became pregnant with Jesus.

The second step of the marriage was for the groom to "take" the bride by going to her house and taking her back with him to live in his home. On the night of the wedding, the groom would be dressed as much like a king as possible, with colorful garments scented with spices, garlands of flowers around his neck, and a crown on his head.[7] Isaiah described a groom when he wrote, "[God] hath clothed me with the garments of salvation, he hath covered me with the robe of righteousness, as a bridegroom decketh himself with ornaments" (Isaiah 61:10). A bride would also be elaborately adorned and wearing any valuable pieces of jewelry the family owned.[8] Ezekiel gave this description of a bride: "I decked thee also with ornaments, and I put bracelets upon thy hands, and a chain on thy neck. And I put a jewel on thy forehead, and earrings in thine ears, and a beautiful crown upon thine head" (Ezekiel 16:11–12).

The groom would travel to the bride's home with a group of invited guests and escort her to his home where the wedding celebration would be held. Before leaving her home, the bride may have been given a blessing by her father or brothers, much like Rebekah in the Old Testament was blessed "be thou the mother of thousands of millions" (Genesis 24:60). The bride left her house with her hair down, with her face veiled, and accompanied by a procession of invited guests, who played music and danced along the way. Those who had been invited to join in the wedding wore a wedding garment and carried a torch or a lamp through the dark streets. The ten virgins in Christ's parable who were waiting for the bridegroom with their lamps were waiting to join in this type of procession.

After this procession, all the "children of the bridechamber" (Matthew 9:15), or those who were invited to the wedding, would gather to praise the new couple and eat the wedding feast. There was no religious ceremony at the feast, but friends and relatives could offer words of wisdom and blessings. These wedding celebrations could go on for a whole week!

# Anna

*"And there was one Anna, a prophetess, the daughter of Phanuel, of the tribe of Aser: she was of a great age, and had lived with an husband seven years from her virginity; And she was a widow of about fourscore and four years, which departed not from the temple, but served God with fastings and prayers night and day. And she coming in that instant gave thanks likewise unto the Lord, and spake of him to all them that looked for redemption in Jerusalem."*

*Luke 2:36–38*

**Forty days after the birth of Jesus** and at the end of her time of purification under the Mosaic law, Mary took Jesus to the temple in Jerusalem and presented him to the Lord (Luke 2:22–23). While Mary and Joseph were in the temple, it was revealed to Simeon, a man who had been promised by God he would live to see Christ, that Jesus was the promised Messiah. While Simeon held Jesus and prophesied of His divine mission, a woman named Anna, a prophetess, came in "that instant" (verse 38) into the temple and also recognized the Christ child.

Anna was a widow "of about fourscore and four years" (verse 37). This means that she was either eighty-four years old or that

she had been a widow for eighty-four years. The scripture is unclear, so either reading might be correct. Personally, I feel that the latter interpretation is most likely correct and that she had been a widow for eighty-four years. This is because Luke tells us that she had only been married to her husband for seven years before he died, indicating to me that she had been widowed for most of her life. Luke also says that she was of "great age," and if we assume that Anna had been married around the age of fourteen (a usual age to get married at the time), she would have been widowed at twenty-one and been a widow for the next eighty-four years. That would have made her at least 105 years old when Mary and Joseph brought Jesus to the temple!

Luke also tells us that Anna "departed not from the temple, but served God with fastings and prayers night and day" (verse 37). The temple grounds in Jerusalem were a huge compound (see "Temple Diagram" on page 129) and it would have been possible for Anna to live within the outer courts, though it may have meant that she was essentially homeless. It seems that she was at a point in her life when she had no other goal or desire than to serve God and worship in the temple.

Anna went to the temple every day, but it impresses me that she went the "instant" Simeon was speaking with Mary and Joseph, just in time to hear and see the promised Messiah. That was no coincidence. For years, she had dedicated her life, and the majority of her time, to serving the Lord. I can only imagine that she must have desired more than anything else to see the face of God.

And she did.

Her story is such a powerful reminder to me that there is no knowledge or experience that is beyond our reach. God has promised that if we knock, we will receive. He doesn't say

> "[She] departed not from the temple, but served God with fastings and prayers."

how many times we will have to knock or how long it will take before He answers the door. He only promises that if we diligently seek Him, like Anna did, we will receive eventually.

When I was in seminary, I had a question about the beautiful, and frustrating, verses in Doctrine and Covenants 93 that explore light, truth, and intelligence. After class, I asked my teacher to explain it to me. He smiled and said, "Heather, that is a big question, and I could explain it to you, but I am not going to. If I did that, I would rob you of the experience of finding it out for yourself." I was frustrated by his answer. I felt he had belittled my request.

Yet over the next several years I found myself coming back again and again to Doctrine and Covenants 93. One day about four years later, I was sitting in my college dorm room studying Doctrine and Covenants 93 for probably the thousandth time when I had a huge spiritual epiphany. I studied until four in the morning. What the Lord taught me blew me away. I have tried to explain it to others since then, but I can't. It was something that the Lord taught me in my soul, way deep down, and it changed the way I looked at the world. I was grateful that my seminary teacher hadn't answered my question the way I wanted. I gained so much more through struggling and searching than I would have if I had been handed the answer to my question on a silver platter.

I have a lot of questions about the gospel, questions I want answers to just as much as I wanted to understand Doctrine and Covenants 93. For a long time, I was taught to put my questions on a "shelf" to be answered someday in heaven. But my shelf got too heavy. It had so many questions on it, I felt like it was going to collapse. So instead, I started putting

my questions on "stairs," and I started to climb toward understanding them.

In my mind, putting a question on a "shelf" suggests passively waiting for an answer that may or may not exist. However, if I put my question on a "stair," I have faith that there is an answer and that I can take steps to reach it. I am committing to climb that staircase, to actively search, question, and struggle toward understanding.

Many of us have questions and desires burning in our hearts. There are things that we want to understand, mysteries of the universe we want unfolded, and heavenly beings we would like to see. Such knowledge is not beyond our reach.

Anna's example of not departing from the temple and continually serving the Lord is a good reminder to all of us on how to receive further light and knowledge. Elder Jeffrey R. Holland advised those who wish to have more faith:

> In moments of fear or doubt or troubling times, hold the ground you have already won, even if that ground is limited. . . . When those moments come and issues surface, the resolution of which is not immediately forthcoming, hold fast to what you already know and stand strong until additional knowledge comes. . . . Jesus said, "If ye have faith as a grain of mustard seed, ye shall say unto this mountain, Remove hence to yonder place; and it shall remove; and nothing shall be impossible unto

you." The size of your faith or the degree of your knowledge is not the issue—it is the integrity you demonstrate toward the faith you do have and the truth you already know.[1]

Luke also calls Anna a prophetess, a title reserved for only a few women in the scriptures. (See "Four Daughters of Philip" on page 205.) A prophetess is someone who bears testimony of Jesus Christ, which is just what Anna did after seeing Jesus in the temple; she "spake of him to all them that looked for redemption in Jerusalem" (Luke 2:38). After many years of searching and service, she had seen the face of God and could not keep the joy of that knowledge to herself.

We too can see the face of God. We too can understand hidden mysteries. We can see into the future. We can know all that God knows. The only qualifications are that we must believe such knowledge is possible and we must have the faith to put in the time and the effort to obtain it.

Like Anna, we have to keep showing up, keep searching, and keep struggling day after day and year after year. Some knowledge and experiences do not come easily. They have to be earned hour by hour, line upon line, until one day, like Anna, we walk into the temple and see the Savior of the world.

# Samaritan Woman at the Well

*"There cometh a woman of Samaria to draw water: Jesus saith unto her, Give me to drink. (For his disciples were gone away unto the city to buy meat.) Then saith the woman of Samaria unto him, How is it that thou, being a Jew, askest drink of me, which am a woman of Samaria? for the Jews have no dealings with the Samaritans. Jesus answered and said unto her, If thou knewest the gift of God, and who it is that saith to thee, Give me to drink; thou wouldest have asked of him, and he would have given thee living water."*

*John 4:7–10*

*While Christ was traveling* through Samaria to Galilee, He approached Jacob's well[1] and, being weary from His long traveling, sat and rested. When a Samaritan woman came to draw water from the well, Jesus said to her, "Give me to drink" (verse 7). This woman was astonished to see a Jewish man at the well but even more astonished to have a Jew ask her for water. The Jews and Samaritans had a long history of violence and hatred toward one another, and both groups viewed the other with disdain. (See "Samaritans" on page 165.) Most Jews so abhorred Samaritans that they considered any food or drink touched by Samaritan hands to be ritually unclean. Many Jews traveling to Galilee even took a route that avoided Samaria altogether. So it is no wonder that this woman, astonished, asked Jesus, "How is that thou, being a Jew, askest drink of me, which am a woman of Samaria?" (verse 9). Then, with

> "Whosoever drinketh of the water that I shall give him shall never thirst."

perhaps a little bitterness in her voice, she concluded, "for the Jews have no dealings with the Samaritans" (verse 9). The Samaritans felt themselves ill-used by the Jews, and many of them—perhaps including this woman—harbored hard feelings toward all Jews.

In response, Jesus told her, "If thou knewest the gift of God, and who it is that saith to thee, Give me to drink; thou wouldest have asked of him, and he would have given thee living water" (verse 10). The woman, now intrigued, asked how He could possibly give her living water when He didn't even have anything to use to draw it up from the well. She also, perhaps with a tinge of accusation, wondered if He thought Himself greater than Jacob, their forefather, who had created the well that had supplied his posterity with water for generations. Christ didn't directly answer but instead told her, "Whosoever drinketh of this water [referring to Jacob's well] shall thirst again: But whosoever drinketh of the water that I shall give him shall never thirst" (verses 13–14). Christ was, of course, speaking of Himself and His divine mission as the Messiah, but the Samaritan woman thought they were still talking about the water that comes out of a well. Perhaps a bit teasingly, she said, "Give me this water, that I thirst not, neither come hither to draw" (verse 15).

Christ could see that this woman did not understand the spiritual undertones of His message, so He changed the topic and said, "Go, call thy husband, and come hither" (verse 16). The woman told Him that she had no husband, to which Christ replied, "Thou hast well said, I have no husband: For thou hast had five husbands; and he whom thou now hast is not thy husband: in that saidst thou truly" (verses 17–18).

This declaration on the part of Jesus astounded the woman and made her see that she was not dealing with any ordinary Jew. She perceived that He was a prophet and consequently asked Him about the doctrinal question of great dispute between the Jews and the Samaritans. She said, "Our fathers worshipped in this mountain [Mount Gezim]; and ye [the

Jews] say, that in Jerusalem is the place where men ought to worship" (verse 20). This woman was evidently troubled by this question and wanted to know how and where she ought to worship. She may have been searching and struggling with certain questions about her faith, which is perhaps the reason Christ singled her out.

This woman's questioning spirit reminds me of Joseph Smith, who approached God with the question about which religious group was correct and which he should join. The Samaritan woman, with her question about where to worship, was asking Christ a similar question: Which group is correct?

In response to her earnest question, Christ gave her an answer similar to the one Joseph Smith received. He told her that the time would soon come when neither Jew nor Samaritan would worship in Mount Gezim or in Jerusalem, but that the true worshippers would "worship the Father in spirit and in truth: for the Father seeketh such to worship him" (verse 23). This woman affirmed her faith in the Messiah (a belief which the Samaritans held more firmly than the Jews[2]) and said, "I know that Messias cometh, which is called Christ: when he is come, he will tell us all things" (verse 25). Christ then did this woman a great honor and told her something that He had not yet even declared plainly to His Apostles: "I that speak unto thee am he [the Christ]" (verse 26).

It is incredible to me that out of all the people to whom Christ could have first revealed Himself as the Messiah, He chose this woman. I have often wondered why Jesus chose her, because she seems an unlikely audience for so grand a declaration. What made her unique was that she asked. Not only did she ask Jesus for the living water, but her question about the correct way to worship indicates that she was searching for answers. I think it this attribute more than anything else that allowed Jesus to reveal to her who He was.

Elder Dieter F. Uchtdorf taught, "We are a question-asking people, we have always been, because we know that inquiry leads to truth. . . . In fact, I'm not sure how one can discover

> *"You will rarely discover a revelation that didn't come in response to a question."*

truth without asking questions. In the scriptures, you will rarely discover a revelation that didn't come in response to a question." He then pointed to Joseph Smith as an example for this drive to question: "Whenever a question arose and Joseph Smith wasn't sure of the answer, he approached the Lord, and the results are the wonderful revelations in the Doctrine and Covenants. Often the knowledge Joseph received extended far beyond the original question. That is because not only can the Lord answer the questions we ask but even more importantly, He can give us answers to questions we should have asked."[3]

The Samaritan woman is an example of how important it is to cultivate a questioning and inquisitive mind. She asked Jesus a simple question but one that she sincerely wanted an answer to. And she got a miraculous answer. It is only when we desire to know more and are willing to go to God with our questions that we receive greater light and knowledge.

I also think it is significant that in this story Christ did not haul the water up for the Samaritan woman; she had to do it herself. It is a reminder to me that for each of us Christ has a well of living water. Within His well are the solutions for all of our problems, the balms for all of our wounds, and the answers for all of our questions. Yet, like the Samaritan woman, we must hunger and thirst after that water. We must come to the well prepared with something to fill. We must make room in our hearts and in our minds for answers and new ideas. We must have faith to let down our water pot into the unknown, to ask and have faith we will receive. Finally, we must have the perseverance to haul up the living water for ourselves, hand over hand, until we gain what we have been striving for.

It was this thirst and desire for more that motivated the Samaritan woman at the well, as well as many of the women Christ taught in His ministry. As authors Jeni and Richard Holzapfel wrote, "Drawing water is a powerful image . . . like the Samaritan woman, other women living in the Jewish Palestine thirsted for living water to quench their parched souls. They stood at the well, hoping to draw life from the ancient traditions of their people or longing to discover an inner well of divine power and life. They wanted to be wellsprings of a new vision and hope, to use their gifts to change their own lives and the lives of their families, friends and neighbors."[4]

Christ's interaction with the Samaritan woman reminds me that His living water stands ready and free for anyone who is thirsty for it. Once obtained, it is water that heals and nourishes individuals, families, and communities for generations. But we must bring the vessels to be filled, and we must do the work to pull up the water.

# Widow of Nain

*"And it came to pass the day after, that he went into a city called Nain; and many of his disciples went with him, and much people. Now when he came nigh to the gate of the city, behold, there was a dead man carried out, the only son of his mother, and she was a widow: and much people of the city was with her. And when the Lord saw her, he had compassion on her, and said unto her, Weep not. And he came and touched the bier: and they that bare him stood still. And he said, Young man, I say unto thee, Arise. And he that was dead sat up, and began to speak. And he delivered him to his mother."*

*Luke 7:11–15*

*This woman lived in Nain,* a village in Galilee about nine miles from Nazareth. She had only one son, a young man, who had recently died. While she and "much people of the city" (verse 12) were taking her son out of the city on a funeral bier, Christ saw her and "he had compassion on her" (verse 13).

In New Testament times, the dead were prepared and buried very soon after death, usually within hours. As one BYU scholar wrote:

When a person breathed the last breath and the heart stopped beating, the eyes of the deceased were reverentially closed, the entire body was washed and anointed with oil, and the hands and feet were then wrapped in linen bands. The body, clothed in a favorite garment, was then wrapped with winding sheets. Spices of myrrh and aloes were placed in the folds of the garment to perfume the body. A napkin was then bound from the chin to the head. The family took the body on a bier to be buried within hours of death, not days. During the first century, many people were laid to rest in rock-hewn tombs, . . . others were buried in the ground.[1]

We don't know if this young man's death was the result of a long drawn out illness or an unexpected accident, but no matter how he died, it is likely that his mother's grief was fresh. She may have only had hours to process the news of his death and all the implications that came with it. As a widow, now with no male to take care of her, this woman's plight may have been hard indeed. The newness of her grief makes Christ's tender words, "Weep not" (verse 13), all the more powerful. He was telling her that even though her grief seemed unbearable, she wouldn't have to mourn much longer. Christ then approached the bier where the dead man's body lay, touched it, and commanded, "Young man, I say unto thee, Arise" (verse 14). Immediately, the woman's son arose from the dead, spoke, and was "delivered" to his mother (verse 15).

When I studied this story, I was touched by the phrase "he had compassion on her" and began to study more closely the word *compassion*. While I studied, I noticed that in the New Testament, Christ was often "moved with compassion"[2] to perform a miracle for someone. I also learned that compassion is not the same thing as pity, sympathy, or empathy. It seems that one of the big differences is that while pity and empathy

> ### "He had compassion on her."

are things that you feel, compassion is something that you do. Compassion in the scriptures is often linked to the word *mercy* and is used to describe the motivation behind great acts of charity and love, like the Atonement. In fact, the outward expression of charity is compassion.

Throughout the scriptures, Christ often says that His "bowels are filled with compassion"[3] toward God's children. The word *bowels* in the original New Testament Greek is *splágxnon* and refers to organs of the body like the heart, lungs, intestines, and womb. All these are parts of the body that swell and then *must* expel something to keep functioning properly. So when Christ says that His bowels are filled or moved with compassion, He is saying that His great love for God's children compels Him to bless them.

The other thing I love about this woman's story is that it is a profound testimony of Christ's love and compassion toward women. In the accounts we have of Jesus raising someone from the dead, all of them are done in the presence of, and usually on behalf of, women. Some of the other examples we have are:

• The raising of the daughter of Jairus was not only performed on a woman (a girl really), but the only people there to witness it were the girl's father and mother and three of the Apostles. (Luke 8:41, 49–56)

• The raising of Lazarus from the dead was done in the presence of many but mainly on behalf of Mary and Martha. (John 11:1–45)

• When Christ rose from His grave, His first witness was Mary Magdalene and the other women who came to prepare His body for burial. (John 20:1–16)

Raising a person from the dead is an incredible miracle for anyone to witness. Yet I can't help but feel that it has special meaning for women, whose bodies create mortal life and who spend so much of their time nurturing and shaping lives. It seems to me that Christ wanted to demonstrate to women that He had power over the grave. He gave them a living testimony that through Him and by Him all the children women bear and nurture on this earth will live again. Reminding them that no sacrifice to bring a child to the world, to nurture a friend, or to love a family member will be in vain. Like Christ told the widow of Nain, we can "weep not." Even though our grief may seem unbearable, Christ has been victorious over death. And there is nothing that can change that.

# Simon Peter's Mother-in-Law

*"And he arose out of the synagogue, and entered into Simon's house. And Simon's wife's mother was taken with a great fever; and they besought him for her. And he stood over her, and rebuked the fever; and it left her: and immediately she arose and ministered unto them."*

Luke 4:38–39

**The story of the mother-in-law** of Simon Peter is told in Mathew, Mark, and Luke and happened early in Christ's ministry. Her healing may have been the first healing miracle that Jesus performed. The scriptures tell us that she was in the home of her son-in-law Simon Peter, the newly called Apostle of Christ, when she "was taken with a great fever" (verse 38). She was sick enough that everyone was worried about her. They called Christ to come, having faith that He could heal her. When Christ came, He rebuked the fever, took her by the hand, and raised her up from her bed.

Immediately afterward, she was able to stand and even began to minister to them, which probably means she provided them with food and care. It is significant that the first thing she did after she was miraculously healed was serve. She didn't run out into the street shouting that she had been healed, nor did she didn't fall down and praise Christ. Instead, she began to serve. She, like many of the women who followed Christ, realized that the best way she could thank Christ for what He had done for her was to serve, not only Him but also all of God's children.

Once in a stake conference, I heard a speaker share an experience about how a ward member had done something incredibly kind for one of her children. Later, she had an opportunity to do something kind for this same ward member, who, when she was finished, asked her how he could repay her. "There is nothing that you can do for me," she told him,

"If you want to say 'thank you,' keep loving and serving my children. That will mean more to me than anything else." She then went on to explain how that experience taught her about the nature of God, how His greatest delight is in His children, and that when we serve others, we are also expressing our love for Him.

We may not have the opportunity to show our gratitude to Jesus Christ by literally serving and ministering to Him, like Simon Peter's mother-in-law did, but we can serve His children. And like King Benjamin from the Book of Mormon taught, "When ye are in the service of your fellow beings, ye are only in the service of your God" (Mosiah 2:17).

# Daughter of Jairus

"There came from the ruler of the synagogue's house certain which said, Thy daughter is dead: why troublest thou the Master any further? As soon as Jesus heard the word that was spoken, he saith unto the ruler of the synagogue, Be not afraid, only believe. And he cometh to the house of the ruler of the synagogue, and seeth the tumult, and them that wept and wailed greatly. And when he was come in, he saith unto them, Why make ye this ado, and weep? the damsel is not dead, but sleepeth."

Mark 5:35–36, 38–39

We may dread it, but we know that the eventual deaths of our parents and grandparents are natural and inevitable. We know we will have to say good-bye one day. The death of a child, though, is a different matter. No one is ever prepared to lose a child. Yet the death of their child was exactly the situation Jairus and his wife found themselves facing.

Jairus was the ruler of a synagogue in Jerusalem and apparently well acquainted with Jesus. When his daughter, a twelve-year-old girl, became deathly ill, he sought out Jesus and begged Him, "I pray thee, come and lay thy hands on her, that she may be healed" (verse 23). Christ agreed to go with Jairus to his house, but on the way He was touched by a woman with an issue of blood (see "Woman With an Issue of Blood" on page 55) and stopped to acknowledge her and her faith. While Christ was speaking with the woman, one of Jairus's servants came and told him, "Thy daughter is dead: why troublest thou the Master any further?" (verse 35).

I can picture the despair that must have come over Jairus at that moment. All hope he had of Christ healing his daughter was gone. Recognizing his feelings, Jesus turned to him and said, "Fear not: believe only, and she shall be made whole" (Luke 8:50). Those words probably gave Jairus hope, even if he didn't understand what Christ had in mind. They continued on to Jairus's home and saw that people were already gathered there to mourn his daughter's death. Seeing their "tumult" (Mark 5:28), Christ said to mourners, "Weep not; she is not dead, but sleepeth" (Luke 8:52). On hearing this declaration, the people "laughed him to scorn" (Mark 5:40). They truly believed that this young woman was past all hope.

Christ then sent all those who didn't believe away and invited only Jairus, his wife, Peter, James, and John into the room where the young girl lay. I imagine that Jairus must have despaired. What could possibly be done for his daughter now? Christ reached out and took the girl by the hand and said, "Talitha cumi" (Mark 5:41), or "Maid, arise" (Luke 8:54). After the Savior spoke, the girl immediately sat up and began to walk. Christ told them to get her something to eat and to keep it secret, "that no man should know it" (Mark 5:43).

Throughout His ministry, Christ often used physical healing to teach spiritual truths.[1] He used His miracles to demonstrate that He had the power to not only to heal physical ailments but to also forgive sin, what we might call "spiritual sickness." With

> *"Be not afraid, only believe."*

advanced technology and medicine in our day, fewer parents face the grief of losing a child to death than in scriptural times. While the physical death of children is much less common in our day, spiritual sickness and death is rampant. We may be able to better relate to the grief of losing a child spiritually—to have a wayward child who has strayed from the gospel path or who has made poor life choices. The grief associated with the spiritual sickness of a family member isn't any less real than

the grief that comes with physical sickness. Sometimes it can even be more anguishing because, unlike physical death where we know we will see our loved ones again, spiritual death leaves us doubting that everything will be okay.

Many parents, like Jairus and his wife, moan in misery while they watch their children suffer. They watch in agony while a beloved son or daughter makes choices that take them further and further away from the safety of the gospel. Some of these parents may even relate to Jairus when he, falling at the Savior's feet, exclaimed, "My little daughter lieth at the point of death" (Mark 5:23). Like Jairus, these parents have great faith in the Savior's power and trust that He can fix what they cannot.

Yet, instead of acting quickly like parents hope, the Savior seems to be in no hurry. In the case of Jairus,

He even stopped to take time to speak to the woman with an issue of blood who had been healed when she touched His garment. It was during this delay, which must have been agonizing for Jairus, that the servant came and told him that his daughter was dead. I know some parents who can relate to Jairus. They started out with great hope that Christ would work a miracle and had faith that their child would be healed. Yet, the years went by and their child grew worse rather than better. They began to feel, as the servant suggested to Jairus, that their child was past hope. Christ's response to Jairus, and to all who find themselves despairing, was simply, "Be not afraid, only believe" (Mark 5:36).

While I was thinking about the story of the daughter of Jairus, a certain friend of mine came to mind. She had made lots of bad choices in her life and, at the time,

Daniel Rona, a fairly well-known Jewish-Mormon tour guide in Israel, has said that he thinks when the Savior said, "Talitha cumi," He was not just saying, "Maid, arise." He was calling her by a term of endearment. Rona explained that in Hebrew the word *Taleh* means "lamb" and that a female lamb is called a *Talita* and is sometimes used as a pet name for young girls. In speaking of Christ, he said, "Don't you suppose that since He lived here [Jerusalem] for eighteen to twenty months that He probably knew the children? Don't you suppose that He had endearing names for the children? . . . What was the little girl's name? I really don't know but I have an idea what she looked like. She had a head of curly hair, and he took her by the hand and said 'little lambykins get up' and she did and came alive again."[3] It is sweet to think that Christ may have known this little girl personally and that He may have even given her a nickname because of her curly hair.

As Daniel Rona pointed out, if Christ could give Peter, a grown man, the nickname "Rocky," it isn't unbelievable that He would give children nicknames as well (Matthew 16:18). This perspective on the word *Talitha* makes Christ's actions toward this young woman incredibly touching and personal. It helps remind me that Christ knows each of us personally and that when our day comes to meet Him, He will know us like He knew this little girl—as a friend.

was close to hitting rock bottom. One day, when I was talking with her in my kitchen, the tattoos, the dyed hair, and the tired lines on her face melted away and I saw *her*. For just a second, I had a glimpse of who she really was—how the Savior must see her—and I was blown away. I realized that underneath all the scars of her mistakes was a beautiful soul. I saw her radiating light and beauty and I felt—for just a moment—how much God loved her. The glimpse faded away, but while I stared at her with new eyes, the words "She is not dead, but sleepeth" resonated through my soul. I realized that even though my friend was currently far away from the light of the gospel and that spiritually she was "at the point of death," she was in reality just sleeping. Her light was dimmed, but it was there, waiting for the Savior's hand and His tender words, "Maid, arise."

The glimpse I had of my friend made me realize that often we lose our faith in people much too quickly. We get bogged down by watching the consequences of their choices and feeling disappointment in their actions. We lose sight of the eternal picture. We forget that to God, who sees the beginning and the end, these wayward children are not lost. He knows exactly where they are and what they need, and some day, in His own time and in His own way, those souls will have the opportunity to be awakened. They will arise. Orson F. Whitney taught:

The Prophet Joseph Smith declared—and he never taught a more comforting doctrine—that the eternal sealings of faithful parents and the divine promises made to them for valiant service in the Cause of Truth, would save not only themselves, but likewise their posterity. Though some of the sheep may wander, the eye of the Shepherd is upon them, and sooner or later they will feel the tentacles of Divine Providence reaching out after them and drawing them back to the fold. Either in this life or the life to come, they will return. They will have to pay their debt to justice; they will suffer for their sins; and may tread a thorny path; but if it leads them at last, like the penitent Prodigal, to a loving and forgiving father's heart and home, the painful experience will not have been in vain. Pray for your careless and disobedient children; hold on to them with your faith. Hope on, trust on, till you see the salvation of God.[2]

Just as Jairus's daughter was not beyond hope, so our children suffering from spiritual sickness and death are not beyond Christ's power. They will have to repent and accept the consequences of their choices, but the power and faith of covenant-keeping parents is a strong force. It will bless their children in this life and the next.

I know that with God nothing is impossible. I have faith that one day my friend will become that woman I glimpsed in my kitchen. I don't know when or how, but I know that one day all those who mock, scorn, and clutter her life with their doubts will be cleared from the house. And then when it is just her, the Savior, and those who love her in the room, she will feel how much she is loved. That love will touch those beautiful parts of her soul that are currently buried in sin, anger, confusion, and doubt. She will awaken and her true self will arise. It may not be anytime soon, but I have hope that it will happen because I know that, like the daughter of Jairus, she is not dead, only sleeping.

> *"She is not dead, but sleepeth."*

# Menstruation

In ancient times, when a girl began to menstruate, she entered a whole new phase of her life. According to the Mosaic law, any woman who had an "issue" of blood was considered unclean until seven days after she had stopped bleeding (Leviticus 15:19–33). This rule meant the whole household, male and female, would have been aware of when a girl was menstruating because, due to her "unclean" status, she would not have been able to help prepare food for other people or perform tasks for others without making them ritually unclean.

The word unclean seems very harsh to our modern ears and I know some women who have had much heartache about it, wondering how God could ever label something so innately a part of them as dirty. This confusion may stem from not understanding what the word unclean means in Hebrew. In Hebrew, the word that is translated as "unclean" in the King James Version of the Bible is tuma. There is not an English equivalent of this word (which is why it can be a hard concept to grasp), but the easiest way to understand the meaning of tuma is to understand that it is the spiritual status that occurs when you have had contact with death. This is because every living thing in the world contains a spark of divinity, a portion of God's power, and when that power departs, it leaves behind a "spiritual vacuum,"[1] or a state of tuma.

For example, the death of a human body results in the strongest form of tuma because men and women are created in the image of God and therefore possess the greatest spiritual power and potential. When the link between the spirit and the body is severed, the body becomes an empty shell, devoid of the power that animated it and gave it life. Furthermore, both the body and the spirit have been cut off from the presence of God, and without the Atonement and Resurrection of Christ, they would be forever in a state of tuma, unclean and cut off from God's presence. In the Mosaic law, there was a set of requirements that a man or a woman had to perform in order to come out of a state of tuma and become clean (see "Childbirth" on page 18).

*Tuma*, or being unclean, could happen to both men and women any time they came into contact with something that had died or had decreased in its manifestation of God's power. For example, a woman who was in the process of giving birth, or who had just given birth, was considered "unclean" (*tuma*) not only because of the "spiritual vacuum"[2] that was created when the extra life within her left, but also because her child, in entering mortal life, has been cut off

from the presence of God. *Tuma* also occurs at the loss of potential life that happens during sexual intercourse and during menstruation.[2] As modern Rabbi Shraga Simmons stated, "After having marital relations, men are in a state of Tuma, because of the loss of the 'building blocks' of life within them (Leviticus 15:16). And women incur this state of Tuma when they menstruate, because of the loss of potential life within them (Leviticus 15:19)."[3]

A woman who has menstruated is in the state of *tuma* because every month when her body prepares to release an egg, she reaches a high level of potential holiness. She has within her body the possibility of new life, and that one little egg contains within it one of the most sublime powers of God: the power to create new life. When this egg is first released, its potential for new life is high. If it is not fertilized, then its potential decreases, the holy power departs, and the lifeless remnants are shed from a woman's body. This loss results in a state of *tuma* because where there was once the potential for new life, there is now just empty space.

This understanding of the menstrual cycle and of menstrual blood is probably how women in Old and New Testament times understood their monthly cycles. They would not have looked on menstruation as being dirty, shameful, or even ordinary. Instead, menstruation was a sign of the continuation of life and would have been rejoiced at, perhaps even seen as an innately spiritual experience. In fact, the bath or washing that a woman had to undergo to come out of a state of *tuma* (or any state of "uncleanliness") was a special bath called a *mikvah*. The *mikvah* was a pool or bath of clear water in which a man or woman would immerse themselves in. The *mikvah* was not intended to wash away impurities or dirt caused by the state of uncleanliness. They had to completely wash their bodies prior to entering the *mikvah*. The purpose of the *mikvah* was to come out reborn, holy and spiritually clean, much the same way that baptism by immersion does today.

It is important to remember that the law of Moses was given as a preparatory law to turn the hearts of the Jews to Jesus Christ. Everything in the Mosaic law bears testimony of the need for a Savior. Menstruation is a monthly blood sacrifice that reminds us that if it were not for Christ, we would be continuously in a state of *tuma*—separated from God's life-giving power—and unable to return to Him. Yet, because of Jesus Christ and the blood that He shed for us, we can be washed clean and become pure and able to return to God's presence.

# Woman with an Issue of Blood

*"And a certain woman, which had an issue of blood twelve years, and had suffered many things of many physicians, and had spent all that she had, and was nothing bettered, but rather grew worse, when she had heard of Jesus, came in the press behind, and touched his garment. For she said, If I may touch but his clothes, I shall be whole."*

*Mark 5:25–28*

*Throughout His ministry,* Christ was often traveling, frequently on His way to visit different towns and cities. Yet the destination was never as important to Him as the journey. He never let His determination to get someplace keep Him from ministering and teaching to those He met on the way. The story of the woman with an issue of blood is one of those examples.

Jesus was approached by a ruler of the synagogue named Jairus, whose daughter was sick. (See "Daughter of Jairus" on page 47.) Jairus knelt before Jesus and begged Him to come heal his daughter. Jesus went with Jairus right away, but "much people followed him, and thronged him" (verse 24). While He made His way through the crowd, a woman touched His robe.

> The word *virtue* in this story does not refer just to chastity, as we commonly use it today. The word in Greek is *dunamis* and means "strength power" or "moral power and excellence of soul." In the New Testament, the word is almost always used to describe the power by which Christ worked His miracles. It is important that we understand that virtue is the power that comes to us when we follow God's commandments and when we understand and respect the power we possess within our bodies. Perhaps this is why we so often link chastity with the word virtue, because the power of procreation is one of the most beautiful and apparent ways in which we are able to use God's power on this earth. Yet, it isn't the only way. When our bodies, our minds, and our souls are clean, strong, pure, and healthy, we are able to be instruments—channels, really—for God's power to flow through us and work miracles.

This woman was "diseased with an issue of blood twelve years" (Matthew 9:20). Under the Mosaic law, an issue of blood referred to menstrual, postpartum, or other vaginal bleeding. The footnote to Matthew 5:25 indicates that an "issue of blood" was what we would call a *hemorrhage*, which means she was probably experiencing intense, abnormal vaginal bleeding. Today, she may have been diagnosed with menorrhagia (or another similar problem), which is heavy menstruation that causes enough blood loss to fill a pad at least every hour for several weeks and makes normal daily activities impossible. Under the Mosaic law, any woman with an issue of blood was considered *tuma*, or unclean, and was "put apart" for at least seven days. (See "Menstruation" on page 52.)

During this time, anything she lay on or sat on was considered unclean and people who touched one of those things would have to wash their clothes and bathe in water to become clean again. Also during this time, if any man was sexually intimate with her, he was also unclean for seven days and had to adhere to the same sort of isolation as the woman.[1] The Mosaic law also specified that if a woman had an issue of blood that lasted longer than seven days, then all the days of her issue were considered unclean and she must be treated as such (Leviticus 15:25). This means that this woman had been unclean for twelve years and that she had to live separated from others for all that time. Her unclean status would also have meant that she was unable to attend the temple or other worship services. She was estranged not only from the people around her but also from her God.

She had done all she knew to get better. She had "suffered many things of many physicians," and she had spent "all that she had, and was nothing bettered, but rather grew worse" (Mark 5:26). I can only imagine that after twelve years of constant blood loss, this woman must have been desperate. No one could help her; she knew she needed a miracle.

So when she heard that Jesus was near, she joined in the throng of people following Him while He made His way to Jairus's house. It is likely that with the amount of blood she had lost she also suffered from severe anemia; it probably took every ounce of her physical strength to even make it to Christ. I can just imagine her, exhausted and suffocated by the crowd, desperate to make it a little bit closer to Him. When she knew she couldn't

> ## "Thy faith hath made thee whole."

go any farther, she fell to her knees saying to herself, "If I may touch but his clothes, I shall be whole" (verse 28). She reached out her hand to briefly brush the fringe of His robe when He passed by.

That was all it took. She didn't have to speak to Him. She didn't have to tell Him what it was she needed. She just had to have enough faith to reach out to Him. For as soon as she touched Him, "the fountain of her blood was dried up," and she "felt in her body that she was healed of that plague" (verse 29). What a miracle. When she touched Him, Christ, "immediately knowing in himself that virtue had gone out of him," stopped and asked, "Who touched my clothes?" (verse 30). Peter, looking around Him, replied, "Master, the multitude throng thee and press thee, and sayest thou, Who touched me?" (Luke 8:45).

When she realized she was healed, this woman tried to hide back in the crowd. She was probably afraid because she had just touched Jesus and made Him, as well as everyone else in the crowd, ritually unclean. Yet, she knew that she had been healed, and she knew that Jesus knew it. When she saw that she could not hide from the Lord, she "came trembling" (verse 47), fell at Christ's feet, and bore testimony to the crowd of the miracle that had happened to her. Instead of scolding her for touching Him and therefore making Him unclean, Christ looked on her with compassion and told her, "Daughter, be of good comfort: thy faith hath made thee whole; go in peace" (verse 48).

This woman's story of faith is especially sweet to me. During the birth of my third child, my placenta failed to detach. After an hour, my midwife looked worried. It was looking like I might need a serious procedure done to get it safely out. My midwife asked my husband if he would give me a priesthood blessing. I remember when he laid his hands on my head, I felt doubtful that a priesthood blessing would be able to fix anything. So it was incredible to feel my body, not even a minute after my husband had finished his blessing, give a strong contraction. I felt all the membranes release and the placenta flow out of me in one complete piece. It was truly a miracle, and as soon as it happened I started to cry, not out of pain but out of gratitude. My heart was overwhelmed. I hadn't thought I had enough faith for something so miraculous happen to me.

Yet while I've pondered on this experience, I've come to see that God doesn't require us to have an unshakable, unwavering, moving-mountains kind of faith in order to work miracles in our lives. Sometimes, just like the woman with the issue of blood, all we need is enough faith to barely touch the hem of Christ's garment. If we can do that, then He can use His miraculous power on our behalf. His power and mercy know no bounds. All we have to do to access it is have enough faith to reach out and touch the hem—just the hem—of His robe.

# *Jesus's Sisters*

*"Is not this the carpenter's son? Is not his mother called Mary? And his brethren, James, and Joses, and Simon, and Judas? And his sisters, are they not all with us? Whence then hath this man all these things?"*

*Matthew 13:55–56*

*Matthew 1:25 tells us that* after Mary had conceived Jesus, Joseph "knew her not till she had brought forth her firstborn son." Apparently this newly married couple chose to abstain from intimacy until after Mary's pregnancy, showing Joseph's tender consideration and an impressive self-control. Yet, it appears that after Jesus's birth, Mary and Joseph had a normal relationship as husband and wife and they had children together. In fact, we know that Mary had at least six other children in addition to Jesus—four sons: James, Joses, Simon, and Judas; and at least two daughters. This is made evident for us when, during Christ's ministry, He returned to His hometown of Nazareth and shocked everyone with His teachings. These people, who had seen Him grow up and knew Him well, wondered, "Whence hath this man this wisdom, and these mighty works? Is not this the carpenter's son? Is not his mother called Mary? And his brethren, James, and Joses, and Simon, and Judas? And his sisters, are they not all with us? Whence then hath this man all these things?" (Matthew 13:54–56).

This verse not only gives us the names of Christ's brothers, but it also lets us know that He had sisters, the plural indicating at least two of them. The people stating that His sisters were "with us" may indicate that they were still living in Nazareth, either in Mary's household or perhaps in their husbands' households. We don't know anything else about Christ's sisters, but, given the evidence we have of Christ's respect for His mother, we can imagine that His sisters received the same type of love from Him. It is also sweet for me to think that these sisters would have been some of the first women Jesus interacted with in His life. They would have been His first introduction to womanhood, and I imagine that He learned much about how to love and understand women based on His interactions with them.

> *"And his sisters, are they not all with us?"*

# Herodias and Her Daughter

*"But when Herod's birthday was kept, the daughter of Herodias danced before them, and pleased Herod. Whereupon he promised with an oath to give her whatsoever she would ask. And she, being before instructed of her mother, said, Give me here John Baptist's head in a charger. . . . And he sent, and beheaded John in the prison. And his head was brought in a charger, and given to the damsel: and she brought it to her mother."*

Matthew 14:6–11

*Herodias was the daughter* of Aristobulus, the first son of Herod the Great. Her brother was Herod Agrippa, who was the king of Judea from AD 32–44.[1] When Herodias was old enough, she married her uncle Herod Phillip and, according to the historian Josephus, they had a daughter named Salome, "after whose birth Herodias . . . divorced herself from her husband while he was alive, and was married to Herod (Antipas), her husband's brother by the father's side, he was tetrarch of Galilee."[2] Herod Antipas was not only Herodias's brother-in-law but also another one of her uncles. (See "Herodian Family Tree" on page 217.)

John the Baptist had publicly criticized Herod Antipas for this marriage, saying, "It is not lawful for thee to have thy brother's wife" (Mark 6:18). Herod Antipas and Herodias, like most of the Herodian family, were Jews and would have been familiar with the law of Moses, which said, "Thou shalt not uncover the nakedness of thy brother's wife" (Leviticus 18:16) and "if a man shall take his brother's wife, it is an unclean thing" (Leviticus 20:21). Herod and Herodias knew that their marriage was not in harmony with correct teachings, but they didn't care—they wanted to be able to live and marry anyway they chose to.

Evidently, this criticism of their marriage made Herodias especially angry and she "had a quarrel against him [John the Baptist], and would have killed him; but she could not" (Mark 6:19). She did manage to have him thrown into prison, but Herod was afraid to kill John. Not only was he worried that the people, who all believed John was a prophet, would get angry, but he also knew that John was "a just man and an holy, and observed him . . . and heard him gladly" (verse 20). So despite Herodias's wishes, Herod didn't have John killed, but rather, to appease her, he kept him imprisoned.

On the day of his birthday, Herod threw a big feast in which Herodias's daughter danced before him and all "his lords, high captains, and chief estates of Galilee" (verses 21–22). The scriptures don't tell us the name of this daughter, but we know historically that Herodias had a daughter named Salome by her first husband. It is commonly believed that Salome was the one who danced for Herod. Oftentimes when this scene is displayed, we imagine Salome as an alluring teenager who charmed Herod with her sexually charged dance. Yet there is nothing in the Bible that indicates that Salome's dance was seductive. In fact, given the timeline of events, it is likely that Salome was a young girl around ten or eleven[3] and that her dance may have been more theatrical or gymnastic in nature than seductive.

This daughter's dance pleased Herod and the other men at the banquet. In his delight, he rashly swore an oath to her: "Whatsoever thou shalt ask of me, I will give it thee, unto the half of my kingdom" (verse 23). On hearing this, the young girl went to counsel with her mother about what she should ask for. This confidence in her mother gives us an idea of how much she trusted and relied on her. It also shows us that, at least on the part of the daughter, there was nothing premeditated or conniving about her dance.

In response to her daughter's inquiry, Herodias, still angry with John the Baptist, instructed her to ask Herod for the head of John the Baptist. It is appalling to me to think about the type of woman Herodias's anger and sin had turned her into. Her depravity went beyond the murder; she told her daughter to request that his head be brought to her—the daughter—on a charger, or large plate.

When Herod heard this, he was "was exceeding sorry" (verse 26). It must have been obvious to him that this girl was being used by her mother to seek the revenge on John the Baptist that he had denied. Yet, because he had sworn an oath in front of the entire party, he didn't feel like he could refuse her request. So he "sent, and beheaded John in the prison. And his head was brought in a charger, and given to the damsel: and she brought it to her mother" (Matthew 14:10–11). I can picture the horror that the daughter felt when she received her "gift." What young girl having a bloody decapitated head brought to her on a plate would not have been traumatized? Herodias's request was grotesque and cruel. Because she was eager to justify her sin and avenge her anger, she used her daughter in a conniving way. It is even sadder to me, though, that her daughter actually went through with her request, becoming partner to her mother's cruelty. It is an example to me of how powerful a mother's influence is on her daughter, for good or for bad.

Elder Ballard taught this truth when, in speaking to mothers, he said,

> We have a family friend who travels often with members of her extended family. Her primary observation after each trip is how much the young women behave like their mothers. If the mothers are thrifty, so are their daughters. If the mothers are modest, so are the girls. . . . Let me assure you that even when you think your daughter is not listening to a thing you say, she is still learning from you as she watches you to see if your actions match your words. As Ralph Waldo Emerson is believed to have said, "What you do speaks so loud that I cannot hear what you say."[4]

It is important for all women, mothers or not, to watch what messages they send to the young women in their lives. We may do or say things out of insecurity, anger, or judgment without realizing that we are sending negative or twisted messages to our young women. I had a friend who once, when I made a disparaging remark about my appearance, reminded me that how I felt about my body would greatly influence how my daughter felt about her own body. She told me, "You are your daughter's primary and strongest example of womanhood. If you want your daughter to love herself and be kind to her body, you must first love yourself and be kind to your body." My friend's reproach helped me see that my influence on my daughter was much more significant than I had realized. While she will always have her agency, much of how she sees the world and herself will be shaped by my example. She will value what I value, she will hold what she see me holding, and she will do what she has seen me do. Unlike Herodias, I hope that the messages I send my daughter will always be righteous and good.

*"And they that had eaten were about five thousand men, beside women and children."*

*Matthew 14:21*

*After Christ received the news* that His beloved cousin, John the Baptist, had been beheaded at Herodias's request (see "Herodias and Her Daughter" on page 63), He went into the wilderness to be alone. By this time it was nearly impossible for Christ to ever be alone; those who wanted to be taught or to have their sick healed were constantly following Him. Christ was in deep grieving, but still He was "moved with compassion" toward the multitude, and "he healed their sick" (Matthew 14:14). His example of serving, even in His difficult moments, is a reminder to me that the best way to deal with my sorrows is to forget myself and focus on others.

After Christ had ministered to the multitude, it was late and the disciples told Jesus to send everyone away to go find their own food. Instead, Christ told them, "They need not depart" (verse 16). When His disciples found five loaves and two fish, Christ blessed them and broke them into twelve baskets. With that bread, the disciples fed all the people who were gathered. Matthew tells us that there were five thousand men but that there were women and children in addition to that number. When I think about these women, some who had children with them, my heart is touched. At the moment they thought Christ was going to turn them away to seek food for themselves in the villages, He told them to stay and He fed them to overflowing. There was so much left over that the disciples needed twelve baskets to collect all the extra bread and fish.

The story of the feeding of the four thousand is very similar. Again, Christ had gone into a remote area and again He was followed by those that "were lame, blind, dumb, maimed, and many others" (Matthew 15:30). Jesus, seeing that they were hungry and that they had been following Him for three days with nothing to eat (think of the poor mothers with children), desired to feed them. This time His disciples found seven loaves and "a few little fishes" (verse 34). He again blessed them and broke them into pieces. The disciples took seven baskets and fed the four thousand men, plus all the women and children. When everyone was full, they again had extra in their baskets.

This miracle is a beautiful reminder that Christ's gospel and kingdom is one of abundance. So often Satan tries to deceive and frighten us by having us believe that this world is one of scarcity where we must compete for blessings and guard what we want and what we need. Christ, on the other hand, repeatedly shows us that God is a God of abundance and that He always has enough: enough mercy, enough love, enough forgiveness, and enough bread for everyone, women and children included.

*"They need not depart."*

# Syrophenician Woman and Her Young Daughter

*"For a certain woman, whose young daughter had an unclean spirit, heard of him, and came and fell at his feet: The woman was a Greek, a Syrophenician by nation; and she besought him that he would cast forth the devil out of her daughter. But Jesus said unto her, Let the children first be filled: for it is not meet to take the children's bread, and to cast it unto the dogs. And she answered and said unto him, Yes, Lord: yet the dogs under the table eat of the children's crumbs. And he said unto her, For this saying go thy way; the devil is gone out of thy daughter."*

*Mark 7:25–30*

**In an attempt to escape** the throngs of people who followed Him, Christ came to a house in the borders of Tyre and Sidon and "would that no man should come unto him" (Mark 7:24, footnote a; from Joseph Smith Translation). His disciples tried hard to help Him get some much-needed rest, keeping everyone away from Him. Even so, somehow a Greek woman from the Phoenician part of Syria came to Christ, begging Him to heal her young daughter, who was "grievously vexed with a devil" (Matthew 15:22).

At first, "he answered her not a word" (verse 23). Eventually this woman's supplications began to annoy Christ's disciples. They begged Him to send her away because "she crieth after us" (verse 23). Apparently, this woman just wouldn't give up. She had faith that Christ could help her and intended to keep asking until someone listened to her. Christ was trying to rest, but when He beheld those who sought Him, "he could not deny them; for he had compassion upon all men" (Mark 7:24, footnote a; from Joseph Smith Translation). Christ's compassion extended to this woman as well and, even though she was a Gentile, He agreed to speak with her.

> *"He had compassion upon all men."*

When she was brought in, she worshipped Him and begged, "Lord, help me" (Matthew 13:25). In response to her plea, Jesus gave what appears to be a very unkind answer: "Let the children of the kingdom first be filled: for it is not meet to take the children's bread, and to cast it unto the dogs" (Mark 7:27, footnote a; from Joseph Smith Translation). Some people have interpreted this passage to be an instance where Christ demonstrated racism or passed unjust judgment based on His cultural background. Calling Christ unkind, racist, or unjust does not mesh well with my understanding of the nature and character of Christ. We know that Christ had been moved with compassion to help this woman and that His attitude toward her was one of love. I think when Christ compared her to a dog and the Jews to children, He was trying to teach her an important truth.

This woman was a Gentile and Christ's mission at that time was to preach the gospel to the Jews. As He told His disciples, "I am not sent but unto the lost sheep of the house of Israel" (Matthew 15:24). We know that Christ would later go teach other sheep, like those in the Americas and in the spirit world, and that eventually the gospel would go to the Gentiles. Yet at this time, Christ's ministry was to first give the gospel to the Jews so that, as Christ taught, "the last shall be first, and the first last" (Matthew 20:16).[1]

Think of it this way.

Imagine that you are sitting at the table with your family. You have worked hard all day and have made the best meal you've ever made in your life. You happily set it before your children only to have them turn up their noses at it and refuse to eat it. You do everything you can to get your children to eat your wonderful meal, but no matter how hard you try they simply

won't eat it. What do you do with your wonderful meal? Will it just go to waste? You look down at your feet and your dogs look up at you with big eyes and eager tongues, ravenously hungry for anything you will give them. So you take your delicious meal, which your children rejected, and give it to them—because they are hungry for it.

Christ's statement to her was actually foreshadowing what would later happen. The Jews (the children) would reject the bread (the gospel) that Christ offered to them. After they rejected the gospel, it would be taken from them and sent to the Gentiles (the dogs), who would embrace it in great numbers because they were hungry and ready for it. This is what started to happen later in the New Testament when the gospel began to spread through the Gentile countries.

It also seems to me that when Christ compared this woman to a dog, He was acknowledging her personal hunger, her ravenous desire, for things of the Spirit. This woman was evidently ready for it, more so than many of the Jews that Christ was trying to teach. Yet Christ knew that the Jews had to be given their opportunity to accept "the bread" first before it would go to those who, like this woman, were ready and hungry for it.

It appears that the Syrophenician woman wasn't offended by His statement because she replied, "Truth, Lord," acknowledging that she understood what He had told her. But she then said something that seemed to impress Christ: "yet the dogs eat of the crumbs which fall from their masters' table" (Matthew 15:27). Christ had just told her that it was not yet time for the Gentiles to have the gospel, but she was undaunted. She had faith, powerful

---

The story of the Syrophenician woman reminds me of the woman mentioned in Christ's parable of the unjust steward. In Luke 18, He gave this parable:

> There was in a city a judge, which feared not God, neither regarded man; and there was a widow in that city; and she came unto him, saying, Avenge me of mine adversary. And he would not for a while: but afterward he said within himself, Though I fear not God, nor regard man; yet because this widow troubleth me, I will avenge her, lest by her continual coming she weary me. (verses 2–5)

Christ's intent with the parable of the unjust steward was to illustrate that if even an unjust judge who didn't fear the Lord would eventually listen to this woman because of her continual crying, how much more would a just and merciful God hear and respond to her cries?

Like the woman in this parable, the Syrophenician woman had a great need and she continually cried after the Lord to hear her. Yet unlike the unjust judge, the Lord did not give in to her because He was wearied with her cries, but because He was filled with love for her. Christ's actions toward the Syrophenician woman are a sweet testament to me that God hears and answers the prayers of His daughters and that He knows the desires of their hearts.

faith, that His power was strong enough that even the "crumbs" from His table would be enough to heal her daughter.

This faith impressed Christ and He told her, "O woman, great is thy faith: be it unto thee even as thou wilt" (verse 28). When she returned home, she found that her daughter was healed and that she had been "made whole" (verse 28) the very hour she had spoken with Christ.

Ultimately what was important was not her nationality but rather her faith. Even though she was a Gentile, she demonstrated incredible faith, and through that faith she was able to call on Christ's power to heal her sick daughter. Her faith was so strong that, perhaps like the Brother of Jared in the Book of Mormon, her request could not be withheld from her.[2] Her example shows me to never underestimate the power of my faith; it is a real power and has much more capacity to influence the world than I realize.

Her reference to crumbs reminds me of Christ's sermon where He taught that He was the "bread of life" and promised that anyone "that cometh to me shall never hunger; and he that believeth on me shall never thirst" (John 6:35). Christ promised in that sermon that anyone, male or female, who came unto Him and believed would be able to partake of the fullness of what He offered. Even though the Syrophenician woman may have asked for "crumbs," a lesser part of the gospel, that isn't what Christ gave her.

A friend of mine wrote,

> As I thought about this notion of crumbs, . . . I was reminded of a phrase that I love from S. Michael Wilcox: "What we must understand about our Father in Heaven is that He only gives bread; He never gives stones. He only gives fish; He never gives serpents. He only gives eggs; He never gives scorpions." And He never gives just crumbs. God gives the Bread of Life to all who seek it. The Master's table is spread, and we are all invited to partake. . . . There is no inequality in God's eternal plan. There is only Bread.[3]

Christ's gospel is not one of inequality or injustice. There is room enough—and bread enough—for all of God's children. While we may not always understand why God does things in the way or order that He does, we can have faith that God's blessings for all of His children are the same. No one gets stuck with "crumbs" because of their nationality, their gender, or their skin color. God's bread is available to all of His children and each of us can receive a fullness. Yet, like the Syrophenician woman demonstrated, receiving those blessings depends on our faith. If we are persistent in our petitions to God and strong in our faith He will always hear us and grant us the righteous desires of our hearts.

# Mary Magdalene

*"And it came to pass afterward, that he went throughout every city and village, preaching and shewing the glad tidings of the kingdom of God: and the twelve were with him, and certain women, which had been healed of evil spirits and infirmities, Mary called Magdalene, out of whom went seven devils."*

*Luke 8:1–2*

**Mary Magdalene is one of the most** intriguing women in the New Testament. This is because she is one of the most frequently mentioned women, yet we know very few details about who she really was or what her role was in Christ's life. In Luke 8:2, it says that she was "Mary called Magdalene." Magdala was a coastal city in Galilee and it is likely that the name Magdalene indicated that she was from there. Also, in Hebrew the word *Magdala* means "tower," and it is possible that "Magdalene" was a nickname meaning "tower of strength."[1] Christ often gave His closest disciples symbolic nicknames, like Simon who was "called Peter" (Matthew 4:18). The word *Peter* meant "rock" and was symbolic not only of his personality but also of his future leadership in the Church. It is interesting to think that perhaps, like He did for Peter, Christ also gave Mary a nickname. I can envision a situation in which Christ, playing off the name of her hometown, gave her the name Magdalene, or in other words, "Mary, a tower of strength."

Mary was certainly a tower of strength and steadiness in Christ's life. She traveled with Him while He taught and her name is always listed first when given in conjunction with other female disciples, indicating that she held some kind of position of leadership or seniority among them. She was also one of the only disciples to never leave Christ during His last days. She was present at the cross and stood with Christ's mother and aunt while they watched Him take His final breaths. After His death, she, along with the "other Mary" (see "Mary, the Mother of James and Joses" on page 139), followed Christ's body to the tomb and watched as it was laid out. They sat and guarded over the tomb for as long as they possibly could before they had to return home to keep the Sabbath. It was she, along with several other women, who came as early to the tomb as they could. And it was to Mary that Christ first appeared after His Resurrection, making her the first witness of this miraculous event. All these glimpses of Mary Magdalene paint for us a picture of a woman whose devotion and love for Christ surpassed that of all His other disciples. She was certainly an important woman in His life.

Yet what might be the most intriguing thing about Mary Magdalene is that when Luke introduces her to us, he tells us that she was among the "certain women, which had been healed of evil spirits and infirmities" (Luke 8:2). Specifically, he tells us that Christ had cast seven devils out of her. Throughout His ministry, Christ repeatedly cast devils out of people. In Matthew 8:16, we read that "they brought unto him many that were possessed with devils: and he cast out the spirits with his word, and healed all that were sick."

Here and elsewhere in scriptures, those who were possessed by devils were often classified among the sick or among those having mental infirmities. For example, Saul had "an evil spirit which was not of God" (1 Samuel 16:15, footnote a; from Joseph Smith Translation) that tormented his mind and made

> "Mary, a tower of strength."

him act out of character. Only the sound of soothing music, specifically David's harp, helped calm and sooth his troubled mind (verse 23). The man out of whom Christ cast a "legion" of devils was so infirm in mind that he could not be bound with chains to keep him from wandering in the mountains. After he was healed by Christ, the people were astonished

to see him clothed and "in his right mind" (Mark 5:1–15).

While we don't know the details of Mary Magdalene's infirmity, we might deduce based on what we know of the others whom Christ healed from evil spirits that she was tormented with some sort of mental infirmity.[2] The fact that she had seven devils cast out of her suggests that her infirmity may have been severe.

It is interesting to me that sometimes God's greatest and strongest servants struggle the most with feelings of darkness and hopelessness. Elder Jeffery R. Holland, in speaking about his own struggle with depression, said that he, and many others, had "taken courage from those who, in the words of the Prophet Joseph, 'search[ed] . . . and contemplate[d] the darkest abyss' and persevered through it—not the least of whom were Abraham Lincoln, Winston Churchill, and Elder George Albert Smith, the latter being one of the most gentle and Christlike men of our dispensation."[3] It seems like those who are close to the Spirit can be targeted heavily by Satan and his forces.

A dear friend of mine, who is one of the most spiritually-minded people I know, struggled with severe depression during and after her fourth pregnancy. She wrote this about her experience:

> Depression felt like hell—like my mind and body had been literally hijacked by demons. I was bombarded with waves of oppressive darkness and misery, but it didn't make any sense to me. I was attending church, reading my scriptures, exercising regularly, eating more healthy foods than I had ever eaten before, I had an amazing husband and three wonderful children, so why was I so ridiculously miserable?

I wrote in my journal a lot during that difficult time. One of those therapeutic entries reads:

> And now I am losing it—again. It seems it doesn't matter how many epiphanies I have, how many priesthood blessings, how many times God reassures me. The demons, anger, and overwhelming gloom just keep coming back. They won't give me more than the most brief rest. . . .

### OTHER WOMEN HEALED OF EVIL SPIRITS AND DEVILS

In addition to Mary Magdalene, two women named Joanna and Susanna were also listed as being among the women whom Jesus Christ had healed from "evil spirits and infirmities" (Luke 8:2–3). We can assume that there were also many other women who had been healed by Christ whose identities we do not know. There are three other accounts of women being healed from evil spirits in the New Testament: the young daughter of the Syrophenician woman, the woman with a spirit of infirmity, and the damsel possessed with a spirit who was healed by Paul.

During this time, I became quite reclusive. I rarely left the house except to go to church or grocery shopping. I excused myself from all but the most necessary social gatherings or activities. I felt guilty and horrible. . . . In my darkest moments, when it seemed that my cries toward heaven were going unheard, I even found myself questioning the existence of God.[4]

While every experience is unique, my friend's experience is not uncommon for those who struggle with depression or other mental illnesses. Her feelings about her body and mind being "hijacked by demons" may have been similar to what Mary Magdalene experienced when she was tormented by the seven devils. Because I have watched my friend struggle through her depression, I can better understand what type of challenges Mary Magdalene may have had and how powerful it would have been to see her healed. I can only imagine the joy she, and all those who loved her, must have felt to finally have those bands of darkness taken from her mind and heart.

The story of Mary Magdalene gives me great hope. She reminds me that there is no sickness—physical or mental—that Christ cannot heal. As Elder Holland reminded us,

> Whatever your struggle, my brothers and sisters . . . [t]rust in God. Hold on in His love. Know that one day the dawn will break brightly and all shadows of mortality will flee. Though we may feel we are "like a broken vessel," as the Psalmist says,

we must remember, that vessel is in the hands of the divine potter. Broken minds can be healed just the way broken bones and broken hearts are healed. While God is at work making those repairs, the rest of us can help by being merciful, nonjudgmental, and kind.[5]

It is also powerful to remember that Christ, the most perfect of all, "descended below them all" (D&C 122:8). In His hours in the Garden, Christ felt all our misery. He felt the chains of darkness wrap around Him and felt the despairing gloom, anger, and fear that threatened to overcome His power. Yet the glory of His Atonement is that He was not overcome by the darkness; He found a way out. Consequently, His message to each of us is "come, follow me" (Luke 18:22). He invites us to turn toward Him and follow Him because He, and only He, knows the way out—out of sin, out of darkness, and out of despair.

It gives me hope to know that Mary Magdalene, who was burdened with the darkness and despair of devils, was able to shake those bonds and become, like her name says, "a tower of strength." She was truly a remarkable woman and stands as a witness to all those who struggle that Christ's power can overcome anything. He is the ultimate healer.

# The *Marys* in the New Testament

*The name Mary was very popular* in first-century Palestine. It is the Greek version of the name Miriam. Miriam was the older sister of Moses and was an important role model for Jewish women. In the New Testament, seven women are named Mary, and the name appears in fifty-one passages.[1] This repetition can make it very difficult to keep track of which Mary is which. I have listed them below by how frequently they are mentioned in the New Testament.

## Mary, the mother of Christ:

She is the easiest Mary to keep track of because her role in Christ's life was enormous and her influence continued throughout His ministry. She is also the most frequently mentioned woman in the New Testament. Prophets knew Mary's name nearly two hundred years before she was born. In the Book of Mormon, Nephi, King Benjamin, and Alma all testified that Christ would be born of a woman named Mary. This makes her the only woman in all of scripture whose name was foretold before her birth, and it places her among a very small group of men whose names were known before their births: Noah, Aaron, Moses, John the Baptist, Jesus Christ, and Joseph Smith.[2]

## Mary Magdalene:

She was one of the women who followed Christ and ministered to Him of her substance. Christ healed her from seven devils, and she was a leader among Christ's disciples. She figures prominently in the story of the Crucifixion and Resurrection. She was among the women who found the empty tomb and was the first person Christ appeared to after His Resurrection. (See "Mary Magdalene" on page 75.)

## Mary of Bethany:

She and her sister Martha were disciples of Christ and they often hosted and fed Him. She sat at Christ's feet and was praised by Him for choosing "the good part" (Luke 10:42). She had a brother named Lazarus, who was raised from the dead by Christ. She anointed Christ's head and feet before His death. (See "Mary of Bethany" on page 117.)

## Mary, the mother of James and Joses:

She is sometimes called "the other Mary" (Matthew 27:61; 28:1). She was another of Christ's female disciples and was at both the cross and the empty tomb. She was the mother of two sons: James the less and Joses, the name of which is the Greek form of Joseph. Tradition often identifies "James the less" (Mark 15:40) as the same "James the son of Alphaeus," who is mentioned as being one of the Twelve Apostles (Acts 1:13). If this is correct, we might suppose that he was called "the less" to differentiate him from another Apostle, James the son of Zebedee, perhaps because he was the shorter or the younger of the two. It is interesting to note that Mary, the mother of Christ, also had two sons named James and Joses (Mark 6:3). It is possible that this is the same woman. If that is the case, it does seem strange that the writers didn't mention she was Christ's mother, making me think that they must be two different women.

## Mary, the wife of Cleophas:

She is mentioned among the women who were at the cross and stood alongside Christ's mother and family while He was crucified. (See "Mary, the Wife of Cleophas" on page 141.)

## Mary, the mother of John Mark:

She was an early Christian woman in Jerusalem whose home was where the Christians gathered to pray for Peter while he was in jail. (See "Mary, the Mother of John Mark" on page 177.)

## Mary of Rome:

She was one of the women living in Rome whom Paul greeted at the close of his epistle to the Romans.

Marys in the New Testament

| | Matthew | Mark | Luke | John | Remainder of New Testament |
|---|---|---|---|---|---|
| Mary the mother of Jesus Christ | 1:16, 18–25; 2:11, 13–14, 20–21; 12:46–50; 13:55 | 3:31–35; 6:3 | 1:26–56; 2:5–8, 16, 19, 22, 27, 34–35, 43–51; 8:19–20 | 2:1–5, 12; 6:42; 19:25–27 | Acts 1:14; Galatians 4:4 |
| Mary Magdalene | 27:57, 61; 28:1–10 | 15:40–41, 47; 16:1–8, 9–11 | 8:2–3; 24:1–11, 22–24 | 19:25; 20:1–3, 11–18 | |
| Mary of Bethany | | | 10:37–42 | 11:1–5, 17–20, 28–34, 39–45; 12:3–9 | |
| Mary the mother of James and Joses | 27:55–56, 61; 28:1–10 (Matthew calls her "the other Mary") | 15:40–41, 47; 16:1–8 | 24:1–11 | | |
| Mary the wife of Cleophas | | | | 19:25 | |
| Mary the mother of John Mark | | | | | Acts 12:12 |
| Mary of Rome | | | | | Romans 16: 6 |

# Susanna and the Unnamed Women Who Followed Christ

*"And Joanna the wife of Chuza Herod's steward, and Susanna, and many others, which ministered unto him of their substance."*

*Luke 8:3*

**From the very beginning** of His ministry, Christ invited women to join with Him and be full participants in His work. In Luke 14, we read how Jesus taught about discipleship: "If any man come to me, and hate not his father, and mother, and wife, and children, and brethren, and sisters, yea, and his own life also, he cannot be my disciple" (verse 26). Christ was teaching them that to be His disciples, they must be willing to put Him first and foremost in their lives, even above their own lives.

It is important to notice that the Joseph Smith Translation of this verse adds "or husband" to the list of those we should be willing to sacrifice for Christ's sake. In the Joseph Smith Translation of the Bible, the verse reads like this:

If any man come to me, and hate not his father, and mother, and wife, and children, and brethren, and sisters, *or husband*, yea and his own life also; or in other words, is afraid to lay down his life for my sake, he cannot be my disciple. (Luke 14:26, footnote b; from Joseph Smith Translation; italics added)

This inspired translation of the verse makes it clear that Christ was not only speaking to men, but that His message of discipleship was also for women. He invited women to join with Him in the work of salvation and to follow Him.

And they did, in droves. We know from the scriptures that there were many women who followed Jesus and "ministered unto him of their substance" (Luke 8:3). Susanna was one

> *"Healed of evil spirits and infirmities."*

of these women, alongside Mary Magdalene (see "Mary Magdalene" on page 75), Joanna (see "Joanna" on page 85), and other "certain women, which had been healed of evil spirits and infirmities" (verse 2). We don't know the details of how

Christ healed Susanna, but we do know that afterward she joined those who traveled with Jesus.

Christ encouraged His Apostles to preach the gospel, taking nothing "save a staff only; no scrip, no bread, no money in their purse" (Mark 6:8), and it is likely that He too traveled in relative poverty. He probably relied upon the generosity and kindness of others for His physical needs like clothing, food, and shelter. The scriptures indicate that many times His physical needs were met by the women who traveled with Him and whom He met on His journeys. These women fed Him, clothed Him, sheltered Him, provided for His needs, and gave freely of what they had to Him.

There are only a few women who are named or mentioned in the New Testament as following or ministering to Jesus. Yet there were probably dozens of other women who also accepted Christ's invitation to be a disciple and who followed Him while He traveled. Luke wrote that when Christ carried His cross to Golgotha, there was "a great company of people, and of women, which also bewailed and lamented him" (Luke 23:27). And Matthew wrote that by the cross "many women were there beholding afar off, which followed Jesus from Galilee" (Matthew 27:55). We know very little about Susanna and these other women who followed Christ, but we can assume that they demonstrated great courage, faith, and humility while they followed the Master.

# Joanna

*"And Joanna the wife of Chuza Herod's steward, and Susanna, and many others, which ministered unto him of their substance."*
*Luke 8:3*

*Joanna left a life of wealth* and prestige to follow Jesus. The scriptures tell us that she was "the wife of Chuza," the steward of Herod Antipas. Chuza's title in Greek is the word *epitropos* and refers to someone who managed a household or an estate.[1] Herod Antipas was the ruler of Galilee and Chuza was probably one of Herod's head servants and may have managed the affairs of his household or his estate. With Chuza holding this position, he and Joanna probably lived in comfort in the palace and would have been intimate with Herod's family and associates.

We don't know when Joanna was first introduced to Christianity, but we do know that at some point Christ healed her from some sort of mental or physical disability. She is listed in Luke 8:2–3 among those women whom Christ had "healed of evil spirits and infirmities" and who traveled with Him while He preached, "ministering" to Him of their substance. (See "Susanna and the Unnamed Women Who Followed Christ" on page 83.) She is also mentioned in Luke 24:10 as being among the women who were at the empty tomb and who returned to bear witness of His Resurrection. Joanna, as a woman of wealth, may have been a generous benefactor of Christ and His mission. Some scholars even speculate that her presence among Christ's followers may explain why they were able to afford an "upper room" for the last supper and expensive ointments and herbs for Christ's embalming.[2]

Joanna's change from a woman of influence and worldly prestige to one who humbly followed Christ is remarkable. It shows us that her desires were firmly rooted not upon things of this life but upon Christ. As Elder Dallin H. Oaks taught that "desires dictate our priorities, priorities shape our choices, and choices determine our actions." He also taught, "The desires we act on determine our changing, our achieving, and our becoming."[3] Joanna's desire to follow Christ shaped her life and showed remarkable courage and strength. Jeni and Richard Holzapefel wrote this about Joanna's courage: "She always remained in danger as a former member of the royal court who now was associating with Jesus, considered by Herod as a traitor to the state. Nicodemus came by night, but Joanna stood with Jesus in broad daylight—at the cross and at the tomb."[4] Joanna was a woman who was not afraid to stand as a witness of Jesus Christ at all times, in all things, and in all places.

> *"Joanna stood with Jesus in broad daylight."*

# Martha

"Now it came to pass, as they went, that he entered into a certain village: and a certain woman named Martha received him into her house. And she had a sister called Mary, which also sat at Jesus' feet, and heard his word. But Martha was cumbered about much serving, and came to him, and said, Lord, dost thou not care that my sister hath left me to serve alone? bid her therefore that she help me. And Jesus answered and said unto her, Martha, Martha, thou art careful and troubled about many things: but one thing is needful: and Mary hath chosen that good part, which shall not be taken away from her."

*Luke 10:38–42*

*Martha is perhaps one of the most* unfairly portrayed women in all of the New Testament. She had the unfortunate circumstance to be "cumbered about much serving" (verse 40) while her sister Mary chose "that good part" (verse 42) by sitting at the Savior's feet. For this apparent mistake, Martha is forever being held up as the example of what not to do: get so caught up in physical things that you neglect the things of the spirit. Poor Martha.

Yet there is one little word that helps illuminate our understanding of Martha. In Luke 10, where we read the story of Mary and Martha, it says, speaking of Martha, "And she had a sister called Mary, which *also* sat as Jesus' feet, and heard his word" (verse 39; italics added). That *also* tells us volumes about Martha. Mary wasn't the good woman and Martha the bad woman; Mary was simply following her sister's example and was also sitting at Christ's feet and learning His word.

Evidence of Martha's discipleship is evident throughout the New Testament. Whenever she appears in scripture, Martha is ministering, serving, following, teaching, and bearing testimony. In fact, Martha gave what is perhaps one of the most plain and bold testimonies of Christ given in the New Testament. After the death of her brother Lazarus, Christ came to her and asked her if she believed that "whosoever

> ## "I believe that thou art the Christ."

liveth and believeth in me shall never die" (John 11:26). She answered Him, "Yea, Lord: I believe that thou art the Christ, the Son of God, which should come into the world" (verse 27).

Martha was a strong woman of faith and we can assume that she had modeled for her sister, Mary, a pattern of discipleship. Yet, like all good women, she had a moment where she found herself overwhelmed by everything that was expected of her. After all, it was her house that Christ was eating at and she felt the responsibility for caring and providing for everyone's physical needs. As President Julie B. Beck said, "We like to talk about Martha as the bad woman and Mary as the good woman, but we know that Martha is the one who invited the Savior into her home—it was her home. Aren't we told to do that? Isn't that a good thing? And some of you even have little plaques that say, 'Christ is the center of our home.' That was Martha. Then she was serving Him, and isn't that a good thing?"[1]

Christ's statement to Martha that Mary was choosing "that good part" was not a reprimand but rather an invitation. He was extending to both Mary and Martha an invitation to do more than fulfill physical needs but to be involved in fulfilling the spiritual needs of God's children.

President Julie B. Beck points this out as the moment that Christ organized the ancient equivalent of the Relief Society. In her remarks at a BYU women's conference, she explained, "Relief Society is a restoration or a bringing back of an ancient pattern and practice of discipleship." Then she explained how one of the first times in the scriptures where we see Christ inviting women to be part of His work is in Luke 10. This is the chapter where Christ organized His Church: First He called His Apostles and outlined their responsibilities. Then the Seventy were called and sent out to share the gospel, cast out devils, and perform miracles. In the same chapter, Christ gave the parable of the good Samaritan and taught that when we serve the Lord with all our hearts and love our neighbors as ourselves, we are qualifying for eternal life. And then, as Sister Beck stated, "Immediately following that is this great, misunderstood story of Mary and Martha. . . . [T]he Savior took this opportunity to invite both Mary and Martha to be official participants in His work of discipleship and He said that this was the 'good part.' It was the needful part that would never be taken away from them. When you read that with a spiritual understanding, . . . you will learn that this was the Savior inviting them officially to be part of His work, not to be bystanders, but to be included in what He wanted to accomplish." Sister Beck then stated, "The Lord can't build His kingdom without Relief Society."[2]

Mary and Martha, like the modern-day women who helped establish the Relief Society in Nauvoo, were being invited by Christ to become full participants in God's work and to be, as Joseph Smith taught, organized "under the priesthood and after the manner of the priesthood."[3] He was inviting them not to stop serving but to use their talents to serve in an even higher capacity. President Lorenzo Snow, in speaking to a group of Relief Society sisters, said, "You have ever been found at the side of the Priesthood, ready to strengthen their hands and to do your part in helping to advance the interests of the kingdom of God."[4] Relief Society is a crucial part of the Lord's Church, and whenever the priesthood has been on this earth, so has God's organization for women. This story of Mary and Martha helps us see that Christ's organization of His Church was only complete once the women were invited and organized into His work.

When Christ said that "one thing is needful" (Luke 10:42), He used the Greek word *heis*. It means "one" and is the same word that Christ used to describe His relationship with His Father: "That they all may be one; as thou, Father, art in me, and I in thee, that they also may be one in us" (John 17:21). We might reread the passage in Luke 10:41 as "oneness with Christ, as He is one with God, is needful," and this oneness is "the good part" that will never be taken away.

It is also beautiful to note that in the dedicatory prayer of the Kirtland Temple, Joseph Smith prayed that the Saints would "be prepared to obtain every needful thing" (D&C 109:15). Those words, similar to the ones used in the story of Mary and Martha, help us glimpse what Christ was extending to them: an invitation to make covenants and to be recipients of all the blessings God has for His children—promises that women can still receive today.

Understanding the story of Martha and Mary helps us better understand the importance of women in God's kingdom and the work that women are called to do in Relief Society. As President Beck said, "This restored pattern of discipleship we have in Relief Society provides an alignment for God's daughters with His purpose and helps us learn our unique duties and responsibilities. It also unifies us with men who hold the priesthood in the Lord's work."[5] When we understand that Relief Society is an integral part of God's work and that God's Church cannot be organized without it, we understand that women's voices, ideas, and contributions are important. Christ's Church was never designed to work without them. From the very start, Christ included women and offered them a place in His work: a place for them to learn, to serve, and to receive all the blessings that God has prepared for all of His children, "that good part" that will never be taken away from them.

# Certain Woman
## of the Company

*"And it came to pass, as he spake these things, a certain woman of the company lifted up her voice, and said unto him, Blessed is the womb that bare thee, and the paps which thou hast sucked. But he said, Yea rather, blessed are they that hear the word of God, and keep it."*

Luke 11:27–28

**This woman was among a company** of people who had just witnessed Christ cast a devil out of a dumb man and heard Him bear testimony that a "house divided against a house falleth" (Luke 11:17). Evidently she was so overcome by what Christ was teaching that she lifted up her voice and called out to Him, "Blessed is the womb that bare thee, and that paps which thou hast sucked" (verse 27). This exclamation, while praising Jesus, was an exuberant recognition of His mother, Mary. This woman's joy went so far that she not only rejoiced in Jesus but also recognized and gave gratitude for the woman who nurtured and taught such a man as Jesus Christ.

In response to this praise of His mother, Christ responded to her, "Yea rather, blessed are they that hear the word of God, and keep it" (verse 28). The full Joseph Smith Translation gives important clarity to this verse. The two verses read like this:

> And it came to pass, as he spake these things, a certain woman of the company, lifted up her voice, and said unto him, Blessed is the womb which bare thee, and the paps which thou has sucked. And he said, Yea, *and* blessed are all they who hear the word of God, and keep it.[1]

This version removes the word *rather* and simply states that "Yea," the womb that bore Him and the paps that suckled Him were blessed. It is just one word, but it makes a big difference in the way we understand what Jesus was saying. The word *rather* makes it sound like Jesus was contradicting this woman's blessing, saying, "Yes, but," much like a teacher might when someone in class blurts out the wrong answer. It is significant to me that Joseph Smith was instructed to remove the word *rather* in this verse, making it clear that Mary's womb and her breasts were blessed and that Jesus recognized that, with no qualifications.

This version also included the word *and*, indicating that Christ was making a comparison between the blessedness of the womb and the paps, and the blessedness of "they who hear the word of God." One of the most pervasive themes that Christ used in His teachings was that of childbirth. He even used it to describe the Atonement and Resurrection.[2] As Katherine H. Shirt wrote,

> It is this image of Christ's spiritual suffering to bring forth spiritual life, as a woman suffers physically to bring forth physical life, that reverberates throughout the scriptures. "Inasmuch as ye were born into the world by water, and blood, and the spirit, which I have made, and so became of dust a living soul," God tells Adam, as recorded in the book of Moses, "Even so ye must be born again into the kingdom of heaven, of water, and of the Spirit, and be cleansed by blood, even the blood of mine Only Begotten; that ye might be sanctified from all sin, and enjoy the words of eternal life in this world, and eternal life in the world to come." King Benjamin declares that because the hearts of his people have been changed through faith in Christ, they have become "the children of Christ, his sons, and his daughters." King Benjamin uses dual imagery. Christ has spiritually begotten them—in other words, he has become their father—and they are born of him, in essence making him their mother as well.[3]

Just as we are born into the world through the body and sacrifice of a woman, we must be born in God's kingdom through the body and sacrifice of Jesus Christ. And like a mother nurses and nourishes her child with her breast, Christ teaches us that if we will come unto Him, He will nourish us with His love, or as Isaiah said, "milk without money and without price." (Isaiah 55:1).

When Christ responded to the statement by the woman of the company about the sacredness of His mother's body, He publicly and unabashedly acknowledged her influence and power. He truly held His mother is the highest regard and understood the sacred nature of her body, and consequently of all women's bodies. He understood that the sacrifice He would make to bring eternal life to God's children was similar to the sacrifice His mother had made to give Him mortal life. That was a sacrifice that He didn't dismiss lightly but rather held in the highest esteem. It is a reminder that we too must respect and value the incredible power that women have to give and nurture life.

# Motherhood

Motherhood was an important job in New Testament times. Jewish lineage was determined through the mother's bloodline; people were only considered Jewish if their mothers were Jewish. This may be one of the reasons that Matthew included examples of women in Jesus's genealogy. Women's participation in public forums was limited, but they had significant influence in the home. Despite how a woman may have been treated elsewhere, in the home, a mother often ruled and was loved, trusted, and respected by her husband, children, and servants. Mothers did important physical and spiritual work. Mothers were entirely responsible for the education of their daughters and for the education of their sons until they were old enough to join in men's work. Paul wrote that Timothy had "from a child . . . known the holy scriptures" (2 Timothy 3:15), an accomplishment that can probably be attributed to the influence of his mother, Eunice, and grandmother, Lois.[5]

The Book of Proverbs gives a tribute to a virtuous wife and mother and shows the type of respect she would have received from her family: "The heart of her husband doth safely trust in her. . . . She openeth her mouth with wisdom. . . . Her children arise up, and call her blessed; her husband also, and he praiseth her" (Proverbs 31:11, 26, 28).

A mother was also entitled to expect that her children would care for her in her widowhood or old age. Christ frequently taught that it was important to "honour thy father and thy mother" (Mark 7:10). He specifically addressed this teaching to the Pharisees, chastising them for the practice of dedicating all their property to the temple, making it *corban*, or dedicated to God, which seemed noble but in practice often left elderly parents without the financial support they deserved.[41] Christ rebuked the Pharisees, saying, "For Moses said, Honour thy father and thy mother. . . . But ye say, If a man shall say to his father or mother, It is Corban, that is to say, a gift, . . . he shall be free. And ye suffer him no more to do ought for his father or his mother; making the word of God of none effect through your tradition" (verses 10–13).

In Christ's eyes, duty to parents took precedence over other obligations or desires. Christ Himself demonstrated this when He hung on the cross and His last thoughts were for the welfare of His mother. Since there is no mention of Joseph, we can speculate that Mary was probably a widow by then. The death of her oldest son would have put her in a hard situation. Perhaps it was this knowledge that prompted Jesus to tell John, His beloved disciple, "Behold thy mother!" (John 19:27), after which John took Mary into his own home to live. It was only after Jesus had attended to the needs of His mother that "all things were now accomplished" (verse 28) and He "gave up the ghost" (verse 30). Even in His last moments on the earth, Christ's thoughts were focused on His mother and her welfare.

# *Woman* with a Spirit of Infirmity

*"And, behold, there was a woman which had a spirit of infirmity eighteen years, and was bowed together, and could in no wise lift up herself. And when Jesus saw her, he called her to him, and said unto her, Woman, thou art loosed from thine infirmity. And he laid his hands on her: and immediately she was made straight, and glorified God."*

*Luke 13:11–13*

*Christ saw this woman* while He was teaching in one of the synagogues on the Sabbath. She had suffered with "a spirit of infirmity" for eighteen years (verse 11). Christ would later specify that "Satan hath bound" her (verse 16), indicating that the root of her infirmity was caused by an evil spirit or a similar influence. We don't know exactly what her physical ailment was or how she had gotten it, but it caused her body to contort so that she was "bowed together, and could in no wise lift up herself" (Luke 13:11).

When Christ saw her, He "called her to him" (verse 12). There are few instances when Christ singled someone out for a blessing without them first requesting it. He must have seen or sensed something in this woman that compelled Him to bless her. Even the fact that He saw her was remarkable because in Jewish synagogues the men and the women sat separately. Sometimes the women even sat behind a screen or a veil so that they could not be seen by the men. It is also likely

> *"Thou art loosed from thine infirmity."*

that this woman was used to people looking away from her, embarrassed by her condition. It surely must have surprised this woman, as well as those around her, when Christ took notice of her.

After she came over to Him, Christ told her, "Woman, thou art loosed from thine infirmity" (verse 12). He laid His hands upon her and instantly she was "made straight" (verse 13) and began to praise God. This healing made the ruler of the synagogue angry because Christ had healed her on the Sabbath day. He may also have been upset that Christ had violated the divisions between men and women in the synagogue. In response to this anger, Christ rebuked the Jews for thinking more of their animals than they did of this crippled woman. He told them, "Thou hypocrite, doth not each one of you on the sabbath loose his ox or his ass from the stall, and lead him away to watering? And ought not this woman, being a daughter of Abraham . . . be loosed from this bond on the sabbath day?" (verses 15–16).

Christ's ability to see this woman and His remark to the Jews that she deserved to be healed because she was a "daughter of Abraham" remind me of the story of Hagar in Genesis 16 in the Old Testament. After a visitation by angel, Hagar gave God a name. She called Him "Thou God seest me" (verse 13), or in other words, "The God that sees me." This is a testimony that she knew that God was aware of her, that He heard her cries, and that He could literally see her.

In a similar way, Christ's ability to see this Jewish woman was a testament to her, and to the Jews, that God is aware of women. A reminder that there is not a woman on this earth who cries out in pain, disappointment, fear, or despair whose voice He does not hear and whose trials He does not see. Christ's actions toward this woman affirmed the worth of women and reminded the Jews that God sees women.

# Woman *Taken in Adultery*

*"And the scribes and Pharisees brought unto him a woman taken in adultery. . . . [H]e lifted up himself, and said unto them, He that is without sin among you, let him first cast a stone at her. . . . When Jesus had lifted up himself, and saw none but the woman, he said unto her, Woman, where are those thine accusers? hath no man condemned thee? She said, No man, Lord. And Jesus said unto her, Neither do I condemn thee: go, and sin no more."*

*John 8:3–11*

**One day Jesus went** "early in the morning" (John 8:2) to the temple. When the people saw Him, they "came unto him; and he sat down, and taught them" (verse 2).[1] While He was teaching, a group of Pharisees came into the temple, carrying with them a woman who had been caught "in the very act" (verse 4) of adultery. The Mosaic law was very harsh on women who were caught, or even suspected of, being adulterous.

The book of Numbers describes a test that a man who had the "spirit of jealousy" (Numbers 5:14) could submit his wife to if he suspected that she had been unfaithful to him. The process often went something like this:

[The husband] brought her to the temple to undergo a test or an ordeal to prove her innocence. . . . In the temple, "before the Lord"—that is, before the altar—she was obliged to drink a potentially poisonous draught composed largely of water, dirt from the temple floor, and the ink scratched from a parchment containing a curse. . . . The drink would supposedly have no effect if she was innocent. If she was guilty, however, her belly would swell and her thigh rot.[2]

Before a woman was subjected to this ordeal, she was often publicly humiliated as well. One scholar described the treatment like this, "The priest seized her garments and tore them down to the waist so as to expose her breasts. . . . The priest then unloosed her hair. . . . All jewelry was removed and she was bound tight (around the breasts) with a cord. . . . Anyone could examine her at this point. . . . Some rabbis believed that all the women in the Court of Women at the time were required to look at her as some type of object lesson. After this degrading experience the priest offered her the bitter water drink . . . and waited for the sign."[3]

A man could submit his wife to this ordeal if he even just suspected that she had been unfaithful to him, whereas a woman could do nothing if she knew her husband had been unfaithful.[4] If this was how a woman who was only suspected of adultery was treated, I can imagine that the treatment given

a woman who was "taken in the very act" must have been especially harsh.

Perhaps this woman was naked from the waist down, tied with a cord, and forced to stand in the middle of the temple for all to see. It seems that since there was no doubt of her guilt, the usual test of bitter water was being forgone and she was

> *"Neither do I condemn thee: go, and sin no more"*

already condemned to die. It was in this sad and humiliating state that she was brought before Jesus.

It is powerful to me that when faced with this woman's humiliation, Christ wrote on the ground with His finger. We don't know what He wrote or why He wrote it, but it lets us know that when everyone else's eyes might have been staring at this woman in her nakedness, Christ kept His eyes averted. In a gesture of consideration for her, He "wrote on the ground, as though he heard them not" (John 8:6) instead of staring at her.

The Pharisees, whose intent in bringing her before Jesus was to snare Him into saying something wrong, continued to press Him. Finally Jesus "lifted up himself" and told them, "He that is without sin among you, let him first cast a stone at her" (verse 7). After saying these words, Jesus sat down and began to write on the ground again.

The power and wisdom of His words are astounding. Christ knew that whatever type of judgment He pronounced upon this poor woman, the Pharisees would argue that He had been unjust and would use His answer against Him. So instead, Jesus turned the tables on them. He challenged them to, instead of judging the woman, judge themselves. He told them to examine their own hearts and search their own souls to see if they were any better off than this poor sinful woman. When the Pharisees and people gathered in the temple were faced with this type of inward reflection, Jesus's challenge pricked their hearts. They were "convicted by their own conscience" and they all left until there were only Jesus and the woman "standing in the midst" (verse 9).

Jesus's invitation for the Pharisees to be their own judges reminds me of how, when we as modern-day members of the Church apply for a temple recommend, the only person who judges the truthfulness of our answers is ourselves. The bishop, in his administration of the questions, acts like Christ. He asks us to examine our own hearts, judge our own motives, and decide if we are worthy to enter the temple and, subsequently, into God's presence. Our responses to the questions are completely on our honor, and God lets us judge ourselves—to our eternal misery or to our eternal happiness. This process is not much different from how our judgment will be when we stand before God to be judged as to whether we are worthy to enter His eternal kingdom. As Romans 14:11 states, "Every knee shall bow to me, and every tongue shall confess to God. So then every one of us shall give account of himself to God."

This responsibility to judge ourselves is perhaps one of the reasons that the scriptures tell us that when the wicked are judged by God, "then shall they confess . . . that the judgment of an everlasting punishment is just upon them" (Mosiah 27:31). It will be hard to argue with the judgment when you are the judge.

After everyone had left the temple, Jesus again "lifted up himself" (John 8:10) to address the adulterous woman. He asked her, "Woman, where are those thine accusers? hath no man condemned thee?" (verse 10). He was making it clear to her that He did not accuse her, nor did He condemn her. Out of everyone in the temple that day, only one person was truly without sin, and that was Christ. He was the only one justified in throwing a stone at her, yet He didn't. Her guilt was plain to see; in her condition, she could hide nothing. She knew, in accordance with the law, that she deserved death. Yet, even faced with her obvious guilt, Jesus offered her what He offers every one of God's children: mercy. Author James L. Ferrell wrote,

> It is true that we are commanded to love and honor others. But what's false is this idea that you or I deserve that love and devotion—that we are somehow entitled to it. The truth is that there is only one thing we truly deserve, and that's to be sent to hell—you . . . me . . . all of us.

> Hell is all we could ever hope for . . . if it weren't for the redeeming power of the Savior's Atonement. It is only his love, offered not because we deserve it but even though we do not, that saves us. We don't want what we deserve, believe me. . . . Our only hope is to receive what we don't deserve—the mercy that brings the gift of eternal life.[5]

No matter what sins we have or have not committed in our lives, each of us are in the same situation as the woman taken in adultery. There will come a day when, like this woman, we will have all our sins revealed and we will stand naked before God. This is because, as Amulek taught in the Book of Mormon, despite our best efforts in this life, when we meet

God, "we shall not be found spotless . . . and in this awful state we shall not dare to look up to our God; and we would fain be glad if we could command the rocks and the mountains to fall upon us to hide us from his presence" (Alma 12:14).

When that day happens we, like the woman in adultery, will not be able to hide. We will have to face God and see all our sins revealed. The beautiful thing is that even though we will be faced with our mistakes and inadequacy, we will not have to be afraid of God. As Amulek continued, "We must come forth and stand before him in his glory, and in his power, and in his might, majesty, and dominion, and acknowledge to our everlasting shame that all his judgments are just; that he is just in all his works, and that he is merciful unto the children of men, and that he has all power to save every man that believeth on his name and bringeth forth fruit meet for repentance" (verse 15).

When we stand before Jesus, our judge, He will treat us much like He did the woman taken in adultery. He will not ignore our sins, but He will not condemn us for them either. He will treat us with love and respect, and if we are willing to accept it, He will offer us mercy. I can imagine Him, as He may have done for the woman in the temple, untying our cords and covering our nakedness with His own robe. He will tell us, like He so tenderly yet firmly told her, "Go, and sin no more" (John 8:11).

The Joseph Smith Translation of this story gives us added insight into this woman's heart. It says that after this encounter with Jesus, "the woman glorified God from that hour, and believed on his name" (John 8:11, footnote c; from Joseph Smith Translation). She had been saved from death and given a divine gift that she did not deserve. She had felt the miracle that happens to those who accept Christ's mercy and Atonement, and had been given a second chance at life.

When I think of her experience, I am reminded of how important it is to judge ourselves, and others, with love and compassion. None of us is perfect and never will be in this life, and so we never have a reason to condemn others for their mistakes. Only Jesus Christ, the one perfect man, has the right to cast stones. Yet, as He demonstrated to the woman in the temple, He will never throw them. His arms are always stretched out wide and His mercy is always extended toward us. His mercy is a gift that none of us deserves but which each of us desperately needs. When faced with the mistakes of others, we would all do well to follow His example, to put down our stones, and to treat others with love and respect.

# Divorce

In most New Testament cultures, men were allowed to divorce their wives, but never were wives allowed to divorce their husbands. According to scholars, "Men could divorce a wife for three main justifications. . . . First, sexual misconduct; second, 'even if she spoiled a dish for him'; and finally, 'even if he found another fairer than she.'"[6] This ease of divorce could not have been good for women, and the obvious double standard reflected the low status of women in society.

Some rabbis maintained that since Moses had given guidelines concerning divorce, God must condone the practice. Jesus stated that it was only "for the hardness of your heart" (Mark 10:5) that Moses gave them directions about divorce. Instead, He taught that "from the beginning of the creation" (verse 6) God intended for men and women to become "one flesh" (verse 8) and that men should not separate what "God hath joined together" (verse 9).

These teachings on divorce went against the normal practice of the day, where women could be divorced with little reason or concern. It seems that these teachings surprised even His disciples, who once they were "in the house" (verse 10) asked Him more questions. To them He clarified that God did not approve of someone getting a divorce just to be remarried to someone else. In fact, He taught, "Whosoever shall put away his wife, and be married to another, committeth adultery against her" (verse 11). What Christ taught next might also have been surprising. He said, "And if a woman shall put away her husband, and be married to another, she committeth adultery" (verse 12).

With these teachings, Christ made it clear that there was no double standard between men and women when it came to marriage and sexuality. Men were expected to be as loyal to their wives as wives were expected to be to their husbands. God holds both men and women to the same standards of sexual purity. Jesus's teaching also demonstrated that a woman had rights within marriage and that she could not be cast aside for another woman without consequence. Most of all, He affirmed the higher law of marriage, one in which husband and wife become "one flesh" and are never "put asunder" (verses 8–9).

# Mother of the Man Born Blind

*"But the Jews did not believe concerning him, that he had been blind, and received his sight, until they called the parents of him that had received his sight. And they asked them, saying, Is this your son, who ye say was born blind? how then doth he now see? His parents answered them and said, We know that this is our son, and that he was born blind: but by what means he now seeth, we know not; or who hath opened his eyes, we know not: he is of age; ask him: he shall speak for himself."*

*John 9:18–22*

*In New Testament times,* if babies were born with disabilities or handicaps, it was often assumed that it was because the parents had sinned. Knowing little of how babies developed or grew in utero, people assumed that the only reason for a child to be born disfigured or disabled was because it was a punishment from God. Having a child with a disability is difficult and I can only imagine how much harder it was when people blamed you and your sins for your child's problems.

In John 9, we read that Christ saw a man who was blind from birth and His disciples asked, "Master, who did sin, this man, or his parents, that he was born blind?" (verse 2). Christ told them that no one had sinned but that he was born blind "that the works of God should be manifest in him" (verse 3). As I have struggled to understand why some people seem to have an unfair percentage of trials and hardship, I have come to understand that it is only as we taste the bitter that we know the sweet. The woman who struggles with infertility reminds us what incredible gifts conception and new life truly are. The child born with crippled legs reminds us what a blessing it is to walk and to run. A girl who is deaf makes us appreciate our ability to hear. And a man who is born blind reminds us how remarkable it is to see. It is truly in our trials, and in the trials of others, that we see the works of God manifest.

After Christ spoke, He went to this blind man and "spat on the ground, and made clay of the spittle, and he anointed the eyes of the blind man with the clay" (verse 6). He then commanded him to go and wash the earth out of his eyes. The man went and did this and, miraculously, he saw. On seeing him healed, his neighbors marveled. He bore testimony to them that it was "a man that is called Jesus" (verse 11) who had opened his eyes. The people took the man before the Pharisees who, when they heard that it was Jesus who had healed him, wouldn't believe that the man had ever been blind.

Trying to prove that he had never been blind, they called in the man's parents to testify. When the parents saw that their son, who had been blind from birth, could see, they were amazed. They said, "We know that this is our son . . . but by what means he now seeth, we know not; or who hath opened his eyes, we know not: he is of age; ask him: he shall speak for himself" (verses 20–21). His parents may have believed that Christ had healed him but perhaps were afraid to admit it because the Jews had said that anyone who believed in Christ would be kicked out of the synagogue. This possible apathy on the part of the parents is sad. They were so afraid of what other people thought of them, and of losing their position in the synagogue, that they refused to stand up for their son or to testify of the miracle that had happened to him.

The son, on the other hand, was not afraid to boldly bear his testimony. Even though the Pharisees mocked and insulted him, he continued to affirm Christ's power and told them, "Since the world began was it not heard that any man opened the eyes of one that was born blind, except he be of God. If this man were not of God, he could do nothing" (verses 32–33, footnote 32a; from Joseph Smith Translation). He was willing to stand firm in his testimony, even when all those around him—including his parents—were too afraid to speak out. Eventually, the Jews did cast him out of their synagogue. When Christ heard of this, He went to the man and told him openly that He was the Son of God. He told him, "For judgment I am come into this world, that they which see not might see; and that they which see might be made blind" (verse 39).

When this man had done as Christ said and had gone and washed the earth out of his eyes, he had not only had his physical eyes opened but also his spiritual eyes. In contrast, the Pharisees, and possibly the blind man's parents, had their hearts and their eyes so focused on things of the earth that they were the ones who remained blind. The parents knew that a miracle had been performed for their son, but they were unwilling to wash away the "earth" from their eyes and see and comprehend who Christ really was. This story reminds me how important it is that we strive to open our spiritual eyes and how, like this man, sometimes it is the "earth" and all its distractions that we must wash away before we can see things as they truly are.

# Mother *of Zebedee's Children*

*"Then came to him the mother of Zebedee's children with her sons, worshiping him, and desiring a certain thing of him. And he said unto her, What wilt thou? She saith unto him, Grant that these my two sons may sit, the one on thy right hand, and the other on the left, in thy kingdom. But Jesus answered and said, Ye know not what ye ask. Are ye able to drink of the cup that I shall drink of, and to be baptized with the baptism that I am baptized with? They say unto him, We are able. And he saith unto them, Ye shall drink indeed of my cup, and be baptized with the baptism that I am baptized with: but to sit on my right hand, and on my left, is not mine to give, but it shall be given to them for whom it is prepared of my Father."*

*Matthew 20:20–23*[1]

***Shortly before Christ*** made His triumphal entry into Jerusalem, a woman simply known to us as "the mother of Zebedee's children" (verse 20) came humbly before the Lord, worshipping Him. She had heard Him teach and had heard Him talk about those who would enter His kingdom. He was on the brink of bringing forth His Father's glory, and the greatest desire of this woman's heart was to be a part of that. Yet as a woman, she must have felt that such a place of honor could never include her. So she bowed down at Christ's feet and asked, "Grant that these my two sons may sit, the one on thy right hand, and the other on the left, in thy kingdom" (verse 21).

This story is often told in a way that makes the mother of Zebedee's children seem like a vain, glory-seeking woman who desires a special place for her sons in God's kingdom above all the other Apostles. Her story is often used as an example of how we should not be proud and aspire for callings or places within God's kingdom. It is true that her sons, the Apostles James and John, were both such mighty men of God that Christ had nicknamed them "Boanerges," which means "the sons of thunder" (Mark 3:17). This woman had every reason to be proud of her sons, but I believe that pride wasn't what motivated her to approach the Savior.

To understand her motivation, you need to look at her through a different lens, remembering that in first-century Palestine, Jewish women had very few rights as individuals. Their status was just above that of a gentile or slave. Most could not read, write, or participate in civic life. They had no voice and very few individual freedoms, and were often just seen as appendages to their husbands and sons. Though she of course had a name, we only know her as "the mother of Zebedee's children." This title indicates that to society, and perhaps to herself as well, the greatest evidence of her worth was embodied in her sons rather than in her as an individual.

In the story in Matthew, it is the mother who initially asked Jesus the question, not James and John. It may be helpful to create a mental image in your mind of the story. Picture Jesus sitting, perhaps under a tree, and the mother and her two

> ## "Lord, is there room for me in your kingdom?"

sons kneeling at His feet, listening expectantly to His answer. Because the passage often uses the pronouns *they* and *ye* to refer to her and her two sons, it is easy to forget that Christ was responding to her request: "Grant that these my two sons may sit, the one on thy right hand, and the other on the left, in thy kingdom."

Christ told her, "Ye know not what ye ask" (Matthew 20:22). This response was not given in reproach. Christ was telling her, "You are asking the wrong thing." Christ was the master of looking past the question and going directly to the heart of the questioner. He knew that the question lying just below the surface of this woman's heart was, "Lord, is there room for me in your kingdom?" Yet, she didn't dare ask that question. Perhaps she couldn't conceive that such a thing could be possible. And so she brought her sons—the greatest evidence she could find of her worth—and begged the blessing through them.

I imagine Christ looking down on this woman with love and sorrow in His eyes, seeing that she was so limited by the confines of her culture that she couldn't imagine her true worth. He saw that she could not comprehend the power and privileges that were available to her, as an individual and as a woman and not simply secondhand through her sons.

Christ helped her to see. He asked, "Are ye able to drink of the cup that I shall drink of, and to be baptized with the baptism that I am baptized with?" To which they responded, "We are able" (verse 22). Then Christ told them, "Ye shall drink indeed of my cup, and be baptized with the baptism that I am baptized with: but to sit on my right hand, and on my left, is not mine to give, but it shall be given to them for whom it is prepared of my Father" (verse 23).

In this passage, Christ beautifully told this woman that there was a place for her—for all women—in His Kingdom. She would "indeed" be able to partake of baptism and participate in His gospel. But the privilege "to sit on my right hand, and on my left" was a gift the Father must bestow. The implied message was that such a position in God's kingdom was available to all who were worthy of it, male and female. Her sons could qualify to sit down on Christ's right hand, but so could she.

Christ's response to her is even more beautiful when we consider what He taught afterward to the other Apostles, who reacted somewhat negatively to His comments. He told them, "Ye know that the princes of the Gentiles exercise dominion over them, and they that are great exercise authority upon them. But it shall not be so among you: but whosoever will be great among you, let him be your minister" (verses 25–26). Christ was gently reminding His Apostles that His kingdom is not like an earthly kingdom where power comes from the top and trickles down. In His kingdom, the power comes from the bottom, from those who are lowly, poor, and humble and radiates up. "And whosoever will be chief among you," He said, "let him be your servant" (verse 27).

This woman had spent her life serving and ministering to others as a daughter, a sister, a mother, and a wife. We also know that she served and ministered to Christ Himself because she is listed among the women who followed Him. (See "Susanna and the Unnamed Women Who Followed Christ" on page 83.) Christ's message to her, and to His Apostles, was a reminder that to those who serve in humility, the Father gives power to sit on His right hand.

Sometimes I feel like many of us are like the mother of Zebedee's children. We are so unaware of our potential as children in His kingdom that we come to Him humbly, mustering up all our strength to ask Him for the grandest blessing we can imagine, only to have Him look at us and say, "You know not what you ask. Let me show you what I see. Let me show you what you are really capable of doing. Let me show you who you really are."

That is the beauty of the gospel of Jesus Christ: It expands our understanding of the world, of eternity, and of ourselves. It helps us see that the Lord always has much bigger plans for us than we do for ourselves. And like the mother of Zebedee's sons, it helps us look past our narrow cultural lenses and glimpse our true selves.

*"Now a certain man was sick, named Lazarus, of Bethany, the town of Mary and her sister Martha. (It was that Mary which anointed the Lord with ointment, and wiped his feet with her hair, whose brother Lazarus was sick.) Therefore his sisters sent unto him, saying, Lord, behold, he whom thou lovest is sick. When Jesus heard that, he said This sickness is not unto death, but for the glory of God, that the Son of God might be glorified thereby."*

John 11:1–14

**When their brother Lazarus became very sick,** Mary and Martha sent word to Jesus. He did not come right away but instead waited two days, saying, "This sickness is not unto death, but for the glory of God, that the Son of God might be glorified thereby" (John 11:4). After a two-day wait, Jesus announced that He would return to Judea, to which His disciples responded with alarm. They knew it would be dangerous for Jesus to return to Judea as the Jews had tried to stone Him the last time He was there. Yet Christ knew He needed to go. He told His disciples, "Our friend Lazarus sleepth; but I go, that I may awake him out of sleep" (verse 11). His disciples were confused, thinking that because Lazarus was sick, sleep would be good for him. It was then Jesus told them plainly that Lazarus was already dead, but that He would perform a miracle "to the intent ye may believe" (verse 15).

When Jesus got close to Bethany, Martha heard that He was coming and "went and met him" (verse 20). She told Him that her brother had been dead for four days and that she knew "if thou hadst been here, my brother had not died" (verse 21). Christ told her that her brother would rise again and asked her if she believed that "whosoever liveth and believeth in me shall never die" (verse 26). Martha responded, "Yea, Lord: I believe that thou art the Christ, the Son of God, which should come into the world" (verse 27). Martha clearly understood who He was and what authority and power He had, but she was bearing testimony of the distant resurrection of the dead. She didn't suspect what great miracle was coming.

When Mary saw Jesus, she fell down at His feet and wept the same words that Martha had: "Lord, if thou hadst been here, my brother had not died" (verse 32). It seems that these two sisters had clung to the hope that Christ could heal their brother, but now that he was dead, they were despondent. When Jesus saw their sorrow, "he groaned in the spirit, and was troubled" (verse 33). And then, in what is one of the most compassionate acts in the scriptures, we read that "Jesus wept" (verse 35).

Jesus's earlier words to His disciples about raising Lazarus from his sleep tell us that Christ already knew that Lazarus would live again, and yet He still wept. Why? Sister Linda S. Reeves answered this question when she taught,

> Apostle James E. Talmage wrote, "The sight of the two women so overcome by grief . . . caused Jesus to sorrow [with them] so that He groaned in spirit and was deeply troubled." This experience testifies of the compassion, empathy, and love that our Savior and our Heavenly Father feel for each of us every time we are weighed down by the anguish, sin, adversity, and pains of life. . . . They do not say, "It's OK that you're in pain right now because soon everything is going to be all right. You will be healed, or your husband will find a job, or your wandering child will come back." They feel the depth of our

Christ's tears also tell what type of man He was. He wept publicly, unashamed of His tears or of the depth of His feeling. He wept openly just like the women. I think one of the things that I love most about attending the meetings of The Church of Jesus Christ of Latter-day Saints is that nowhere else in my life have I ever seen so many grown men cry. Every time I see a man shed tears when he bears testimony, when he shares a spiritual experience, or when he speaks of his family and wife, I remember those words: "Jesus wept." It is a beautiful to me that the gospel embraces and cultivates men who are like the Savior, men who are not ashamed to weep.

suffering, and we can feel of Their love and compassion in our suffering. . . . Whatever sin or weakness or pain or struggle or trial you are going through, He knows and understands those very moments. He loves you! And He will carry you through those moments, just as He did Mary and Martha.[1]

Christ's tears were not for Lazarus but for Mary and Martha. He saw how much they had loved and thus how much they had suffered. His tears were for their sorrow.

Christ knows and feels all the sorrow that women experience on this earth. He sees how deeply we love and consequently how deeply we grieve. Even if He knows that our story will end happily, He doesn't minimize the reality of the pain and the sorrow that we feel. He mourns with us when we mourn and comforts us when we stand in need of comfort. His tears for Mary and Martha are a precious reminder that when we weep, we never do it alone.

# Death

At the death of a loved one, it was customary for people to be wailing and mourning and often women took the lead in this demonstration of grief. These wails began immediately after a person died and could be loud and long. Sometimes women who were especially good at these mourning practices would be hired to mourn at a death.[2] To show their grief, people would also tear their clothes, wear sackcloth, beat on their breasts, or weep.[3] When Jesus arrived at the house of Jairus shortly after the death of his daughter, He must have encountered this type of situation. The scripture says there was a "tumult, and them that wept and wailed greatly" (Mark 5:38).

Bodies were not preserved and were buried within twenty-four hours after death. In preparation for burial, the face would be covered with a napkin (a square piece of cloth) and the body would be completely wrapped in strips of linen. When Lazarus arose from the dead, he was described as coming forth, "bound hand and foot with graveclothes" (John 11:44).

Spices and other herbs were also wrapped in between the layers of cloth. When Jesus was taken down from the cross, Nicodemus and Joseph of Arimathea brought "a mixture of myrrh and aloes" and wound Christ's body "in linen clothes with the spices, as the manner of the Jews is to bury" (John 19:39–40).

After the body was prepared, it was laid on a funeral bier with poles at each corner. Men carried this bier on their shoulders to the tomb where the body was to be laid. This is how the son of the widow of Nain[4] would have been "carried out" (Luke 7:12) when Jesus saw them leaving the city. Poor people were buried in graves, but wealthy people were buried in family tombs carved into the rocks. Jesus was buried in a tomb because Joseph of Arimathea, a wealthy disciple, gave his newly carved tomb to Jesus. According to BYU scholars,

> Burial in a rock-hewn tomb usually consisted of two separate and distinct burials. The first burial was the simple placement of the body in the tomb either in a niche—shafts cut as deep as a body in the burial chamber—or on an arcosolium—a bench or shelf cut out of the wall of a tomb. The second burial occurred about a year later when family members reentered the tomb, carefully took the bones of the deceased (once the flesh had completely decomposed), and placed them in a specially prepared, separate container known as an ossuary (from Latin *os*, "a bone"). These chests were placed in small niches in the tomb for permanent burial.[5]

After a burial it was customary for there to be a mourning feast in which food would be prepared for the family and friends. We see remnants of this custom in the story of Lazarus when "many of the Jews came to Martha and Mary, to comfort them concerning their brother" (John 11:19). It seems that the purpose of these types of gathering were to comfort the mourners in their time of need, perhaps much like the traditional luncheon provided for the family after LDS funerals.

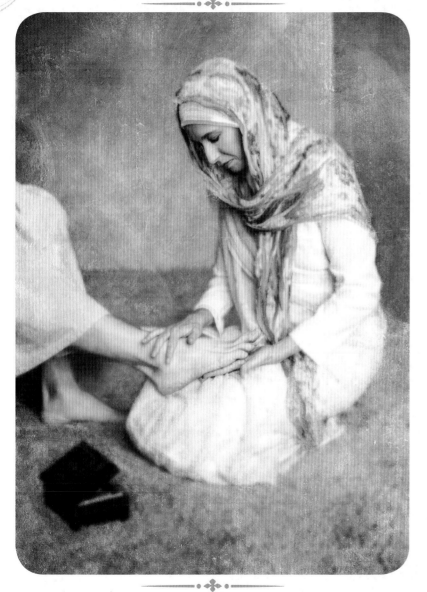

# Mary of Bethany

*"Then took Mary a pound of ointment of spikenard, very costly, and anointed the feet of Jesus, and wiped his feet with her hair.... Then saith one of his disciples, Judas Iscariot, Simon's son, which should betray him, Why was not this ointment sold for three hundred pence, and given to the poor? ... Then said Jesus, Let her alone: for she hath preserved this ointment until now, that she might anoint me in token of my burial. For the poor always ye have with you; but me ye have not always."*

*John 12:3–8, footnote 7a; from Joseph Smith Translation*

*Christ's female disciples* seemed to recognize and understand His mission better than did some of His Apostles. While His Apostles understood that He was the Son of God and was endowed with great power, they were still expecting that His deliverance would be political. They expected that, like Moses, Christ would free the Jewish people from oppression, get rid of Roman rule, and make them a great and free nation. This may have been why Peter, when Christ was arrested in Gethsemane, drew out his sword and cut off an opponent's ear. He was ready for the fight he thought was coming. Instead, Christ refused to fight and healed the man's ear with His touch. This unwillingness to fight, or even to defend Himself, confused some of the Apostles and may have been the reason that some of them deserted Him in His final hours.

On the other hand, Christ's female disciples seemed to understand that Christ was not going to be a political Savior but rather a spiritual Messiah. While neither the women nor the men fully understood the extent of Christ's work or what He meant when He said He would rise again, the story of Mary of Bethany and her anointing of Jesus shows us just how much these women did understand about Christ's mission.

Six days before Passover, and thus six days before His death, Christ went to Bethany and had dinner with Martha, Mary, Lazarus (who had been raised from the dead), and several of His Apostles. During the meal, Mary brought in an alabaster box that contained "a pound of ointment of spikenard, very costly" (verse 3). She broke open the box and began to anoint Christ with it. Matthew and Mark both say that she anointed His head, while John specified the feet.[1] I think, given the spiritual significance to both of these parts of the body, it is likely that she did both.

Spikenard was a very fragrant ointment made from the root and spike of the nard plant, which came from the mountains in Northern India.[2] It was very rare and expensive. The amount that Mary used on Christ was worth more than three hundred pieces of silver (Mark 14:5), which was the equivalent of a year's wages. In today's market, it would be as though Mary spent $30,000–40,000 on her gift. It is no wonder that Judas and some of the others murmured at her extravagance, saying that it might "have been given to the poor" (verse 5). It was a shocking tribute.

Mary did another shocking thing: she let down her hair and wiped Christ's feet with it. It may have been improper for a respectable woman to let down her hair in front of men, and washing the dust and dirt off of Christ's feet was a job for the lowest slave in the household (sometimes a master would even wipe his hands on the slave's hair). This was a

> ## "Why trouble ye the woman?"

remarkable position for Mary, a free woman, to assume.[3] Only the greatest love and deepest respect could have prompted her to humble herself like that. Seeing her actions, the others began to criticize her, but when Jesus "understood it," He told them, "Why trouble ye the woman? for she hath wrought a good work upon me" (Matthew 26:10).

I find it significant that before Christ washed the feet of His disciples, Mary washed and anointed the feet of Christ. I wonder how many of the Apostles, while they watched Christ wash their feet, remembered what they had seen six days earlier when Mary, in her great act of humility, washed the feet of the Savior. Mary seemed to truly understand what the Savior meant when He taught, "Whosoever of you will be the chiefest, shall be servant of all" (Mark 10:44).

Mary also understood what the Apostles did not at this time fully comprehended: that Christ was going to die. It seems that she and Christ were the only ones who knew the reason for her actions because Jesus had to explain to them, "Let her alone: for she hath preserved this ointment until now, that she might anoint me in token of my burial" (John 12:7, footnote a; from Joseph Smith Translation). The words anoint and token are powerful words and help us

understand that Mary's actions were not just motivated out of kindness, but that she was performing sacred work for the Savior. This was no ordinary gift.

In Ancient Israel, both kings and temple priests were anointed with perfumed oil.[4] In the Old Testament, there are several accounts of prophets crowning kings by anointing them with oil on their heads. For example, when David was anointed as king, he was anointed with "holy oil" (Psalm 89:20). Priests who officiated in the temple were also given an anointing by having holy oil placed on their heads.[5] This oil was used as a symbol of being endowed with power from God. In fact, the word *Messiah* means "anointed one." It is significant that the only account we have of Christ being ceremoniously anointed is by Mary.[6]

Her anointing becomes even more symbolic when we remember that

## SINFUL WOMAN WHO WASHED CHRIST'S FEET WITH HER HAIR

In Luke 7, there is also the story of "a woman in the city, which was a sinner" (verse 37), who came and stood at Christ's feet, weeping and washing His feet with her tears. She kissed His feet and then dried them with her hair and anointed them with ointment. Christ allowed her to do this. The Pharisees scoffed and said, "This man, if he were a prophet, would have known who and what manner of woman this is that toucheth him" (verse 39). Christ did know who she was and what she had done, but instead of rebuking her, He commended her for her faith. He said, "Her sins, which are many, are forgiven; for she loved much" (verse 47). And He told her, "Thy faith hath saved thee; go in peace" (verse 50).

Some of the details of this story are similar to the story of Mary anointing Christ, but this event happened early in Christ's ministry whereas Mary's anointing took place just before His death. The placement of this story makes it likely that Luke was writing about a different woman and a different event. However, given how similar the stories are, it is possible that details from both stories were mixed together. It is also interesting to think that Mary's behavior to Christ at the time of His anointing may have reminded people of the actions of this sinful woman, perhaps one of the reasons the disciples criticized her.

later, in the haste to bury Christ before the Sabbath, He was not given a proper burial or the anointing that should have accompanied it. (See "Susanna and the Unnamed Women Who Followed Christ" on page 83.) Mary's anointing was the only proper anointing Christ would get before His death and was, in fact, preparing Him for His Resurrection.

What Mary did was so significant that Christ commanded, and it is recorded in all three accounts of the story, that "this which she has done unto me, shall be had in remembrance in generations to come, wheresoever my gospel shall be preached" (Mark 14:8, footnote a; from Joseph Smith Translation). It is unfortunate that we don't talk more about the story of Mary anointing Christ, especially when Christ was so emphatic that her story be remembered through all generations. Her story is a powerful testament to the exalted way in which Christ viewed women and to the type of spiritual power and understanding that the women who followed Him had. They truly understood what His divine mission was and it is beautiful to think that Christ—the King of kings and High Priest of priests—was anointed for His death and His Resurrection by a woman.

# Daughters of Jerusalem

"*And there followed him a great company of people, and of women, which also bewailed and lamented him. But Jesus turning unto them said, Daughters of Jerusalem, weep not for me, but weep for yourselves, and for your children.*"

*Luke 23:27–28*

**When Christ made His triumphal entry** into Jerusalem, He was greeted and followed by a great multitude of people, including many women who had followed Him from Galilee. While Christ rode into Jerusalem on a donkey, they spread out their garments in front of Him and cut down branches and "strawed them in the way" (Matthew 21:8). While they followed Him into the city, they cried, "Hosanna to the Son of David: Blessed is he that cometh in the name of the Lord; Hosanna in the highest" (verse 9).

It was Passover time and Jerusalem would have been crowded with people who were there to worship at the temple. Some scholars estimate that Herod's temple could have accommodated almost four hundred thousand pilgrims and that there could have been hundreds of thousands of extra people in the city at Passover time.[1] This means that the crowd that thronged Jesus when He made His entry into Jerusalem could have been enormous. Truly an entrance fit for a king.

This triumphal entry was a stark contrast to how Christ would leave the city almost a week later as a criminal condemned to die, carrying His cross to Golgotha. When He made this

> "*But may Christ lift thee up.*"

sad exit from Jerusalem, many women again followed and "bewailed and lamented him" (Luke 23:27). On seeing their grief Christ turned to them and said,

Daughters of Jerusalem, weep not for me, but weep for yourselves, and for your children. For, behold, the days are coming, in the which they shall say, Blessed are the barren, and the wombs that never bare, and the paps which never gave suck. Then shall they begin to say to the mountains, Fall on us; and to the hills, Cover us. For if they do these things in a green tree, what shall be done in the dry? (Luke 23:28–31)

Christ had just performed the Atonement and had felt the full weight of all the wickedness, sorrow, and pain that the daughters of the world would face. He knew what awaited them in the future and that the wickedness of men would only increase. He knew that women would suffer and that there would come a day when even their incredible ability to create new life would be abused and unappreciated. Knowing this, He told the women that they shouldn't weep for Him but instead for what they and their children would face. He was saying to them, "If they can do this to me, the Son of God, what will they do to you?"

Sometimes I think about all the things that women and children suffer on this earth and my heart gets unbearably heavy. It seems that women, often because of their ability to create and nurture new life, bear an unequal portion of the world's suffering. All over the world they are treated as objects, raped, enslaved, undervalued, ignored, and even prevented from being born. Their suffering makes me weep. Yet, when I feel this sorrow creep into my heart, it helps me to remember what Mormon told his son after writing about the atrocities suffered by the Nephite and Lamanite women. He wrote, "May not the things which I have written grieve thee, to weigh thee down unto death; but may Christ lift thee up, and may . . . the hope of his glory and of eternal life, rest in your mind forever" (Moroni 9:25). In those moments, when the suffering of women seems too much to bear, I remember that Christ, through His glorious Atonement and Resurrection, has "swallowed up" (Mosiah 16:8) all their pain and sorrow. It gives me hope to think that one day all the wrongs of our mortal existence will be righted and that women will again, as they did in Jerusalem so long ago, lay down their clothes in adoration and cry out in gratitude, "Hosanna! Hosanna!" for the mercy and love of their King.

# Widow Who Gave Two Mites

*"And there came a certain poor widow, and she threw in two mites, which make a farthing. And he called unto him his disciples, and saith unto them, Verily I say unto you, That this poor widow hath cast more in, than all they which have cast into the treasury: For all they did cast in of their abundance; but she of her want did cast in all that she had, even all her living."*

*Mark 12:42–44*

*In the last weeks of His life,* Jesus often taught His disciples in the temple. The Temple Mount in Jerusalem was a bit like our modern-day Temple Square in Salt Lake City. The outer gates consisted of a huge walled-in area in which anyone, Jew or Gentile, could enter. This area was called "the court of the gentiles" and was where goods relating to the temple were sold.[1] Farther toward the center of the mount stood the inner walls of the temple courtyard. Its gates were guarded to ensure that only ritually pure Jewish men and women entered into this part of the temple.

The first court in this part of the temple was called the "court of the women" because this was as far into the temple as Jewish women were allowed to go. The court of the women had several chambers: the treasury of the temple; chambers for storing wood, oil, and wine used in the temple; the chamber of the leper; and the chamber for Nazarite vows. Beyond the court of the women was the "court of the men of Israel" where only Jewish men were allowed to enter. This court surrounded the temple itself and was where the burnt offerings were sacrificed. Men and women could both climb the steps to the gate of this court in order to offer their sacrifices, but women were not allowed to actually enter. It is significant that whenever Jesus taught in the temple, He always did it in the court of the women. His message was for both men and women, and He ensured that they both had equal access to His teachings.

During one of the times when Jesus was teaching in the court of the women, He looked up and "beheld how the people cast money into the treasury: and many that were rich cast in much" (verse 41). While He watched, He saw a certain poor widow come and cast "in two mites, which make a farthing" (verse 42). A mite was the smallest bronze coin used by the Jews and, much like our modern penny, was an insignificant sum of money. Yet despite her meager offering, Jesus proclaimed, "This poor widow hath cast more in, than all they which have cast into the treasury" (verse 43). The treasury of the temple consisted of thirteen trumpet-shaped boxes where people placed their tithes and paid different offerings like the temple tax, contributions for purification rites, donations for the poor, or freewill offerings.[2] On any given day, the court of the women would have echoed with the sounds of donations filling the treasury.

So how is it that by giving her two mites, this woman's offering was considered to be more than everything that had been cast into the treasury? As Jesus explained, it had to do with faith and, more specifically, with consecration. He said, "For all they did cast in of their abundance; but she of her want did cast in all that she had, even all her living" (verse 44).

Someone watching this widow donate her mites may have wondered, "Why even bother?" Two mites was hardly enough money to buy a single stick of incense for the altar. The temple would function perfectly fine without it. So why give it, especially when she needed it so badly?

Yet, this is just the point Jesus was trying to teach His disciples. It doesn't matter if you have heaps of gold, time, talents, or energy to donate to the Lord's work or if you only have two mites' worth to give, the entrance price into God's kingdom is the same for each of His disciples, rich or poor. He asks for everything we have. Absolutely everything.

This is what the rich young man whom Jesus met could not understand. He asked Jesus what he should do to gain eternal life. In response Jesus told him to keep the commandments, to which he replied, "Master, all these have I observed from my youth" (Mark 10:20). Jesus then "beholding him loved him, and said unto him, One thing thou lackest: go thy way, sell whatsoever thou hast, and give to the poor, and thou shalt have treasure in heaven: and come, take up the cross, and follow me" (verse 21). When the young man heard what Jesus said, he was sad "and went away grieved: for he had great possessions" (verse 22).

The rich young man's desires, even though he had followed the commandments and had a testimony of Jesus, were still focused on the things of the world. His heart was not in the right place and so he wasn't able to give what the Lord asked of him.

On the other hand, it is obvious that the desires of the widow at the temple were firmly rooted in God. There was nothing on earth that was going to hold her back from being united with Him.

Her heart was focused on the riches of heaven and not on the things of this world. As Elder Neal A. Maxwell explained,

> Everything depends—initially and finally—on our desires. These shape our thought patterns. Our desires thus precede our deeds and lie at the very cores of our souls, tilting us toward or away from God. . . . [O]nly by aligning our wills with

God's is full happiness to be found. Anything less results in a lesser portion.[3]

I believe we tend to think the widow gave her last two mites in dejection and hopelessness. Yet, I think the opposite is probably more accurate. Instead of seeing her bowed down with shame and woe, we should see her enter the court of the women and approach the treasury with her head held high and faith in her eyes. She gave because she had faith that God would take care of her. With her offering, she placed her fate squarely in the arms of the only man who could help her—the Almighty God. It is beautiful that out of all the people in the temple that day, Jesus noticed *this* widow. He, out of all the people there, was the only one who truly knew what great a sacrifice had been made that day.

Just as He saw this poor widow, God sees us and understands the desires of our hearts. He knows what will make us happy and wants to bless us. Yet, often times His ability to bless us is dependent upon the degree to which we are willing to consecrate ourselves to Him. The more we give of ourselves, and the more we focus on what God wants rather than what we want, the more He is able to bless us.

Throughout our lives, God will ask each of us to consecrate in different ways. He may ask for our time, our health, our family, our future plans, our wealth, our comfort, or perhaps our pride. Most important, He will ask that we give ourselves, because that is really the only thing we have to give. Elder Neal A. Maxwell taught this when he said,

> The submission of one's will is really the only uniquely personal thing we have to place on God's altar. The many other things we "give," brothers and sisters, are actually the things He has already given or loaned to us. However, when you and I finally submit ourselves, by letting our individual wills be swallowed up in God's will, then we are really giving something to Him! . . . Consecration thus constitutes the only unconditional surrender which is also a total victory![4]

Consecration is never easy. That is how you know you are doing it right. The Lord specifically tells us that when we feel we are lacking, our sacrifices are the most valuable.

Consecration, in all its forms, requires exercising more faith than you have ever had to muster before. It requires letting go of worldly constructions of happiness and having faith that God knows what you need better than you do. Still, even with great faith, consecration often feels like the stupidest, scariest jump off a cliff you have ever taken in your life. You just have to have the faith that God is waiting with open arms to catch you.

This is the lesson that this humble widow understood. Giving her last two mites could not have been easy for her, but she did it with a firm faith that she would gain something far better, even "all that my Father hath" (D&C 84:38). The same promise is true for each of us; we just have to have the faith to open our clenched fists and let those two mites go.

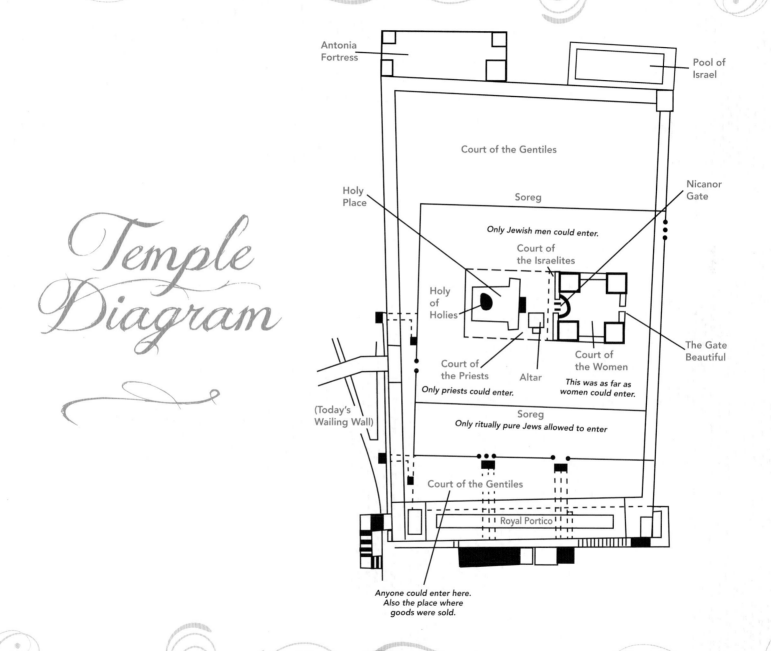

Temple Diagram

Antonia Fortress

Pool of Israel

Court of the Gentiles

Soreg

Nicanor Gate

Holy Place

*Only Jewish men could enter.*

Court of the Israelites

Holy of Holies

Court of the Priests

Altar

Court of the Women

The Gate Beautiful

*Only priests could enter.*

*This was as far as women could enter.*

(Today's Wailing Wall)

Soreg

*Only ritually pure Jews allowed to enter*

Court of the Gentiles

Royal Portico

*Anyone could enter here. Also the place where goods were sold.*

# Damsel and Maid at the Door

*"And as Peter was beneath in the palace, there cometh one of the maids of the high priest: And when she saw Peter warming himself, she looked upon him, and said, And thou also wast with Jesus of Nazareth. But he denied, saying, I know not, neither understand I what thou sayest. . . . And a maid saw him again, and began to say to them that stood by, This is one of them. And he denied it again."*

*Mark 14:66–70*

*Most of us are familiar* with the story leading up to Christ's Crucifixion. After holding the Passover meal, Christ and several of His Apostles retired to the Garden of Gethsemane where Christ completed the Atonement. When Christ and His Apostles were leaving the garden, Judas met them with a host of men armed with weapons. Peter drew his sword to defend Christ and cut off the ear of Malchus, one of the servants of the high priest. Christ healed Malchus's ear and then allowed Himself to be bound and taken before the high priest. Peter and John followed, but only John was allowed in because he "was known unto the high priest" (John 18:15). This left Peter standing outside the door of the palace, but John spoke to the "damsel" (verse 17) who kept the door and she let Peter in.

It was a common practice of the day to have a young female slave, probably twelve to fourteen years old, in charge of watching the door. (See "Rhoda" on page 173.) This damsel saw Peter with a group of people warming themselves around a fire in the palace and she "earnestly looked upon him" (Luke 22:56). She approached him, saying, "And thou *also* wast with Jesus of Nazareth" (Mark 14:67; italics added). It appears that she was acquainted with John, whom she had let through the door, and recognized Peter as also being one of Christ's disciples. She seemed certain of his identity, but Peter tried to deny it, saying, "I know not, neither understand I what thou sayest" (Mark 14:68).

It seems to me that if this damsel knew who John was, and so easily recognized Peter, that it is likely she may have been among those who listened to Jesus and perhaps was even numbered among His disciples. If in fact she did have faith in Christ, I can only imagine how her faith may have been shaken to hear Peter—the senior Apostle—deny his association with Christ so publicly and adamantly.

Not long after Peter denied Christ to the damsel and those standing around the fire, he went out onto the porch of the

palace. Once he was on the porch, another "maid"[1] saw him. Again, he was easily recognized. She boldly told the people around her, "this fellow was also with Jesus of Nazareth" (Matthew 26:71). Like the first young woman, this maid didn't seem to question Peter's identity; she knew him to be one of the Apostles. Yet once again, Peter tried to deny it, this time with an oath, saying, "I do not know the man" (verse 72).

After this second denial, another group of people approached Peter. Among them was one of the kinsmen of Malchus, the man whose ear Peter cut off, who insisted that Peter was one of Christ's followers, "for thy speech bewrayeth [reveals] thee" (verse 73). After this confrontation, Peter began "to curse and to swear, saying, I know not the man" (verse 74). As soon as he was finished, he heard the cock crow and remembered what Christ had told him and what he had so adamantly refused to believe, that "before the cock crow, thou shalt deny me thrice" (verse 75). When the realization of his mistake hit him, Peter "went out, and wept bitterly" (verse 75).

We don't really know why Peter denied Christ. It could have been that he was afraid or that he had a moment of doubt. Regardless, this story exposes Peter's human weakness. Despite his important role as Christ's Apostle, and despite the fact that he would later become the prophet of the Christian church, we see that he was capable of making mistakes—big mistakes. The maid and the damsel at the door were eyewitnesses to his unfortunate display of weakness and poor judgment. When faced with the reality of Peter's faults, they had a choice to make. They could condemn Peter and use his actions as a reason to justify their anger or opposition to the Church, or they could look past Peter's mistakes and forgive him.

We don't know what choice these young women made, but we do know that Christ chose to forgive him. In John 21 after Christ had been resurrected, we read that He asked Peter three times, "Lovest thou me?" (John 21:15–17), giving him the opportunity to redeem himself by repeating three times,

> ## "Thou also wast with Jesus of Nazareth."

"Thou knowest that I love thee" (verses 15–17). Even though Peter had denied Him and left Him alone at the time of His greatest need, Christ knew Peter's heart. He knew that he was a good man and that he was trying his hardest to do what was right, but that he was human and that he had weaknesses and faults to overcome.

President Spencer W. Kimball once said,

> I do not pretend to know what Peter's mental reactions were nor what impelled him to say what he did this terrible night. But in light of his proven bravery and courage and his great devotion and his limitless love for his Savior, could we not give him the benefit of the doubt and at least forgive him as his Savior seems to have done? Almost immediately Christ had elevated him to the highest post in His Church, endowed him with the total keys of that kingdom.[2]

The story of Peter's denial is a good reminder that there will be times when each of us is faced with obvious evidence that those we respect, sustain, or follow have faults and make mistakes. Even the very best people in the Church are still human and are still capable of having poor judgment, saying the wrong thing at the wrong time, or being unkind. When faced with human folly, sin, or error, we, like these two women at the door, have a choice in how we react. We can judge and condemn, or we can be like Christ and forgive those who have hurt us and betrayed us. No one is perfect, and it is best to always give someone the benefit of the doubt—just like I hope these two young women did for Peter.

# *Wife* of Pontius Pilate

*"When he was set down on the judgment seat, his wife sent unto him, saying, Have thou nothing to do with that just man: for I have suffered many things this day in a dream because of him. . . . When Pilate saw that he could prevail nothing, but that rather a tumult was made, he took water, and washed his hands before the multitude, saying, I am innocent of the blood of this just person: see ye to it."*

Matthew 27:19, 24

**After He was betrayed,** Jesus Christ was brought before Pilate, the Roman governor of Jerusalem. Pilate listened to the accusations the Jewish elders made against Him and plainly asked Christ, "Art thou the King of the Jews?" Jesus answered, "Thou sayest" (Matthew 27:11). Pilate marveled at what Jesus had said and was impressed by how He refused to answer or defend any of the accusations brought against Him by the Jewish leaders. While Pilate was sitting in judgment, trying to decide what to do in the case of Jesus, his wife sent him a message saying, "Have thou nothing to do with that just man: for I have suffered many things this day in a dream because of him" (verse 19).

It would have been unusual during this period of history for a woman to send counsel to her husband, especially when he was sitting on the judgment seat in an important case. It was brave of her to send such a message. She must have felt that what she had to say was important and urgent. We don't know the details of her dream, but it appears that she had received a distinct and powerful witness that Jesus was indeed a "just man." The scriptures say that she had "suffered many things" because of what she had learned in her dream. I can imagine the struggle that must have gone on in her heart while she contemplated what to do with the message she had been given.

We don't know how much her message influenced Pilate's actions. Yet, after he received her message, Pilate told the Jews that he could find no fault with Christ. He offered to release Jesus to the people on the Passover, as custom allowed, but instead the Jews chose to release the prisoner Barabbas. When it became apparent that the Jews were intent on crucifying Jesus, Pilate "washed his hands before the multitude, saying, I am innocent of the blood of this just person" (verse 24). He knew that Christ was innocent, perhaps because of his wife's message, and even though he still didn't have the courage to stand up for Him, he knew that he didn't want Jesus's blood on his hands.

Regardless of the influence her message may have had upon Pilate's actions in Jesus's trial, her actions were impressive. As a wealthy Roman, she had likely heard about Jesus before, but it is unlikely that she had ever had the chance to meet Him. Her testimony of His innocence and goodness may have been based solely off the revelation and dream she had been given.

With only that one witness, she had the faith and the courage to do what many of Christ's Apostles and closest disciples did not—to stand up for Him in His darkest moment.

Most of us are in a position similar to Pilate's wife. It is unlikely that we will see or meet Jesus Christ on this earth, and yet we are each asked to stand as witnesses for Him. Often the only ways we can know for sure that Jesus is the Messiah is to rely on the promptings and revelations we receive from God and to listen to the testimonies of those who have seen Him, like the prophets and people in the scriptures. God will speak to us, just as He spoke to Pilate's wife, and give us knowledge in a way we can best understand it.

Doctrine and Covenants 90:11 says, "Every man shall hear the fulness of the gospel in his own tongue, and in his own language." The scripture is referring to the literal teaching of the gospel through missionary work, but I think it is also a good explanation of how God speaks to us. God will teach us and speak to us in whatever "language" we will be most

receptive to. This means that revelation will come to us as a still small voice, as a thought that won't go away, as a burning in our bosoms, as a wave of emotion, as a comment made in a class, as a photo in a book, as a child's remark, or, like the wife of Pontius Pilate discovered, as a dream.

A friend once shared an insight into receiving personal revelation that changed the way I approach spiritual learning. She wrote,

> Several of my good friends are currently struggling with anxiety and depression. This week, one of them said to me that she can't feel God anymore. She can't feel His presence or answers. This is terrifying to her. She is beginning to question everything.
>
> Medication has helped a little bit, but she still feels numb. . . . She wondered out loud to me today, "if a medication can block me from feeling the Spirit, then maybe the Spirit is not real. Maybe it is just a hormone."
>
> Of course I believe that this was her depression and doubt and fear talking, but it switched a light bulb on for me. . . . I used to be that way. I needed to feel a burning in my bosom with tears brinking to know I was feeling the Spirit, or to feel that I was being guided and led along. I now see that only having one way of receiving personal revelation is problematic. If one's feelings

suddenly become hijacked by depression or chemistry, a person may feel spiritually abandoned—drowning in a choppy sea....

I have learned in [recent] years that God and his angels communicate with you in whatever ways you open to. Or rather, whatever you'll realize is communication. A few years ago I opened my self up to all kind of metaphysical communication and I got it. Boy did I get it. If I told you all the ways I know I am led along throughout the day, you might laugh. I often do especially . . . when I stop in the middle of a meditation for no reason and read a scripture that ends up being a missing link to something. Why did I stop? I didn't feel "prompted." I didn't feel a burning in my bosom. I didn't feel anything. I just thought, I want to pick up my scriptures right now.... [That] is personal revelation. [1]

It is important that we learn to recognize all the ways that God speaks to us and that we trust what He tells us. Sister Julie B. Beck, a former general Relief Society president, taught,

> The ability to qualify for, receive, and act on personal revelation is the single most important skill that can be acquired in this life. . . . It requires a conscious effort to diminish distractions, but having the Spirit of revelation makes it possible to prevail over opposition and persist in faith through difficult days and essential routine tasks. [2]

It would have been easy for Pontius Pilate's wife to brush off her dream and think of it as just another strange experience. But she didn't. She recognized that God was giving her a message and she acted on what she had learned. She may not have realized it at the time, but her simple action influenced one of the most important trials in history.

When we open our hearts and our minds to receive personal revelation, we will be astounded at the many different ways the Lord finds to speak to us. Like the wife of Pontius Pilate, we don't have to see or meet Jesus Christ to know of His divinity. It is possible for all people, no matter where or when they lived, to receive a testimony of Him and know—not just feel or believe—that He is indeed the Son of God. This knowledge may not come to us with our mortal eyes, it may not even come when we are awake, but it always comes to those who are willing to receive it.

> "Have thou nothing to do with that just man."

# Mary, the Mother of James and Joses

*"There were also women looking on afar off: among whom was Mary Magdalene, and Mary the mother of James the less and of Joses, and Salome; (Who also, when he was in Galilee, followed him, and ministered unto him;) and many other women which came up with him unto Jerusalem."*

*Mark 15:40–41*

*This Mary is also known as* "the other Mary" (Matthew 28:1). When your name was as common as the name Mary was in the ancient world, there were bound to be times when people used an adjective to distinguish you from all the other Marys. Those of us who have common names, like Heather, understand this. In high school, three of my friends were also named Heather, so I had my share of being called "the other Heather."

This designation may have been especially necessary because whenever this Mary is mentioned in the New Testament, she is always connected with Mary Magdalene. (See "The Marys in the New Testament" on page 79.) They must have been good friends. She, like Mary Magdalene, was a dedicated disciple. She is mentioned in Matthew and Mark[1] as being one of the women who stood afar and watched while Christ was crucified. When Christ's body was brought down from the cross and His body laid in the tomb, she and Mary Magdalene followed and "beheld where he was laid" (Mark 15:47) and remained "sitting over against the sepulchre" (Matthew 27:61), watching guard over Christ's body until the very last moment. When they could stay no longer without breaking the Sabbath, they returned home and "rested the sabbath day according to the commandment" (Luke 23:56).

This must have been the darkest of days for Christ's disciples while they, grieving and confused, contemplated all that they had lost. Their sorrow would have been magnified by the fact that, in their haste to bury Christ before the Sabbath began, He had been hastily wrapped and hastily buried. This last injustice must have been especially disturbing to the women who loved Him and had cared for His physical needs while He was alive. It must have taken every ounce of willpower they had to sit at home when all they wanted to do was be at the tomb.

As soon as the new week "began to dawn" (Matthew 28:1), they hurried back to the tomb. One thing that impresses me most about these women's faith was that they approached the tomb knowing a large stone had been rolled in front of the entrance, which would have made it impossible for them to enter. This problem didn't seem to factor into their decision to go forward with their plan. They seemed to have faith that the stone would be moved; their question wasn't "how" but simply, "*Who* shall roll us away the stone from the door of the sepulchre?" (Mark 16:3; italics added).

## "The other Mary."

Mary's faith wasn't weak or wavering, but it was forward-looking and confident. Her love for the Savior, and her willingness to serve Him even in death, allowed her to be witness to the most miraculous event to ever take place on the earth—the Resurrection of Jesus Christ. While we may not know much about Mary, the mother of James and Joses, we can see that she was a remarkable woman and a devoted disciple of Jesus Christ.

# Mary, *the Wife of Cleophas*

*"Now there stood by the cross of Jesus his mother, and his mother's sister, Mary the wife of Cleophas, and Mary Magdalene."*

John 19:25

**This Mary is only mentioned once** in the New Testament. She is among the women who stood by the cross. Her presence at the cross, as opposed to being among the women who watched from afar, indicates that she was among Christ's inner circle of followers and perhaps even a relative.

The grammar in John 19:25 is unclear; it can be read either as "his mother's sister who *was* Mary the wife of Cleophas" or as "his mother's sister, *and* Mary the wife of Cleophas." Many scholars argue that the second rendering is more likely correct and that John was writing about two different women. They point out that it would be highly unusual for two daughters within the same family to be named Mary.[1]

Regardless, Mary, the wife of Cleophas, was included among some of the women closest to Jesus. She was witness to the final moments of His life and stood beside His mother while she watched her beloved Son suffer and die. Even though we don't know much about her, I believe that her presence at the cross tells us that she was a devoted and beloved disciple of Christ.

# Jesus's Aunt

*"Now there stood by the cross of Jesus his mother, and his mother's sister, Mary the wife of Cleophas, and Mary Magdalene."*

John 19:25

*We don't know much about this woman* except that she was the sister to Mary, an aunt to Jesus, and that she stood at the cross in the final moments of Christ's life. She would have been with Jesus from the beginning to the end. She would have known of Mary's miraculous conception and of the challenges and gossip she must have faced throughout her life. She would have seen Christ grow from "grace to grace" (D&C 93:13) and become the man He was. She would have watched while He was ridiculed and threatened, and finally she would have watched when Jesus turned to His mother and cried, "Woman, behold thy son" (John 19:26) and took His final breaths.

Her presence at the cross indicates that perhaps more of Christ's family than just His mother accepted Him and followed His teachings. Our families can be either our greatest critics or our greatest supporters. Joseph Smith's family was a bulwark of faith and support for him throughout his life. His father, mother, brothers, and sisters stood by him through all of his ups and downs, never wavering in their faith and support. It is encouraging to me to think that Christ may have also had a family like Joseph Smith, one that rallied around Him and supported His mission with their whole hearts. While we can't know for sure, His aunt's presence at the cross suggests that perhaps He did.

# Salome

*"There were also women looking on afar off: among whom was Mary Magdalene, and Mary the mother of James the less and of Joses, and Salome; (Who also, when he was in Galilee, followed him, and ministered unto him;) and many other women which came up with him unto Jerusalem."*

Mark 15:40–41

**Salome is mentioned** among the women who ministered to Christ when He was in Galilee and who came up with Him to Jerusalem when He made His triumphal entry into the city. In Mark 16, she is also named alongside Mary Magdalene and Mary, the mother of James and Joses, as coming "very early in the morning" (verses 1–2) to anoint Christ's body with spices. Salome was one of the women who followed Jesus as He traveled and ministered to His physical needs (see "Susanna and the Women Who Followed Christ" on page 83). Her concern for His physical needs even carried over after His death. When Christ's body was brought down from the cross, it was the women who followed it and saw "the sepulchre, and how his body was laid" (Luke 23:55). In their haste to bury Christ before the Sabbath began, Joseph of Arimathea and Nicodemus quickly wrapped Him with linen and spices in "the manner of the Jews" (John 19:38–40). It must have caused these women grief to see their beloved Christ so hastily prepared for His burial. So, once again

concerned for the physical welfare of His body, Salome arose very early on the morning after the Sabbath and came with the other women to the tomb, bringing spices with which to give Jesus a proper burial. It is powerful to me that because she was actively caring for the physical needs of another—what some might call "women's work"— Salome was among the first witnesses to the one of the greatest moments in history—the Resurrection of Jesus Christ.

It is also important to note that in Matthew's account of the Resurrection, he does not name Salome but lists three women—Mary Magdalene; Mary, the mother of James and Joses; and the mother of Zebedee's children. (See "Mother of Zebedee's Children" on page 109.) Some scholars conclude that Salome and the mother of Zebedee's children were the same woman. Other scholars, however, think that this conclusion would be an "over harmonistic" reading of the gospels and that they were two separate women.[1] She should not be confused with the daughter of Herodias (see "Herodias and Her Daughter" on page 63), who also may have been named Salome.

The name Salome is also interesting because it is a shortened version of the name Shelamzion, which means "peace of Zion." From 76 to 67 BC, a woman named Salome Alexandra (whose full name was Shelamzion) ruled Judea, one of only two female rulers in the country's history.[2] Salome Alexandra reigned over a time of peace and was well liked by many of her subjects. This can be evidenced by the fact that Salome was the second most common girls name in Judea (the first being Mary) around the time of Christ.[3]

Regardless of her identity, Salome was companion to two of Christ's most faithful female disciples: Mary Magdalene and Mary, the mother of James and Joses. She followed and ministered to Jesus during His life and even after His death —faithful and committed to Him in a time when many of His disciples abandoned Him, an indication that she was a woman of courage and faith.

# *Women* at the Empty Tomb

*After the birth of my second son,* I had a powerful spiritual experience. I got in the shower to clean up after the birth. While I rubbed soap over my belly, I began to think how strange it was that just earlier that morning, in the same shower, I'd rubbed soap over a pregnant belly. Now it was empty. I thought to myself, "Wow! Where did it all go?" And then the words "He is not here" pierced my heart, and I found myself remembering the story of the women at the empty tomb. Specifically, I remembered words written by my friend Robyn:

> As the women approached His tomb, they said to each other: "Who shall roll us away the stone from the door of the sepulchre? And when they looked, they saw that the stone was rolled away: for it was very great. And entering into the sepulchre they saw a young man . . . and he saith unto them, Be not affrighted: Ye seek Jesus of Nazareth, which was crucified: he is risen; he is not here; behold the place where they laid him."
>
> The empty tomb symbolizes the power of Christ and new life through the Atonement. It symbolizes joy and wonder and even possesses mysterious significance. In like manner, the mother's empty womb symbolizes the power of creation made possible through Heavenly Father. It is a sacred event, as are the Atonement and resurrection of the Lord and Savior, Jesus Christ. The empty womb symbolizes physical life offered to a spiritual being, offering joy, wonder, and mysterious significance—mysterious because it is easy to ask, "How is this done?" The only answer can be through God, through His infinite wisdom and power.[1]

While I stood in the shower and stared at my deflated stomach, I had a powerful realization that both the womb and the tomb are places of transformation and those who enter emerge as new beings. The womb is a place where bones, sinews, muscles, organs, and nerves are all organized and ordered. A person enters the womb as only a few cells and miraculously emerges nine months later as a mortal being with millions of cells. In a similar manner, the tomb (death) is also a place of transformation. A person enters it with a mortal body that will corrupt and decay, yet, because of Christ, one day that body will be organized and ordered again and will emerge as an immortal being.

The image of resurrection being a literal birth is very powerful for me, because even with all our medical advances, we know very little about how human life is created or the process that governs labor and birth. Whenever I have witnessed a birth, I have found myself in awe at the incredible miracle of life. How can a living, breathing person possibly be created out of only the materials housed within a woman's body? It makes me cry, as Robyn said in her essay, "Lord, how is it done?"

Giving life is truly miraculous and if I didn't know that women do it—and have done it for thousands of years—it would be hard for me to believe that such a miracle was even possible. I feel that same way about resurrection. The whole process is so mysterious to me. How is there any way that a human being who has been dead for thousands of years, whose bones have turned to dust, can be reconstructed and reunited with its spirit? It seems impossible and makes me question doubtfully, "Lord, how is it done?"

Just like the miracle of mortal birth is possible, the miracle of resurrection is also possible.

Christ, with His empty tomb and left-behind clothes,[2] is a testament of that. Both birth and resurrection are free gifts, one given to us by our mortal mothers and one given to us by Jesus Christ. They are gifts that no matter how hard we try, we will never be able to repay.

It will always be beautiful to me that on the morning of His Resurrection—His spiritual birth—Christ's first interactions were with women. Not only were women the first witnesses of the empty tomb, but they were also the first to touch Christ. As one BYU scholar wrote,

> Jesus appeared to Mary Magdalene before any of the other disciples. The King James Version translates the words of the Savior to Mary Magdalene as, "Touch me not; for I am not yet ascended to my Father." This has caused some to suppose that Mary was forbidden to physically touch the resurrected Christ until He reported to His Father in Heaven. The Greek verb, however, that is translated as "touch me not" could be translated as "stop touching me." The implication is that in her joy at seeing Jesus alive again, Mary Magdalene has grabbed the Savior and is hugging Him.

## WHO WAS AT THE TOMB?

Reading through all four Gospels and trying to keep track of who was at the empty tomb can be confusing. We don't know the exact number of women who were at the tomb because each of the Gospel writers mentions different women. The only one mentioned in all four accounts is Mary Magdalene, though Mary, the mother of James and Joses (also called "the other Mary"), is mentioned in three of the accounts. Hopefully the chart on page 151 will help you keep track of them easier.

The Joseph Smith Translation may lend support for this understanding in light of the fact that it changes this verse to "Hold me not." Mary Magdalene certainly provides the first eyewitness of Jesus in bodily form, and she may also provide the first sure witness of His physical, resurrected body.[3]

We read in Mark's account that after the women found the tomb empty, they were sent by an angel to tell the disciples of the miracle. On their way, the women were stopped by the resurrected Christ. On seeing their beloved Jesus alive, these women "came and held him by the feet, and worshipped him" (Matthew 28:9). These women were the first of Christ's disciples to touch Him and to see the nail prints in His feet (and presumably in His hands). They were first to know that He was again a living, breathing man.

Christ would later appear to many of His other disciples, and others would touch the marks in His feet, but it is significant to me that the women had that first privilege. Women, who sacrifice so much to create mortal life, were the first to proclaim to the world the joyful news of the Resurrection. What more glorious message could come to women than to know that no sacrifice, no heartache, and no effort they make to create and nurture life will be in vain; that through Jesus Christ there will be no end to life.

| Matthew 28:1 | Mark 16:1 | Luke 24:10 | John 20: 1–3, 11–18 |
|---|---|---|---|
| Mary Magdalene<br><br>The other Mary | Mary Magdalene<br><br>Mary, the mother of James and Joses<br><br>Salome | Mary Magdalene<br><br>Joanna<br><br>Mary, the mother of James<br><br>Other women that were with them | Mary Magdalene |

# Women *Gathered in Prayer with the Apostles*

*"And when they were come in, they went up into an upper room, where abode both Peter, and James, and John, and Andrew, Philip, and Thomas, Bartholomew, and Matthew, James the son of Alphaeus, and Simon Zelotes, and Judas the brother of James. These all continued with one accord in prayer and supplication, with the women, and Mary the mother of Jesus, and with his brethren."*

*Acts 1:13–14*

*Directly after Christ's ascension into heaven,* the Apostles returned to Jerusalem (they had been on the Mount of Olives) and "went up into an upper room" (Acts 1:13). All eleven of the remaining Apostles[1] were gathered together in this room, as well as Jesus's brothers, Mary the mother of Jesus, and "the women," presumably the women who followed Him. Together this group in the upper room "continued with one accord in prayer and supplication" (verse 14). The scriptures don't specify, but this may have been the same "upper room" where Jesus had spent His last Passover, washed the feet of His Apostles, and administered the first sacrament.[2] If it was the same room, it would have been a sacred spot for these disciples. It is significant to me that when the Apostles prayed "with one accord," they included women in that circle.

We don't know what they were praying or supplicating for, but we know that these disciples had much to consider. The resurrected Christ had just instructed them for forty days. I imagine that they were much like the Nephites who, after their visit with Jesus Christ, "did pray for that which they most desired . . . that the Holy Ghost should be given unto them" (3 Nephi 19:9). I think that this desire for the Holy Ghost must have been in the hearts of these Christian disciples as well because not long after this meeting in the upper room, they received the gift of the Holy Ghost on the day of Pentecost.

The word *Pentecost* is a transliteration of the Greek word *pentekostos*, which means "fifty." It was fifty days after the death of Christ that the disciples were once again gathered "with one accord" in a house.[3] While they were praying there "came a sound from heaven as of a rushing mighty wind, and it filled all the house where they were sitting" (Acts 2:2). After this, "they were all filled with the Holy Ghost, and began to speak with other tongues, as the Spirit gave them utterance" (verse 4).

The scriptures do not expressly mention that women were present on the day of Pentecost. However, they were present earlier when the disciples prayed with "one accord," so I think it is safe to assume that they would have been included this time as well. When Peter bore his testimony to the people of Jerusalem that day, he quoted a verse of scriptures that talks about women exercising spiritual gifts. Speaking of the disciples who were miraculously speaking in tongues, he proclaimed that "these are not drunken. . . . But this is that which was spoken by the prophet Joel. . . . I will pour out of my Spirit upon all flesh: and your sons and your daughters shall prophesy. . . . And on my servants and on my handmaidens I will pour out in those days of my Spirit; and they shall prophesy" (verses 15–18).

Peter's choice of this particular scripture, which specifically focuses on the ability of women to prophesy, suggests that the people of Jerusalem heard women as well as men speak in tongues and prophesy.

It is powerful to me to picture these female disciples not only engaged with the Apostles in prayer and worship but also being recipients of powerful spiritual manifestations of the Holy Ghost. The presence of these women in the upper room, and at the day of Pentecost, makes it clear that Christ's teachings on the value and importance of women were not lost at His death. The Apostles and early Church members understood and valued women's voices and contributions, and the development of women's spiritual gifts have always been a part of Christ's Church on the earth.

# Sapphira

*"But a certain man named Ananias, with Sapphira his wife, sold a possession, and kept back part of the price, his wife also being privy to it. . . . But Peter said, Ananias, . . . thou hast not lied unto men, but unto God. And Ananias hearing these words fell down, and gave up the ghost. . . . Then Peter said unto her, How is it that ye have agreed together to tempt the Spirit of the Lord? behold, the feet of them which have buried thy husband are at the door, and shall carry thee out. Then fell she down straightway at his feet, and yielded up the ghost. . . . And great fear came upon all the church, and upon as many as heard these things."*

*Acts 5:1–5, 7, 9–11*

*Sapphira and her husband, Ananias,* were members of the Christian church in Jerusalem after Christ's Resurrection. After the death of Christ, the Apostles began to boldly teach the gospel and perform miracles. The rulers in Jerusalem conspired against them but were unable to stop their work. After the miracle of the Pentecost, many were converted and were filled with the Holy Ghost to such a degree that they were "of one heart and of one soul" (Acts 4:32) and they began to live with all things in common, what we might call the law of consecration. Those who had lands or houses sold them and brought the money to the Apostles to be redistributed.

After covenanting to live this law, Ananias sold a portion of his land. Instead of giving all of the money he made to the Church, he, with Sapphira "being privy to it" (Acts 5:2), kept back part of the money. When Ananias presented his offering before the Apostles, Peter perceived that he was withholding money. Peter confronted him about it and asked, "Why hast thou conceived this thing in thine heart? thou hast not lied unto men, but unto God" (verse 4). When Ananias heard Peter's words, he fell down and "gave up the ghost" (verse 5).

Some young men carried out his body and buried it. Three hours later, Sapphira came in and, not knowing what had happened to her husband, she also lied to Peter about the price of the land they had sold. Peter then told her, "How is it that ye have agreed together to tempt the Spirit of the Lord? behold, the feet of them which have buried thy husband are at the door, and shall carry thee out" (verse 9). After these words were spoken, she fell down at Peter's feet and "yielded up the ghost" (verse 10).

I can only imagine that after the word of their deaths got out, people were pretty scared by it. Can you imagine if the consequence of lying was always instant death? I know that I wouldn't dare tell even a little white lie if there was a chance I'd be struck down right then and there!

Obviously, the story of Sapphira and Ananias is an extreme case, but I think their story illustrates an important spiritual principle: when we break promises—especially promises to God—part of our spiritual self dies. President Gordon B. Hinckley said, "In our time those found in dishonesty do not die as did Ananias and Sapphira, but something within them dies. Conscience chokes, character withers, self-respect vanishes, integrity dies."[1] If we could just see what our choices do to the health of our spirits, as we can see what our actions do to our bodies, we would probably make much better choices.

In a world where honesty and integrity are becoming archaic values, it is important that we cultivate honesty in ourselves and within our families. Being honest gives us spiritual strength. It also prepares us to be honest with God and to honor some of the biggest promises we make on this earth—covenants.

A covenant is a promise between God and man. Relief Society General President Linda K. Burton taught, "Making and keeping covenants means choosing to bind ourselves to our Father in Heaven and Jesus Christ. . . . In that binding contract, the Lord sets the terms and we agree to keep them. Making and keeping our covenants is an expression of our commitment to become like the Savior."[2]

Throughout our lives, we will make several different covenants with God—when we are baptized, when we receive the endowment, and when we are sealed. These covenants are sacred promises we make to the Lord, and honoring and respecting them are crucial to our spiritual well-being. When we break them, like Sapphira demonstrated, we cannot avoid

> "If we could just see what our choices do to the health of our spirits, . . . we would probably make much better choices."

the consequences—spiritual or temporal. For as Paul taught, "God is not mocked; for whatsoever a man soweth, that shall he also reap" (Galatians 6:7).

Understanding this about covenants can help us not only change our own behavior, but it can also help us teach the children in our lives about honesty. When they see us choosing to be honest, in all our dealings, it not only teaches them to be honest with others but also how to be honest with God. If they don't learn how to keep simple promises to their fellow men, they may find that they are unprepared to keep important promises to God. As Ananias and Sapphira showed us, such a situation would be tragic. Sister Linda S. Reeves taught, "When all is said and done, what will matter to our Father in Heaven will be how well we have kept our covenants and how much we have tried to follow the example of our Savior, Jesus Christ."[3] I hope we can learn from the story of Sapphira and Ananias and learn to keep our promises—with men and with God—and not make the same sad mistakes they did.

# Widows *Who Were Neglected*

*"And in those days, when the number of the disciples was multiplied, there arose a murmuring of the Grecians against the Hebrews, because their widows were neglected in the daily ministration."*

Acts 6:1

**As the early Christian Church grew,** it expanded to include people of many backgrounds and experiences. While this growth must have been exciting to the Apostles and members of the Church, it also brought challenges. In Acts 6:1 we read that the Greek disciples were concerned that the Jewish disciples were neglecting the Greek widows, specifically in the "daily ministration." Perhaps these women were not receiving the same Church welfare support as Jewish widows or perhaps they were not being included in the administration of the sacrament or other ordinances. This inequality bothered the Greeks, and they were concerned for the physical and spiritual welfare of their women.

These Greek disciples were sometimes called "Hellenized Jews" because they spoke Greek and followed Greek customs.[1] Linguistic and cultural barriers between the Greek and Hebrew members may have made meeting the needs of both groups of people difficult. I can relate to the situation in which these early believers must have found themselves. When my husband and I were first married, we lived in an area that had a large Hispanic population. My husband and I made friends with a Hispanic family (a single mother with four small children) that lived in the apartment below us and invited them to Church. Our ward was mostly English speaking and our Hispanic neighbors hardly spoke any English at all. It didn't take my husband and I long to realize that our ward, because of the cultural and linguistic barrier, was going to struggle to give this family the support they needed. Our ward was wonderful, though, and many people reached out and found creative ways to include them and love them. Later we were able to help this family connect with the Spanish-speaking branch in our stake. Our ward had done a good job of reaching out, but it really helped this family to have the support of people who spoke their language and who understood their culture. I imagine that these early Hebrew and Greek Saints might have found themselves in a similar situation.

In response to the Greeks' concerns about their widows being unfairly treated, the Apostles gathered the people together and told them, "It is not reason that we should leave the word of God, and serve tables" (Acts 6:2). The Apostles understood that their responsibility was to the "ministry of the word" (verse 4). They did not have time to mediate disputes within the Church, especially when they were not familiar with the customs or needs of different groups of believers. Instead, they told the people to find seven men "of honest report, full of the Holy Ghost and wisdom, whom we may appoint over this business" (verse 3). The seven men chosen were Stephen, Philip,[2] Prochorus, Nicanor, Timon, Parmenas, and Nicolas (verse 5). These men were set apart to oversee different areas of the Church and make sure all the needs of the Saints, wherever they lived, were being met. They may have functioned much like a the modern-day Area Seventies do, whose responsibility is to care for specific groups of Saints in different areas of the world and report back to the Apostles about the people's unique needs and challenges.

This is an important example to remember when we experience inequality or injustice among Church members or in Church practices today. God would not have us murmur and create animosity among members, but rather He would have us work in cooperation with priesthood leaders to discover how God would correct the situation. The early Apostles, after counseling with the Lord, found a solution that not only addressed the issue with the Greek widows, but that also met the needs of *all* the women in the Church. When we follow that same pattern of working cooperatively with priesthood leaders, not only do we create peace, but we also open up the door for God to give us greater revelation and direction in how His Church should operate on the earth.

# Widowhood

In the patriarchal society of the New Testament, a man's inheritance usually went to his sons or his daughters (if he had no sons) but rarely to his wife. This meant that on the death of her husband, a woman was economically dependent upon her sons. If they were not old enough to care for her yet, or if they did not fulfill their responsibility to her, this could leave a woman in dire poverty. A woman who lost her sons in addition to her husband would have been in a very hard situation. This is perhaps one of the reasons that Jesus had compassion on the widow of Nain (see page 41) and raised her son from the dead.

Not all widows were poor. If a woman was well provided for by her sons, widowhood might actually enlarge her sphere. A widow could sometimes assume male roles that would normally be frowned upon for a woman, like engaging in business and interacting openly with men. In this way, widowhood could actually open opportunities to her that would otherwise be off limits. Still, it seems that most widows had difficult lives. As one author noticed, common words often used with the term widow in the Bible are "weeping, mourning, and desolation. . . . Poverty and indebtedness. . . . Indeed, she was frequently placed alongside the orphan and the landless immigrant as representative of the poorest of the poor in the social structure of ancient Israel."[3]

Properly caring for widows is a recurring theme in the scriptures. Caring for widowed women was seen as a responsibility of the early Christian Church. We don't know exactly how the Church provided that support, but perhaps it was similar to how Christ instructed the early Latter-day Saints to provide for their widows. In Doctrine and Covenants 83 He said:

> Women have claim on their husbands for their maintenance, until their husbands are taken; and if they are not found transgressors they shall have fellowship in the church. And if they are not faithful they shall not have fellowship in the church; yet they may remain upon their inheritances according to the laws of the land. . . . And the storehouse shall be kept by the consecrations of the church; and widows and orphans shall be provided for, as also the poor. (D&C 83 2–3, 6)

It seems that some similar sort of system must have existed among the early Saints. In one of his letters to Timothy, Paul instructed him in the proper care for widows who were "widows indeed" (1 Timothy 5:3). Widows hold a special place in God's heart. As James wrote, we cannot practice the "pure religion" of Jesus Christ unless we "visit the fatherless and widows in their affliction" (James 1:27)

# Samaritan Women
## Baptized by Philip

*"But when they believed Philip preaching the things concerning the kingdom of God, and the name of Jesus Christ, they were baptized, both men and women."*

Acts 8:12

*In an attempt to flee persecution,* Philip went to Samaria and preached to the people there. The people with "one accord" (Acts 8:6) listened and believed in the things that he taught them. Many believed because of the miracles Philip was able to perform, specifically casting out unclean spirits and healing the lame. The only barrier to Philip's success was a man named Simon, who "used sorcery, and bewitched the people of Samaria, giving out that himself was some great one" (verse 9). All the Samaritans held Simon in high regard and believed that he had great power from God. When they saw Philip do great miracles in the name of Jesus Christ, they recognized his power and authority and were converted. Even Simon, amazed by the works that Philip was able to do in the name of Christ, was baptized. I think these Samaritan men and women demonstrated spiritual sensitivity in being able to see past deception and recognize real power and truth.

This story is also interesting because when Christ met the Samaritan woman at the well (see page 37), He told His disciples that "one soweth, and another reapeth" (John 4:37). It makes me wonder how many "seeds" Christ sowed among the Samaritans during His two-day visit with them and how the influence of the woman at the well may have prepared the Samaritans to recognize and accept the gospel when it was brought to them. In that sense, Philip reaped, or harvested, the seeds that Jesus had planted. It's a good reminder to me that we never know what seeds the Lord has already planted and who is prepared to receive His gospel.

> "*They were baptized, both men and women.*"

# Samaritans

Samaritans figure prominently in the New Testament. It is important to understand who they were and how they were viewed and treated by the Jews. When the ten tribes were carried away captive, the area of Samaria was repopulated by those living in neighboring areas. These people worshipped idols but began to adopt Jewish practices and teachings into their worship, and eventually they become more observant to the Mosaic law than the Jews. When the Jews who had been carried away captive were eventually granted permission from Cyrus, the Persian king, to return to Jerusalem, the Samaritans were eager to be recognized as Israelites and to be included in Jewish worship. Yet the Jews viewed them as being a tainted race because of their intermarriage with surrounding tribes.

The Samaritans believed that they, during the Jews' exile, had preserved the true scriptures, the true priesthood authority, and the true form of temple worship. They had built a temple on Mount Gezim and claimed that they, not the Jews, were the legitimate heirs to the priesthood because they were descendents of Ephraim and Manasseh.[1] These differences resulted in animosity and violence between the two groups. The Jews destroyed the Samaritan temple on Mount Gezim in 128 BC[2] and reduced the Samaritans' land to a fraction of what it had been before.[3]

By the time Christ came, tensions between the Samaritans and the Jews had eased, but the groups were still not friendly with each other. The Samaritans, despite the ruined temple, still worshipped and offered sacrifices on Mount Gezim and were contemptuous of the Jewish temple in Jerusalem. James E. Talmage wrote that they "accused the Jews of adding to the word of God, by receiving the writings of the prophets; . . . favored Herod because the Jews hated him, and were loyal to him; . . . had kindled false lights on the hills, to vitiate the Jewish reckoning by the new moons, and thus thrown their feasts into confusion, and, in the early youth of Jesus, had even defiled the very Temple itself, by strewing human bones in it, at Passover."[4] The Jews weren't much better. According to Talmage, the Jews also treated the Samaritans poorly: "They had been subjected to every form of excommunication; by the incommunicable name of Jehovah; by the Tables of the Law, and by the heavenly and earthly synagogues. The very name [Samaritan] became a reproach.'"[5] In their courts, the Jews would not recognize the testimony of a Samaritan, nor would they even touch or eat food that had been prepared by Samaritan hands.[6]

It is significant to me that Christianity—the gospel of Jesus Christ—was the first influence to truly overcome these deep-rooted cultural animosities. Christ's gospel brought peace and bridged the gap between the Jews and the Samaritans. They found their common ground in understanding that they were all children of the same God.

# *Candace,* Queen of the Ethiopians

*"And he arose and went: and, behold, a man of Ethiopia, an eunuch of great authority under Candace queen of the Ethiopians, who had the charge of all her treasure, and had come to Jerusalem for to worship."*

*Acts 8:27*

**This woman is mentioned briefly** in the context of her slave, a eunuch, who had traveled to Jerusalem to worship. A eunuch was a slave man who had been castrated. Eunuchs were often used as slaves in the royal courts of women because they were thought to be harmless, as they often didn't have sexual desire for women and were unable to sire children. This particular eunuch, who was in charge of all of her treasure, appears to have been a Jew because he was reading Isaiah when he met Philip. (See "Four Daughters of Philip" on page 205.) Philip taught him about Jesus and baptized him not long after.

Candace, or Kandake as it can also be translated, is not actually a first name but rather a title that means "great woman" or "queen mother." It was a title passed down to each reigning queen and someone would have referred to "the Candace"

just as they may have referred to "the Pharaoh" or "the Caesar."

The Candace ruled over the people of the ancient African kingdom of Kush, which is also sometimes called Nubia or Ethiopia in the scriptures. It was situated just outside of Egypt along the Nile in what is now modern day Sudan. It is interesting that two of the rulers we hear of from this part of the world, the Queen of Sheba[1] and the Candace, were both women. This is because this part of the world had a strong tradition of female leaders. According to one scholar, at least twenty-one queens were recorded as the sole regents of Ethiopia until 9 AD.[2] This pattern of female leadership likely arose because the people believed that their king was a god and thus held in such high esteem that he was not allowed to be touched or spoken of and was not to be bothered with mortal affairs. As a result, it was most often his queen or his mother who managed the affairs of the kingdom. These women were strong, capable women who were also formidable military leaders and were well respected by both their subjects and other rulers.

As the treasurer of the Candace, the eunuch that Phillip met and baptized would have been a man of considerable power and influence. Ethiopian Christians claim that after his conversion he returned to Ethiopia, shared his faith with the queen, and then established the Christian church there—a fulfillment of the words spoken by David that "Ethiopia shall soon stretch out her hands unto God" (Psalm 68:31). While we can't know for sure if this story is true, we do know that Christianity flourished in Ethiopia and that many people there were converted to the teachings of Jesus Christ. Such a wide-spread conversion makes the probability that the Candace, whoever she was, may have believed in Christ and encouraged the spread of His teachings throughout her land.

# Tabitha

*"Now there was at Joppa a certain disciple named Tabitha. . . . And it came to pass in those days, that she was sick, and died: whom when they had washed, they laid her in an upper chamber. . . . [A]nd all the widows stood by him weeping, and shewing the coats and garments which Dorcas made, while she was with them. But Peter put them all forth, and kneeled down, and prayed; and turning him to the body said, Tabitha, arise. And she opened her eyes: and when she saw Peter, she sat up. . . . And it was known throughout all Joppa; and many believed in the Lord."*

Acts 9:36–37, 39–42

**Tabitha, also known by** her Greek name Dorcas, is introduced to us in Acts 9 as "a certain disciple" (verse 36) living in the costal town of Joppa. She was known as a woman who was "full of good works and almsdeeds" (verse 36), which is the giving of money, clothes, food, and other things to the poor. Later we read that she had made garments and coats for many of the widows in Joppa. This tells us that not only was she skilled with her hands and in the making of textiles, but that she also chose to use her talents to bless others.

We don't know how old Tabitha was or what her circumstances were, but somehow she became sick and died. Since the people

of this time period had no way to preserve the dead, they buried bodies within hours after death.[1] The Saints in Joppa had heard that the prophet Peter was in Lydda, which was just twelve miles from Joppa. So two men went there to ask "that he would not delay to come to them" (verse 38). It seems telling that these disciples would think it appropriate—and even urgent—to notify Peter of Tabitha's death and that he left what he was doing and went with them to Joppa. Such actions suggest that Peter may have been well acquainted with Tabitha or that she held some sort of position of respect within the Church.

When Peter got to Joppa he found Tabitha's body laid out in the upper chamber of the house, which was thronged by widows mourning her loss. These widows stood by him, weeping and showing him the clothes and coats that Tabitha had made while she was with them. It is evident from the way she was mourned that her life touched and influenced many others.

After shooing everyone out of the room, Peter knelt down and prayed. He turned toward her body and said, "Tabitha, arise" (verse 40). She opened her eyes and, when she saw Peter, sat up. Peter reached out his hand, helped her stand, and "presented her alive" (verse 41) to the Saints and widows who were gathered in the house. I can only imagine their astonishment at seeing Tabitha alive. They probably had not called Peter to the house expecting a miracle. They likely thought that he wanted time alone with her to mourn, not to bring her back to life. Understandably, news of this miracle quickly spread throughout Joppa and the surrounding areas and caused many people to believe in Christ. The fact that she is identified by both a Hebrew name, Tabitha, and a Greek name, Dorcas, indicates that she and her story were well-known to both the Jews and the Gentiles. It seems that her example as a woman of good works, who was also the recipient of a remarkable miracle, really touched people's hearts and helped spread the gospel.

Tabitha's story reminds us, as the well-known saying goes, to "preach the gospel at all times. When necessary, use words." For all we know, Tabitha never preached the gospel or ever formally shared her testimony of Jesus Christ. It is beautiful to think that it may have been through her everyday good deeds that Tabitha was able to soften the hearts of those around her and prepare them to receive the gospel. Through her reputation as woman of "good deeds" and through the miracle surrounding her, many came to know and follow Christ.

Today missionary work often follows that same pattern manifested in Tabitha's story. In parts of the world that are hostile to or suspicious of Christianity, missionaries often "preach" the gospel through humanitarian efforts, charities, and one-on-one service to individuals and families. Often these missionaries are forbidden by law or cultural custom to formally proselyte or teach the gospel. Yet through their service, people come to taste the love of Christ. Their hearts are softened and prepared to receive the gospel.

Just like Tabitha's story demonstrated, we never know who is watching us or how our kind words or deeds may prepare someone to receive the gospel and believe in Jesus Christ. For as Alma taught, "By small and simple things are great things brought to pass" (Alma 37:6).

> *"By small and simple things are great things brought to pass."*

# Rhoda

*"And as Peter knocked at the door of the gate, a damsel came to hearken, named Rhoda. And when she knew Peter's voice, she opened not the gate for gladness, but ran in, and told how Peter stood before the gate. And they said unto her, Thou art mad. But she constantly affirmed that it was even so."*

Acts 12:13–15

*Rhoda is among the few* young women mentioned of the New Testament. She is called a "damsel" (Acts 12:13), which indicates that she was a young girl who was not yet married. Another damsel spoken of in the New Testament was the daughter of Jairus, who was twelve years old. (See "Daughter of Jairus" on page 47.)[1] It would be a good guess to say Rhoda was around the same age.[2] In Acts 12 Rhoda was gathered with the Jerusalem Christians at the home of Mary, the mother of John Mark (see page 177), at the time of the Passover. This was a time of intense persecution for the Saints. Herod Agrippa had just killed James the Apostle in order to please the Jews, and the Prophet Peter had been imprisoned. Herod intended to turn Peter over to the people and execute him after Easter.

The Saints were terrified and prayed "without ceasing" (verse 5) for Peter. Acts 12:12 tells us that they were gathered in the home of Mary, the mother of John Mark, to pray on Peter's behalf.

We don't know which day Peter was imprisoned since the scriptures only say it was during Passover. Since the Passover lasted for seven nights, it is possible that these Saints spent days in prayer.

On the night before Easter, an angel appeared to Peter, broke the chains off his hands, and ordered him to dress. The angel told Peter to follow him out of the prison. Peter passed safely by the two guards sleeping inside his cell and the fourteen other guards surrounding his cell. The symbolism of Peter being freed from his prison on Easter morning is a beautiful reminder of the freedom Christ's Resurrection gives each of us.

The angel guided Peter out into the street and left him. When Peter "was come to himself" (verse 11), he marveled at what had just occurred and headed toward the house of Mary, the mother of John Mark. The fact that Peter headed toward Mary's house immediately following his release tells us that he knew that would be the place where the Saints would be gathered, a place where he would be welcomed with open— and safe—arms.

When Peter approached Mary's house, he knocked at the door of the gate. Rhoda was the first to "hearken" (verse 13) to his knock. Given the dangerous situation in which the Christians found themselves, she did not dare to open the gate but rather inquired through the closed door who was there. When she recognized Peter's voice, she was so excited that she forgot to open the gate and ran back to tell everyone else. I love how Steven C. Walker wrote about this in his article for the *Ensign*: "Little Rhoda became so excited at meeting Peter at her door that 'she opened not the gate for gladness, but ran in . . .'—leaving the prophet of the Lord, who only moments before had prison gates opened for him by angels, cooling his heels outside."[3]

I can only imagine that those were some nerve-wracking moments for Peter, who was currently the most wanted person in Jerusalem. Yet Rhoda's excitement was understandable. She had been praying, for days perhaps, that the Lord would save the Prophet Peter. I can imagine her praying with all the strength of her young heart for such a miracle. And then, perhaps even in the midst of her prayer, she heard a knock, and when she answered the door there was the very prophet she had been praying for. What an answer to her prayer!

When she ran back and told the group, who was gathered to pray, that Peter was at the gate, they didn't believe her. "Thou art mad" (verse 15), they told her, thinking that there was no possible way Peter could be running around Jerusalem free. Rhoda hadn't even seen him; she had merely heard his voice. Yet she knew the voice of the prophet—she didn't need to see to believe—and so she "constantly affirmed" (verse 15) that he was there.

I admire Rhoda's faith and her tenacity. She stuck firm to what she knew to be true, even when others were mocking and criticizing her. She didn't back down and she didn't deny what she had heard. She knew the voice of the prophet and she could not and would not deny it. What amazing integrity and strength for so young a woman! The people gathered decided that Rhoda must have seen Peter's ghost since he was supposed to have been killed that morning. Yet Peter continued knocking, and eventually they opened the gate and were astonished to see that what Rhoda had said was true.

The parallel here between Rhoda and the women who met Christ at the empty tomb is powerful. (See "Women at the Empty Tomb" on page 149.) Christ rose from the prison of death on Easter morning and the first to know of His deliverance were the women who came to His tomb. Peter was delivered from his prison, and saved from death, as Easter morning drew near. The first person to know of his miraculous deliverance was a woman, a young woman, who was the first to hearken to his knocks. Just as the women at the empty tomb were not believed when they bore testimony to the Apostles of Christ's Resurrection, neither was Rhoda believed when she bore testimony that Peter was alive and physically standing outside the gate. It is beautiful to me that in both of these instances, women were the first witnesses.

Peter didn't stay long with the Saints, only long enough to tell them that their prayers had been answered and that he was safe. He commanded them to "go shew these things unto James, and to the brethren," and then he departed and went to Caesarea to avoid recapture.

This experience must have taught Rhoda a powerful lesson. She would have learned that God hears and answers prayers, specifically her prayers. She learned that sometimes, when there is nothing you can do to fix a problem, the best thing to do is to pray. I think sometimes, as we grow older, we forget how to pray with perfect faith. We are often more like the Saints gathered in the house, praying for a miracle but not really believing that Peter could actually be outside the gate. Instead, if we were praying with Rhoda-like faith, we would be sitting by the door, listening and watching for the miracle, ready to rejoice and share the news when it happened. Like the women who witnessed Christ rise from the dead, Rhoda reminds us that miracles do happen.

> *"With God, nothing is impossible."*

# Mary, *the Mother of John Mark*

*"And when he had considered the thing, he came to the house of Mary the mother of John, whose surname was Mark; where many were gathered together praying."*

Acts 12:12

**In Acts 12 we read of a Mary** who was the "mother of John, whose surname was Mark" (verse 12), the same Mark who authored the Gospel of Mark.[1] Colossians 4 also tells us that Mark (here called Marcus) was the "sister's son to Barnabas" (verse 10), who was Paul's mission companion, and "sister's son" is a long way of saying that Mark was Barnabas's nephew. This means that Barnabas and Mary were brother and sister. This family relationship may explain why Mark traveled with Barnabas and Paul on their missionary travels.[2]

When Mary is first mentioned in Acts 12, it was a time of great persecution and danger for the Christian Church in Jerusalem. Herod Agrippa had "stretched forth his hands to vex certain of the church" (Acts 12:1). He had killed the Apostle James and had imprisoned Peter, the prophet of the Church. Many of the Saints gathered together at Mary's home to pray on Peter's behalf, and it was to her home that Peter went after his miraculous release from prison. (See "Rhoda" on page 173.) The fact that she had a home large enough for the Saints to gather in and that she employed at least one servant indicates that she may have been a wealthy woman.[3]

Despite the peril, Mary opened her home to the Saints and to the fugitive prophet. She would have clearly understood the risk she was taking, but she did it anyway. Her actions tell us that she was smart, brave, and fully converted to Jesus Christ. She understood the power that protects those who follow Jesus Christ and was willing to risk all that she had, including her life and her home, for her faith.

> *"She understood the power that protects those who follow Jesus Christ."*

# Devout and Honorable Women of the Jews and Greeks

*"But the Jews stirred up the devout and honourable women, and the chief men of the city, and raised persecution against Paul and Barnabas, and expelled them out of their coasts."*

Acts 13:50

*"And some of them believed, and consorted with Paul and Silas; and of the devout Greeks a great multitude, and of the chief women not a few. . . . Therefore many of them believed; also of honourable women which were Greeks, and of men, not a few."*

Acts 17:4, 12

Elder D. Todd Christofferson taught, "From age immemorial, societies have relied on the moral force of women. . . . Women bring with them into the world a certain virtue, a divine gift that makes them adept at instilling such qualities as faith, courage, empathy, and refinement in relationships and in cultures."[1] Women exert their moral force in many different ways: they teach and nurture children; they serve and influence their communities; they stand as guardians of virtue and righteous living; and they advocate for changes in their nations.

Elder Christofferson also stated, "While certainly not the only positive influence at work in society, the moral foundation provided by women has proved uniquely beneficial to the common good."[2] It is interesting to notice that woman's influence over society is so prevalent that we even refer to the

> *"Women bring with them into the world a certain virtue."*

land where something originated from as the "motherland," and someone's native language as their "mother tongue." The foundations of societies and nations are forged by women and the choices they make, whether for good or for bad.

This "moral force" can be seen among the Greek and Jewish women that Paul encountered on his missionary journeys.

While Paul and Barnabas were traveling, they came to Antioch and began to preach. They taught in the synagogue and were well received at first by both Jews and "religious proselytes" (Acts 13:43), or Gentile converts to Judaism. Not long after Paul and Barnabas arrived, word of them spread, and soon nearly the entire city was gathered to hear what they were preaching.

This sudden popularity filled the Jewish leaders with envy and they began to speak out against Paul and Barnabas. Despite their efforts, many people continued to believe in Jesus Christ. The Jews, seeing that their attempts were failing, began to stir up the "devout and honourable women" (verse 50) and the chief men of the city. Only when these devout and honorable citizens began to take a stand against Paul and Barnabas were the Jews able to gather enough opposition to expel them from their city. These "devout and honourable" Jewish women were exerting their moral force, their ability to influence the choices that a whole society made. Unfortunately in this case, these women chose to use their moral force to turn people away from Jesus Christ rather than bring them closer to the truth.

Later in their journey, Paul and Silas (another of Paul's missionary companions) taught in Thessalonica, the capital of Macedonia. They began to have great success, but again the Jewish leaders became envious and started to "set all the city on an uproar" (Acts 17:5). Paul and Silas feared for their life and even had to be smuggled out of the city at night to Berea, a nearby city. Here Paul found that the people were "more noble" (verse 11) and better prepared to hear his words. The "honorable women which were Greeks" (verse 12) were among the first to believe Paul, and their faith and example helped convert others. Like the Jewish women of Antioch, these Greek women were exerting their moral force, but unlike the Jewish women, their choices helped turn their community toward Christ.

The stories of these women help remind us that women's voices and opinions have much more weight and influence in the world than we realize. There is great power generated when devoted and committed women raise their voices for or against a cause. Elder Bruce C. Hafen shared this true story from the history of Australia that demonstrates the power of women's influence:

In its early decades as a British colony, Australia was a vast wilderness designated as a jail for exiled convicts. Until 1850, six of every seven people who went "down under" from Britain were men. And the few women who went were often convicts or social outcasts themselves. . . .

In about 1840, a reformer named Caroline Chisholm urged that more women would stabilize the culture. She told the British government the best way to establish a community of "great and good people" in Australia: "For all the clergy you can dispatch, all the schoolmasters you can appoint, all the churches you can build, and all the books you can export, will never do much good without . . . 'God's police'—wives and little children—good and virtuous women."

Chisholm searched for women who would raise "the moral standard of the people." She spent twenty years traveling to England, recruiting young women and young couples who believed in the common sense principles of family life. Over time, these women tamed the men who were taming the wild land; and civil society in Australia gradually emerged. . . . Eventually, thousands of new immigrants who shared the vision of these "good and virtuous women" established stable families as the basic unit of Australian society more quickly than had occurred "anywhere else in the Western world." . . .

These women made Australia a promised land that flowed with a healthy ecosystem of milk and honey. And the milk, literally and figuratively, was mother's milk—the milk of human kindness. That milk nurtures those habits of the heart without which no civil society can sustain itself.[3]

Women's influence is a force that has the power and ability to change and shape the world. It has the ability to soften hearts, touch lives, teach, nurture, inspire, grow, and create individuals, families, communities, and nations. Women's influence is the thread that holds the fabric of the world together. This force has been so prevalent in the history of the world that, as Elder Christofferson said, "perhaps we have begun to take it and [women] for granted."[4]

Even if at times the world may take women's influence for granted, it is vitally important that women understand their power and that they choose to use it in the right way. The choices women make and the way they teach and nurture future generations matters immensely. Their influence and voices can often be a determining factor in whether a society chooses truth and light or dwindles in darkness and unbelief. The story of these Greek and Jewish women reminds us that the moral force of women is a real power, and that we should never underestimate the influence women can have on the world, especially a group of righteous women. That might be one of the most powerful forces in the world.

> *"Never underestimate the influence women can have on the world."*

# Eunice and Lois

*"When I call to remembrance the unfeigned faith that is in thee, which dwelt first in thy grandmother Lois, and thy mother Eunice; and I am persuaded that in thee also."*

*2 Timothy 1:5*

*"Then came he to Derbe and Lystra: and, behold, a certain disciple was there, named Timotheus, the son of a certain woman, which was a Jewess, and believed; but his father was a Greek."*

*Acts 16:1*

*Eunice was not your run-of-the-mill* first-century Jewish woman. She lived in Derbe and Lystra (which is now part of modern-day Turkey) and was a Jewess married to a Greek man. We don't know much about why Eunice was in the marriage she was in. Parents arranged most marriages and, as Jews believed, it was important to marry within the covenant. It would have been usual for a Jewish woman to be married to a Gentile man.[1] Part of me likes to imagine that she had a highly romantic story—a young Jewish girl falls madly in love with a dashing Greek man and forsakes her family, her country, and her religion to run off with him to Turkey. That's probably not even remotely close to the truth, but it would make for a good novel.

No matter what her story was, she was in an unusual position for a first-century Jewish woman, and her circumstances must have been different from the women around her. In view of this, her story is a valuable one for women who are in relationships where their partner is of a different faith or their partner has lost his faith or become "inactive" in the gospel.[2]

Eunice was also the mother of Timothy, Paul's beloved missionary companion and a leader in the early Christian Church. Eunice and Lois, Timothy's grandmother,[3] converted to Christianity and taught Timothy the gospel. In his Epistle to Timothy, Paul mentioned "the unfeigned faith that is in thee, which dwelt first in thy grandmother Lois, and thy mother Eunice; and I am persuaded that in thee also" (2 Timothy 1:5). The word unfeigned means "genuine" or "sincere" and indicates that Eunice and Lois were truly converted and committed to the gospel of Jesus Christ. It was their example that inspired Timothy and prepared him to become the great missionary that he was.

In 2 Timothy 3:15, Paul wrote to Timothy, "From a child thou hast known the holy scriptures, which are able to make thee wise unto salvation through faith which is in Christ Jesus."

This remark seems to indicate that Timothy had been taught the scriptures from his childhood. Since his father was Greek, we can assume that it was his mother and his grandmother who taught him.

Modern women who have the scriptures at their fingertips may not comprehend the significance of this accomplishment. In Eunice and Lois's day, scripture reading was a purely male

> *"She was a mother who knew."*

activity. The Torah, which was the scriptures of the time, was kept in the synagogue and only men were allowed to handle or read from it. Most women would have been illiterate, and some Jews believed that it was improper and obscene to teach women the scriptures. It is remarkable that Eunice was able to find a way to teach her son the scriptures. It must have been important to her and probably required a great deal of time and sacrifice on her part. Yet she was a mother who knew. She knew what was important and focused on teaching those truths to her son. President Julie Beck taught:

Mothers who know are always teachers. . . . A well-taught friend told me that he did not learn anything at church that he had not already learned at home. His parents used family scripture study, prayer, family home evening, mealtimes, and other gatherings to teach. Think of the power of our future missionary force if mothers considered their homes as a pre-missionary training center. Then the doctrines of the gospel taught in the MTC would be a review and not a revelation. That is influence; that is power.[4]

Eunice and Lois were women who knew, and through their influence and teaching, they raised one of the greatest missionaries in the history of the world. Timothy was prepared and ready to serve and share the gospel from a young age, thanks to the example and teachings of the women in his life. He may not have been in the ideal family situation, but his mother had strong faith, focused on what was important, and did the very best she could.

Eunice is a good example for all women, no matter their situations, who are struggling day by day to raise and nurture children in the gospel and to love and sustain their husbands. She was one of the first "missionary moms" and reminds us that a righteous woman who loves the Lord and does her best will accomplish great things—even if she has to do them by herself.

# Lydia

*"And a certain woman named Lydia, a seller of purple, of the city of Thyatira, which worshipped God, heard us: whose heart the Lord opened, that she attended unto the things which were spoken of Paul. And when she was baptized, and her household, she besought us, saying, If ye have judged me to be faithful to the Lord, come into my house, and abide there. And she constrained us."*

Acts 16:14–15

*Lydia has the distinction* of being the first European convert to Christianity. She was among the group of women Paul first taught when he arrived in the city of Philippi in Macedonia. Paul and his companion Silas traveled to Philippi because a man had come to Paul in a dream and said, "Come over into Macedonia, and help us" (Acts 16:9). Spurred on by this dream, they had faith they would find people prepared to hear the message of Jesus Christ, and they did.

One of the first successes they had as missionaries was with Lydia, who was among a group of women gathered along the river "where prayer was wont to be made" (verse 13). Acts 16:14 tells us that even though Lydia was a Gentile, she "worshipped

God" and apparently observed the Sabbath. With her limited understanding, she was doing the best she knew how, and her heart was seeking truth. The description given in Doctrine and Covenants 123:12 fits her well: "For there are many yet on the earth . . . who are only kept from the truth because they know not where to find it." So when she heard Paul preach of Jesus Christ, her "heart the Lord opened, that she attended unto the things which were spoken of Paul" (Acts 16:14).

Lydia was a "seller of purple" (verse 14), which means she was a merchant (and perhaps maker) of purple dye. Purple dye was expensive and only royalty or the rich could afford the

> ## "Come to my house, and abide there."

color. As a vendor of luxury goods, she was probably well-to-do herself and seemed to be independent since no husband or male relation is listed. She also had a household under her care. After she was baptized, she entreated Paul and his companions to come and live at her house while they were in Philippi. She told them, "If ye have judged me to be faithful to the Lord, come to my house, and abide there" (verse 15). Lydia seems to be a woman who was used to getting her way, because the same verse says that she "constrained us," meaning that she wouldn't take no for an answer.

Lydia's home became the center of the Church in Philippi, where the members met and worshipped (see verse 40). Like many of women of God throughout the scriptures, she opened her home to God's messengers and made room for them.[1] The Lord taught latter-day missionaries that this is how they would recognize true disciples: "Whose recieveth you recieveth me; and the same will feed you, and clothe you, and give you money. And he who feeds you, or clothes you, or gives you money, shall in nowise lose his reward. . . . [B]y this you may know my disciples" (D&C 84:89–91). Lydia's willingness to invite the missionaries into her home and to minister to their physical needs was a sign of her discipleship and love for God.

Lydia's example of opening her home to the missionaries reminds me of how our bishop has been encouraging us to have the full-time missionaries in our homes, not just to feed them but to allow them to teach us and bless our homes. The bishop has promised us that as we invite them into our homes, our families will be blessed and we will be guided in the work the Lord has for us to do. Like Lydia, our willingness

to invite God's messengers into our homes, and to share the gospel, is an indication of the depth of our conversion to Jesus Christ.

It is also interesting that Lydia's home later sheltered Paul and Silas after their miraculous deliverance from prison (see Acts 16:20–39). The scriptures say that "they went out of the prison, and entered into the house of Lydia: and when they had seen the brethren, they comforted them, and departed" (verse 40). Lydia's home was truly a place of refuge and shelter from the world. She had a Christ-centered home. Elder Richard G. Scott taught:

> As you center your home on the Savior, it will naturally become a refuge not only to your own family but also to friends who live in more difficult circumstances. They will be drawn to the serenity they feel there. Welcome such friends into your home. They will blossom in that Christ-centered environment. . . . One of the greatest blessings we can offer to the world is the power of a Christ-centered home where the gospel is taught, covenants are kept, and love abounds.[2]

The power of a Christ-centered home should never be underestimated. Our ability to influence people, soften hearts, and change the world for the better through our example and our way of life is more powerful than we realize. Women, especially young mothers, often feel their sphere of influence is limited and question their ability to share the gospel. Lydia's story illustrates that one of the most powerful things you can do to share the gospel is to simply open your home. Open your home to the missionaries; open your home to

The most famous purple dye came from Tyre and was made from the shells of predatory sea mollusks called "murexes." When crushed, these shells created a beautiful purple that was said to not fade over time but rather deepen with age. It took twelve hundred murex shells to create 1.4 grams of dye, only enough to color the trim of one garment.[3] So purple was an expensive color. One historian, Theopompus, said that "purple was constantly sold for its weight in silver."[4] Tyrian purple was a sign of power. In imperial Roman times, anyone outside of the ruling classes was forbidden to wear purple.[5] Purple also had religious significance and it is supposed that during Christ's time, the outer curtains and inner veils of the temple were dyed with Tyrian purple.[6]

Thyatira, where Lydia was from, was also famous for their dye works and the red and purple dye they produced. Archeologists believe that Thyatirian purple was produced from madder-root instead of murex shells, which may have made it cheaper and more accessible for people to buy, but it was still expensive. Thyatira had highly organized trade guilds that had a lot of power and influence in the city. The guilds were closely connected to pagan worship practices, so membership in these guilds would have been difficult for Christians.[7] An ancient inscription discovered in Thyatira commemorates the Dyers' Guild.[8] It is interesting to think that Lydia may have been a member of this guild and that her joining the Christian Church may have changed how she ran her business. She was one of the first women to be a Christian and a businesswoman!

family, friends, acquaintances, and strangers who need what you have. Invite them in and let your example of righteous living, your joy in your family, and your love for Jesus Christ radiate over them like a beam of sunshine. As Elder Scott promised, this light will touch them, help awaken their faith, and help them bloom in their testimonies of Christ.

No matter what your situation is, never underestimate your ability to change the world or your influence as a disciple of Christ. The example of your Christ-centered home is much more powerful than you realize.

> "The example of your Christ-centered home is much more powerful than you realize."

# Damsel Possessed
## with a Spirit of Divination

*"And it came to pass, . . . a certain damsel possessed with a spirit of divination met us. . . . The same followed Paul and us, and cried, saying, These men are the servants of the most high God, which shew unto us the way of salvation. And this did she many days. But Paul, being grieved, turned and said to the spirit, I command thee in the name of Jesus Christ to come out of her. And he came out the same hour."*

Acts 16:16–18

**While Paul and Silas were teaching** in Philippi (see "Lydia" on page 187), they were followed by a "certain damsel possessed with a spirit of divination" (Acts 16:16). Damsel refers to a young girl, and it is probable that this girl was no older than twelve. Apparently she was a slave whose masters used her ability of soothsaying to make money. A soothsayer is a "diviner," or "one who professes to foretell the future,"[1] but soothsaying is not the same as having the gift of prophecy. Being able to prophesy is a gift of the Spirit, and someone exercising the gift of prophecy always bears testimony of Christ and of truth. Soothsaying is Satan's counterfeit, and while a soothsayer's predictions are sometimes correct, the power behind the prediction originates from evil influences and does not edify or enlighten.

When this damsel saw Paul and his associates, she followed them for "many days" (Acts 16:18) and cried, "These men are the servants of the most high God, which shew unto us the way of salvation" (verse 17). Despite the evil spirit possessing her, she bore testimony of the true God and His prophets. Perhaps she truly did have the gift of prophecy, but her masters and the evil spirit possessing her were twisting that spiritual gift into an evil counterfeit. In my own life, I have seen righteous people invite Satan into their heart, and he is able to use their strengths—their intelligence, their creativity, their love for others—for his evil purposes. Satan takes strengths and makes them weaknesses.

Paul was deeply grieved on account of this young girl. It must have broken Paul's heart to see her and her gifts being abused by her masters. When he couldn't stand it any longer, he turned and addressed the evil spirit that was in her and told it, "I command thee in the name of Jesus Christ to come out of her" (verse 18). The spirit didn't leave immediately, but we read that it left her that "same hour" (verse 18).

When the damsel's masters saw that they could no longer use her to make money, they were angry at Paul and Silas and threw them in jail. Eventually, Paul and Silas escaped from jail (and converted the jail keeper and his family) and left Philippi. (See Acts 16:19–40.) We never hear what happened to this damsel after she was freed and her masters could no longer use her. I hope that Lydia and the other Saints in Philippi found her, taught her about Jesus Christ, and showed her how to use her gift in a way that would edify and build the kingdom of God.

# Damaris

*"Howbeit certain men clave unto him, and believed: among the which was Dionysius the Areopagite, and a woman named Damaris, and others with them."*

Acts 17:34

*When Paul preached in Athens,* he had very little success. Only two converts are mentioned by name: Dionysius the Areopagite and a woman named Damaris. Paul fled to Athens after being persecuted and chased out of Thessalonica and later Berea (Acts 17:1–13). His traveling companions, Silas and Timothy, remained in Berea, and the plan was for them to meet up with him later. While Paul was waiting for them, he was very troubled by the idolatry of the people in Athens and began to preach to them in the synagogues and in the market place (verses 16–17).

Then a very unusual opportunity presented itself. The Epicurean and Stoic philosophers heard him preaching and took him to Areopagus, also known as "Mars' hill" (verse 22), where the high court of appeals for criminal and civil cases met. The philosophers wanted him to preach to the men that gathered there, saying, "May we know what this new doctrine, whereof thou speakest, is? For thou bringest certain strange things to our ears: we would know therefore what these things mean" (verses 19–20). These men weren't interested in hearing truth but rather gathered in the Areopagus for entertainment and novelty. For as Acts tells us, "All the Athenians and strangers which were there spent their time in nothing else, but either to tell, or to hear some new thing" (verse 21).

Paul stood on Mars' Hill and preached to them about the true nature of God. He had seen on their altars an inscription to the "Unknown God" whom the Greeks worshipped. He bore testimony of this God and of His power. He said, "God that made the world and all things therein, seeing that he is Lord of heaven and earth, dwelleth not in temples made with hands; neither is worshipped with men's hands, as though he needed any thing, seeing he giveth to all life, and breath, and all things. . . . For in him we live, and move, and have our being; as certain also of your own poets have said, For we are also his offspring" (verses 24–25, 28). He also called them to repentance and bore testimony of the Resurrection. Epicureans believed that the soul was as mortal as the body, so many mocked Paul when they heard his teachings about resurrection. It was only a select group who asked to hear more and who "clave unto him, and believed" (verse 34), among whom was Damaris.

The fact that Damaris appears to have been at the Areopagus has given rise to speculation about her identity. The Areopagus was a civil council and only men were allowed to participate in it. Furthermore, Athenian women were not given much of an education beyond what they needed to know in order to manage slaves and their household. Their sphere of influence was mostly limited to their domestic duties, and they did not have the freedom to participate in civics or academics. This makes some scholars wonder if perhaps Damaris was a foreign woman visiting Athens, thus explaining her presence at the Areopagus.[1] Or perhaps Damaris was a hetaira, an ancient Greek courtesan who was highly educated.[2] Hetairai were often independent and influential women who, in their roles as "companions," took active part in the symposia and other male-dominated spheres, like the Areopagus.[3]

It is possible that Damaris may not have even been at the Areopagus and that she was converted as Paul taught "in the synagogue with the Jews, and with the devout persons, and in the market daily with them that met with him" (verse 17). She may also have encountered Paul in some other social setting and believed what he taught. Some scholars speculate that, because their names are listed together, she may have been the wife of Dionysius the Aeropagite (one of the judges of the Aeropagus), and that her husband taught her the gospel.[4]

While the identity of Damaris is largely a mystery, the one thing we do know about her is that out of all the Athenians who heard Paul's testimony, she was among the few who did not mock him but instead believed. It is a tribute to her that

she was able, amidst all the popular ideas of her day, to recognize truth and not be deceived by the philosophies that surrounded her. She was brave enough to embrace that truth and cleave unto it, even when people were mocking.

Her example is important in a day when many in the world are not interested in seeking what is true or right, but rather they are interested in what is politically correct, progressive, and entertaining. I think in our day, some people spend their time much like the Athenians did, doing "nothing else, but either to tell, or to hear some new thing" (verse 21) on blogs, Facebook, Twitter, Pinterest, Instagram, and all the other social media sites we visit. The Internet is our modern-day Areopagus where we gather to discuss ideas, pass judgments, share opinions, keep up-to-date on events, and be entertained. Just like in Damaris's day, there is much good to be found in such interactions, but we need to be careful about the type of information we seek out and listen to. Elder Adrián Ochoa taught:

I want to extend a word of warning about one very strong sign of the times. My professional life put me on the forefront of technology, so I recognize the value it has, especially in communication. So much information of man is now at our fingertips. But the Internet is also full of much that is filthy and misleading. Technology has augmented our freedom of speech, but it also gives an unqualified blogger false credibility based on the number of viewers. This is why now, more than ever, we must remember this eternal principle: "By their fruits ye shall know them." . . .

My dear brothers and sisters, if you ever come across anything that causes you to question your testimony of the gospel, I plead with you to look up. Look to the Source of all wisdom and truth. Nourish your faith and testimony with the word of God.

## THE NATURE OF GOD

The testimony that Damaris may have heard Paul give at the Areopagus was centered on the true nature of God (Acts 17:21–32). Understanding the true nature of God is the basis for any strong testimony. Without understanding who God is and what He is like, it is easy to have your faith swayed by winds of doubt and the doctrines of men. Gospel practices or doctrines that appear confusing through worldly lenses often become clear as we come to understand the nature of God better and see things as He sees them.

When I have struggled with questions about the doctrine, history, or practices of the Church, diving deeper into the scriptures, and especially studying the nature of God, has helped me to find answers. There are thirteen pages in the Topical Guide under the heading of "God" that touch upon every imaginable facet of His nature and workings among men. This resource is a treasure trove. If you have doubts, write your questions and concerns down and start working through those thirteen pages. I promise that as you start to understand the nature of God, you will begin to see as He sees, and your questions will be answered.

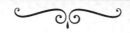

There are those in the world who seek to undermine your faith by mixing lies with half-truths. This is why it is absolutely critical that you remain constantly worthy of the Spirit. The companionship of the Holy Ghost is not just a pleasant convenience—it is essential to your spiritual survival. If you will not treasure up the words of Christ and listen closely to the promptings of the Spirit, you will be deceived.[5]

It is important that as disciples of Christ we cultivate the gift of discernment and rely on the Spirit to help us distinguish between truth and cleverly disguised lies or half-lies. Like Damaris, as we listen to the voices of God's chosen servants and follow what they teach, we can, even the midst of mocking voices, embrace truth and bear testimony of the one true and living God.

# Priscilla

*"And found a certain Jew named Aquila, born in Pontus, lately come from Italy, with his wife Priscilla; (because that Claudius had commanded all Jews to depart from Rome:) and came unto them. And because he was of the same craft, he abode with them, and wrought: for by their occupation they were tentmakers."*

Acts 18:2–3

*Priscilla and her husband, Aquila,* were tent makers originally from Rome, who had been forced from their home because of persecution against Jews. At the time they met Paul, they were in Corinth because Claudius, the Roman emperor, had commanded that all the Jews leave Rome. According to the Roman historian Suetonius, this happened because of "disturbances at the instigation of Chrestus," which referred to conflicts that had occurred between believing and non-believing Jews about the gospel of Christ.[1] Because of these "disturbances," Priscilla and Aquila were forced to leave their home and become what we might call today refugees or displaced persons.

Despite the hard circumstances of their move, it seems that Priscilla and Aquila did well in Corinth. When Paul arrived there, he lived and worked with them because he was "of the same craft" (Acts 18:3), meaning that he was also a tent maker by trade. Tents are a common theme throughout the scriptures. The Tabernacle in Moses's day was a tent rather than a building, Abraham pitched his tent while he traveled in Canaan, and Lehi dwelt in a tent during his wanderings in the wilderness. Ancient people often pitched their tents for long periods of time, but unlike houses, tents were not permanent structures. They could be taken down easily to move to a richer part of land, to escape conflict, or simply to follow a command of God. Symbolically, dwelling in a tent might mean being moveable and teachable, having your heart open to where the Lord wants you to go. Some of God's greatest "instruments" were people, like Sarah and Abraham, and Lehi and Sariah, who were willing to dwell in tents and whose hearts were set on the Lord and not tied up in homes, riches, or their own comfort.

I find it significant that Priscilla and Aquila were tent makers. Even though we know they had houses, where the Church often met, they seem to epitomize what it means to "dwell in a tent": to be willing to go where the Lord needed them. They began their missionary service with Paul in Corinth, but

The name Priscilla is the diminutive form of the name Prisca, which means "venerable" in Latin. The only time that Priscilla is referred to by her proper name is in Paul's second letter to Timothy where he wrote, "Salute Prisca and Aquila, and the household of Onesiphorus" (2 Timothy 4:19). We don't know why Paul used her proper name here when every other time he wrote about her he used Priscilla, but I think the fact that Paul used both of her names shows how close of associates and friends they were. I can imagine they felt an added measure of closeness being unified not only by their work in the gospel, but also in their trade of tent making. It is sweet to me to see evidence of this friendship in Paul's use of the name Prisca.

they later traveled with him to Ephesus. In Ephesus, they again established the Church "in their house" (1 Corinthians 16:19).[2] They also met Apollos, an eloquent man "instructed in the way of the Lord" (Acts 18:25) who was preaching in the synagogue. Priscilla and Aquila "took him unto them" (verse 26). They taught him the true gospel and he became an influential missionary in the early Church. Apollos was probably not the only missionary whom they influenced, because Christian tradition remembers Priscilla as a powerful teacher who was influential in not only sharing the gospel but also in training other missionaries.[3]

Later, after the edict banning Jews was lifted, Priscilla and Aquila traveled back to Rome and once again established the Church "in their house" (Romans 16:5). When Paul wrote his letter to the Romans, he addressed Priscilla and Aquila first in a long list of people in Rome whom he wanted to send greetings to. He also called them his "helpers in Christ" (verse 3). The Greek word translated as "helper" means "coworker" and is the term that Paul often used to describe those who

were actively engaged in missionary work with him. Paul's use of this word lets us know that not only were Priscilla and Aquila hosting and managing the Church in their home, but they were actively sharing and teaching the gospel.[4]

Even so, their missionary work was not always easy. Paul wrote that they "have for my life laid down their own necks" and that not only did he thank them but also "all the churches of the Gentiles" (verse 4). We don't know what Priscilla and Aquila did to deserve this high regard or what danger they underwent for Paul and the gospel, but evidently they had risked a lot for both. This little tidbit really whets my curiosity and makes me wish we knew more about the lives and adventures of Priscilla and Aquila. They were evidently not only bold missionaries, but brave ones as well.

Priscilla and Aquila remind me much of modern-day husband and wife missionary couples who travel the world bravely preaching the gospel of Jesus Christ. Like their ancient counterparts, these modern-day missionary couples leave behind their

homes, their families, their occupations, and their comforts in order to go where the Lord needs them. They are willing to "dwell in a tent," to go where the Lord would have them go and do what the Lord would have them do. It is this humility and faith that makes them, like Priscilla and Aquila of old, powerful instruments in the Lord's hands.

> *"They have for my life laid down their own necks."*

# Wives and Children of Tyre

*"And when we had accomplished those days, we departed and went our way; and they all brought us on our way, with wives and children, till we were out of the city: and we kneeled down on the shore and prayed."*

Acts 21:5

**On Paul's final missionary journey,** while he was traveling back to Jerusalem, his ship stopped to unload cargo in the coastal city of Tyre. Paul was happy to discover Christian disciples there and "tarried" (Acts 21:4) with them for seven days. At the end of the seven days, Paul told them that he had to leave and continue on his journey to Jerusalem. Yet "through the spirit," these Tyrian Saints told Paul that "he should not go up to Jerusalem" (verse 4). Perhaps the Holy Spirit had told them that Paul would not be safe there and had instructed them to warn Paul about his choice. Despite the Spirit's warning, Paul decided to continue on his journey. As the people of Tyre had feared, when Paul arrived in Jerusalem, he was arrested and imprisoned. This imprisonment in Jerusalem would eventually result in Paul's trip to Rome and his martyrdom.

Knowing the character of Paul, we can assume that the choice he made to go to Jerusalem was guided by the Spirit and was a correct one. Yet it is significant to me that these Tyrian Saints, among whom were women, had received revelation from the Holy Ghost about what awaited Paul at the end of his journey. They had the gift of prophecy (see "Four Daughters of Philip" on page 205) and they had not been afraid to use it to warn Paul about what lay ahead.

It is also beautiful to note that when Paul and his companions left Tyre, all the Saints accompanied him "with wives and children" (verse 5) until they were out of the city. When the group reached the seashore, they all knelt down on the sand and prayed together. Can you imagine what an awesome sight that must have been to see a group of Christians—men, women and children—kneeling together in public prayer on behalf of their beloved leader? Their hearts must have been heavy. They had felt the Holy Spirit witness to them that this might be the last time they would ever see Paul, and they had a foreboding of what must lay ahead. I can image that as Paul's ship sailed away, if the song had been written back then, they might have sung together,

> God be with you till we meet again;
> Keep love's banner floating o'er you;
> Smite death's threat'ning wave before you.
> God be with you till we meet again. . . .
> Till we meet at Jesus' feet.
> ("God Be with You Till We Meet Again," Hymns, no. 152)

All they could do was send him with their prayers and their blessings, hoping that the Lord would watch over and protect him.

# Four Daughters of Philip

*"And the next day we that were of Paul's company departed, and came unto Caesarea: and we entered into the house of Philip the evangelist, which was one of the seven; and abode with him. And the same man had four daughters, virgins, which did prophesy."*

Acts 21:8–9

**On Paul's travels back to Jerusalem,** he stopped in a coastal city called Caesarea, where he lodged with Philip, who is called "the evangelist" (Acts 21:8), and his four daughters. Paul recorded that these four daughters—all of whom were young unmarried women—prophesied. Throughout the scriptures, several other accounts are given of women who were known for their ability to prophesy and were referred to as prophetesses. In the Old Testament, Deborah is spoken of as a judge and prophetess, and Moses's older sister Miriam, as well as a woman named Huldah, is called a prophetess.[1] Isaiah calls his wife a prophetess, and in the New Testament, Anna (see page 33) also bears the title of a prophetess.[2] This title does not refer to these women being ordained to the priesthood or their position as the prophet, but rather indicates that they possessed the gift of prophecy. As Elder Dallin H. Oaks explained:

As we read in the Book of Revelation, "The testimony of Jesus is the spirit of prophecy." The Prophet Joseph Smith relied on this scripture in teaching that "every other man who has the testimony of Jesus" is a prophet. Similarly, the Apostle Paul states that "he that prophesieth speaketh unto men to edification, and exhortation, and comfort." Thus, in the sense used in speaking of spiritual gifts, a prophet is one who testifies of Jesus Christ, teaches God's word, and exhorts God's people. In its scriptural sense, to prophesy means much more than to predict the future.

The scriptures often use the word *prophet* and its derivatives in the broad sense of one who teaches and testifies of God. . . . It is important for us to understand the distinction between a prophet [or a prophetess], who has the *spiritual gift of prophecy,* and *the* prophet, who has the *prophetic office.*[3]

A prophetess (or a prophet) is someone who testifies of Jesus Christ through the power of the Holy Ghost. Even though the word is not specifically used to describe them, the four daughters of Philip can also be considered prophetesses. The ability to prophesy is listed among the gifts of the Spirit. Doctrine and Covenants 46 states that "to every man is given a

Philip is called "the evangelist, which was one of the seven" (Acts 21:8). Philip was among the seven men selected by the Apostles to administer to the specific needs of the poor and those who were from different cultural backgrounds. (See "Widows Who Were Neglected" on page 159.) He was also the same Philip who met and baptized the eunuch from Ethiopia. (See "Candace" on page 167.) When he is mentioned in Acts 21, he is identified as the evangelist, which is a very interesting designation. The Bible Dictionary says, "Joseph Smith taught that 'an Evangelist is a Patriarch, even the oldest man of the blood of Joseph or the seed of Abraham. Wherever the Church of Christ is established in the earth, there should be a Patriarch for the benefit of the posterity of the Saints.'"[6] This means that Philip was probably not a traveling minister like the current usage of the term evangelist connotes, but that he may have been the patriarch of the Church. In this office, he may have performed many of the same duties as a modern-day patriarch, perhaps giving blessings and declaring lineages.

gift by the Spirit of God. To some is given one, and to some is given another, that all may be profited thereby" (verses 11–12). In the list of gifts, the gift to prophesy is sandwiched between the gift to work miracles and the gift to discern spirits: "And to others it is given to prophesy" (verse 22). Elder James E. Talmage of the Quorum of the Twelve wrote, "No special ordination in the Priesthood is essential to man's receiving the gift of prophecy. . . . [T]his gift may be possessed by women also."[4]

In fact, the Lord promises that in the last days,

> I will pour out my spirit upon all flesh; and your sons and your daughters shall prophesy, your old men shall dream dreams, your young men shall see visions: And also upon the servants and upon the handmaids in those days will I pour out my spirit. (Joel 2:28–29)

Not only is the gift of prophecy available to women, but the Lord wants all of His children to use it. In the book of Numbers, we read about how a young Israelite man came to Moses complaining that two of the elders, Eldad and Medad, were prophesying in the camp. The young man evidently felt that they had no right to be prophesying and Joshua, who would be Prophet after Moses, agreed with him and said, "My lord Moses, forbid them" (Numbers 11:28). Instead, Moses turned to him and exclaimed, "Enviest thou for my sake? Would God that all the Lord's people were prophets, and that the Lord would put his spirit upon them!" (verse 29).

All of God's children can, and should, become prophets and prophetesses, to be witness of Christ and to bear testimony of truth. Yet, like any spiritual gift, the ability to prophesy must be developed through faith and obedience to the promptings and teachings of the Holy Ghost.

Several years ago, I learned a lesson about how important it is to develop

your spiritual gifts. My husband and I were on vacation with some friends, and between our two families we had seven kids under the age of six. One night after rounding up all the kids, we all knelt together for family prayer. I offered the prayer. As I prayed, I had the most unusual feeling come over me. I had the distinct impression that I could (and should) pronounce a promise and a blessing upon all those little children: a promise that God loved them and that not one of those seven precious souls would be lost to the adversary's power. I was being asked to prophesy.

The feeling was overwhelming and it scared me. I had never before pronounced a promise or a blessing upon anyone, and I wasn't sure if I was "allowed" to. So even though the prompting had come strongly, and the words to say had come into my mind, I didn't say them. I was scared of the power that was being offered to me. Afterward, I was sad. I felt like I had missed an important spiritual opportunity, and I wished more than anything that I had spoken those words. Later in the privacy of my room, I said them, but I felt like the opportunity to speak them as a promise and a blessing had passed. I still hope that the Lord will grant that blessing to those children, despite my weakness.

That experience taught me that as a disciple of Christ who has made sacred covenants, I have access to spiritual power and gifts beyond myself. Through Christ, I have the ability to work miracles, to heal, to cast out devils, to bless, and to prophesy. That night I realized that I hadn't taken the time to fully identify and develop my spiritual gifts, and so I wasn't prepared to use that power when the opportunity came. In my mind, I had confused things like working miracles, healing, prophesying, and blessing as being synonymous with the priesthood authority, available only to men, but they aren't. They are gifts, gifts of faith, and they are available to all who follow Christ. Elder Bruce R. McConkie declared at the dedication of the Nauvoo Monument to Women:

Where spiritual things are concerned, as pertaining to all of the gifts of the Spirit, with reference to the receipt of revelation, the gaining of testimonies, and the seeing of visions, in all matters that pertain to godliness and holiness and which are brought to pass as a result of personal righteousness—in all these things men and women stand in a position of absolute equality before the Lord. He is no respecter of persons nor of sexes, and he blesses those men and those women who seek him and serve him and keep his commandments.[5]

As we teach our young women, it is valuable to remember the story of the daughters of Philip. The purpose of the Young Women program is to help young women develop their own personal testimonies and patterns of discipleship, hence the reason they focus on *Personal* Progress. Young womanhood is a time for them to learn to identify, develop, and practice their spiritual gifts. This time of inward focus and dedication is to prepare them for the greater mission of Relief Society, which focuses on charity—serving and testifying to others. The Lord needs young women who understand their spiritual powers and influences, and are ready to use them the moment they join Relief Society.

We want our young women to be like the daughters of Philip, who had spent time cultivating their spiritual gifts and whose personal testimonies of Jesus Christ were so strong that they prophesied with power. We can help the young women in our lives learn to develop their spiritual gifts and use them with confidence and strength. Then perhaps in a way similar to Moses, the desire of our hearts might be, "Oh, would God that all the Lord's daughters were prophetesses!"

> *"The Lord needs young women who understand their spiritual powers and infuences, and are ready to use them."*

# Paul's Sister

*"And when Paul's sister's son heard of their lying in wait, he went and entered into the castle, and told Paul."*

Acts 23:16

*While Paul was in Jerusalem,* he was arrested and taken before the high priest Ananias. During this encounter, there arose such a great contention among the Pharisees and Sadducees that the chief captain took Paul away to a castle because he was afraid that "Paul should have been pulled in pieces" (Acts 23:10). The next day, more than forty of the Jews banded together and swore an oath to not eat until they had slain Paul. Somehow Paul's nephew (the son of Paul's sister) heard of their plan. Alarmed, he went to Paul and told him of the threat to his life. Paul had his nephew tell what he had heard to the chief captain, who, believing him, made plans to move Paul to a safer location that night.

While we don't know any details about Paul's sister, we might assume that, since Paul was a Pharisee and his father had also been a Pharisee, Paul's sister and her family were also of the same political affiliation. In fact, we might even deduce that one of the reasons Paul's nephew knew what the Pharisees and Sadducees were planning was that he had been among them. Regardless, this young man's willingness to risk his life to save the life of his uncle is impressive. It indicates that even if Paul's family didn't have the same Christian belief that he did, their family unity and love was strong.

# DIFFERENCES BETWEEN PHARISEES, SADDUCEES, AND ESSENES[1]

In Christ's time, there were several major political and religious sects. The gospel writers speak of these groups assuming that their readers are familiar with the philosophies of these groups. They refer to them like we might refer to someone as a Republican, Democrat, or Socialist. If you aren't aware of the Jewish political sects of Christ's time, it can be hard to make sense of some of the scriptures in the New Testament. Hopefully the chart below can be a starting place for understanding these groups better.

| | Pharisees | Sadducees | Essenes |
|---|---|---|---|
| Social Class | Middle class | Aristocratic | Middle class |
| Number during Christ's Time[2] | 6,000 | Very few (Number unknown) | 4,000 |
| Authority | Scholars of the law | Claimed priestly lineage | Claimed priestly lineage |
| Practices | Taught in synagogues. | Influential in the temple and the Sanhedrin. | Felt the temple and synagogue practices were corrupt. Instead they worshipped in the wilderness of Judea. |
| Political Philosophy | Progressive | Conservative | Socialist |
| Attitude toward Scripture | Believed in the Torah as well as the oral law, which were writings by Rabbi's that explained or interpreted the law. | Only believed in what was written in the Torah. Rejected the idea of an oral law or tradition. | Believed in the Torah. The Dead Sea Scrolls are believed to be written by a group with Essene roots. |

|  | Pharisees | Sadducees | Essenes |
|---|---|---|---|
| *Main Beliefs* | Believed God was a spiritual being. Also believed in man's agency and that people would receive consequences for their actions, in this life or the next. Were very strict in their observance of the law and avoided contact with Gentiles. | Didn't believe that people had a spirit or that there would be consequences (good or bad) after death. | Organized brotherhoods and often led monastic and celibate lives in the desert. Had strict dietary laws. |
| *Resurrection* | Believed that the spirit was immortal and that there would be a physical resurrection after death. | Rejected the idea of a physical resurrection and the immorality of the spirit. | Believed in the immortality of the soul but not the idea of a physical resurrection. |
| *Christ's Attitude toward Them* | Christ didn't so much disagree with their teachings as He did with their pride and their hypocrisy. He told them, "Now do ye Pharisees make clean the outside of the cup and the platter; but your inward part is full of ravening and wickedness" (Luke 11:39). See Luke 11; Matthew 23; Mark 7. | Christ rebuked their questions about the scriptures by saying, "Do ye not therefore err, because ye know not the scriptures, neither the power of God?" (Mark 12:24). When Christ cleansed the temple, it was the Sadducees He was mostly chasing out for their corrupt temple practices. | They are not specifically mentioned in the New Testament, but it is likely that John the Baptist was familiar with them since he dwelt in the wilderness. Perhaps Christ also encountered them during his forty-day fast in the wilderness. |

# Drusilla & Bernice

*"And after certain days, when Felix came with his wife Drusilla, which was a Jewess, he sent for Paul, and heard him concerning the faith in Christ."*

Acts 24:24

*"And on the morrow, when Agrippa was come, and Bernice, with great pomp, and was entered into the place of hearing, with the chief captains, and principal men of the city, at Festus' commandment Paul was brought forth."*

Acts 25:23

*Drusilla and Bernice are unique* because they are among the few women in the New Testament who are also well-documented historical figures. They were the daughters of Herod Agrippa and the great granddaughters of Herod the Great. Drusilla was the youngest of Herod Agrippa's children and Bernice was his middle daughter. These two women are mentioned to us briefly in Acts in connection with Paul's trial in Jerusalem, but their story has application to modern women today.

In Acts 24, we read that upon returning to Jerusalem after years of missionary travel, Paul was persecuted by Jewish leaders and accused of sedition (see Acts 21–24). He was taken into custody and brought before Felix, the Roman governor. Felix agreed to listen to Paul while he defended himself against Jewish accusers (see Acts 24:1–20). Later, Felix, who "came with his wife Drusilla, which was a Jewess," sent again for Paul so that he could hear "him concerning the faith in Christ" (Acts 24:24).

It appears that Felix and Drusilla were intrigued by Paul's story and message. They had heard of Jesus and were probably curious to know more about His followers and their beliefs. Likely, they viewed Paul as an interesting character and were ready to be educated, and perhaps even entertained, by his message. What they probably weren't prepared for was the way that Paul's testimony would shake them. Acts 24:25 says, "As he [Paul] reasoned of righteousness, temperance, and judgment to come, Felix trembled."

It appears that Paul's message struck a chord within Felix's heart (and perhaps Drusilla's as well) that made him fear and tremble. It was a well-known fact that Felix had seduced Drusilla and that she had left her first husband (to whom she may have still been legally married) in order to marry Felix.[1] It is likely that as Paul spoke to them, the weight of their sins fell upon them and they trembled to think of the consequences that would befall them if what Paul was saying were true.

Yet the fear that came over Felix was not enough to induce him to change. He told Paul, "Go thy way for this time; when I have a convenient season, I will call for thee" (verse 24). He basically said, "Wow, what you are saying hits home for me, but I am not ready or willing to change. Maybe later when it is more convenient."

It is sad for me when I think about Felix and Drusilla going on with their lives, having heard the truth and feeling of its power but being too proud, scared, or lazy to make the changes needed to receive the blessings Christ had to offer. They exchanged worldly pleasure and physical gratification for eternal glory and joy—and that is sad.

Later, Drusilla's brother and sister, Agrippa and Bernice, also reacted the same way to Paul's teachings. When Felix's governing term in Judea was over, he left Paul in prison for several years to appease the Jews. When Festus, the new governor, was established, King Agrippa and Bernice came to visit him. At this time, Bernice had been widowed twice and had two small sons in her care. She was living with her brother Agrippa and co-ruling with him as Queen of Judea.[2]

While Bernice and Agrippa were visiting, Festus told them about Paul (who was still in jail) and they expressed interest in hearing him speak. Festus arranged for Paul to be brought out, and the next day, Agrippa and Bernice came "with

Drusilla and her son Agrippa are two of the few historical figures documented as perishing in Pompeii during the eruption of Mount Vesuvius in 79 AD.[4] One reason that Drusilla and her son (and most of the inhabitants of Pompeii) perished in the eruption of Mount Vesuvius was because they were not aware of the warning signs. Historical evidence shows that leading up to the eruption, there were signs of an impending eruption (earthquakes, plumes of gas and smoke), but the people of the day did not recognize them for what they really were. As a result, the vast majority of the population was taken by surprise and perished in the eruption. In a similar way, Drusilla also failed to recognize and act upon the warning signs given to her by Paul. She heard his message of repentance and forgiveness, but she failed to see it for what it really was and missed out on the safety and security the gospel offers.

great pomp" (Acts 25:23) and listened as he told the story of his conversion and bore testimony of Jesus Christ. At the end of his speech, Paul could tell that what he had said touched Agrippa, because he stated, "King Agrippa, . . . I know that thou believest" (Acts 26:27). Agrippa admitted to Paul, "Almost thou persuadest me to be a Christian" (verse 28).

There is that word again: *almost.* Once again, the truthfulness of Paul's testimony had touched them, but once again his listeners wouldn't allow the truth of his words to change their hearts. They were like the people who Christ says "hath blinded their eyes, and hardened their heart; that they should not see with their eyes, nor understand with their heart, and be converted" (John 12:40). Drusilla and Felix, and Bernice and Agrippa opened their ears to Christ's message but refused to open their hearts to let His message change them.

Many of us may be doing the exact same thing. Do we, like Drusilla and Bernice,

spend our time hearing the message of the gospel without ever allowing it to change us? Do we, out of habit, go to church every week, read our scriptures, say our prayers, and listen to the prophets but still never do the work required to become truly converted? Elder Dallin H. Oaks taught,

> The Apostle Paul taught that the Lord's teachings and teachers were given that we may all attain "the measure of the stature of the fulness of Christ." This process requires far more than acquiring knowledge. It is not even enough for us to be convinced of the gospel; we must act and think so that we are converted by it. In contrast to the institutions of the world, which teach us to know something, the gospel of Jesus Christ challenges us to become something. . . . It is not enough for anyone just to go through the motions.[3]

The story of Bernice and Drusilla teaches us that it isn't enough to just know the truth; we must also be willing to put in the hard work to become converted. We must be willing to forsake our sins—large and small—and become different from who we were before. Such changes are never easy and they are never convenient, but they are what really matter most in this life. Drusilla and her sister Bernice may have heard, but they weren't willing to let Christ's message go any further than their ears, and in the end, they passed up what truly matters.

*"It isn't enough to just know the truth."*

# Herodian Family Tree

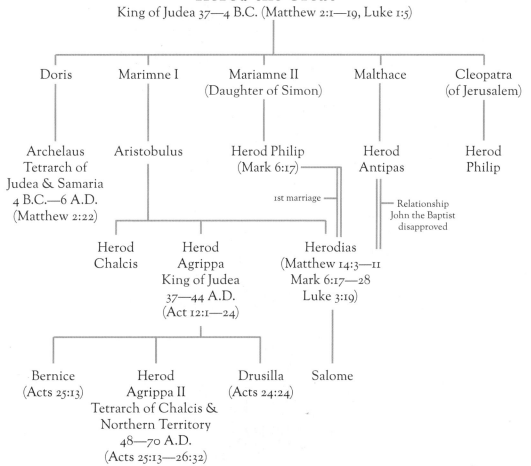

**Herod the Great**
King of Judea 37—4 B.C. (Matthew 2:1—19, Luke 1:5)

| Doris | Marimne I | Mariamne II<br>(Daughter of Simon) | Malthace | Cleopatra<br>(of Jerusalem) |
|---|---|---|---|---|

Archelaus
Tetrarch of
Judea & Samaria
4 B.C.—6 A.D.
(Matthew 2:22)

Aristobulus

Herod Philip
(Mark 6:17)

Herod
Antipas

Herod
Philip

1st marriage

Relationship
John the Baptist
disapproved

Herod
Chalcis

Herod
Agrippa
King of Judea
37—44 A.D.
(Act 12:1—24)

Herodias
(Matthew 14:3—11
Mark 6:17—28
Luke 3:19)

Bernice
(Acts 25:13)

Herod
Agrippa II
Tetrarch of Chalcis &
Northern Territory
48—70 A.D.
(Acts 25:13—26:32)

Drusilla
(Acts 24:24)

Salome

# Phebe

*"I commend unto you Phebe our sister, which is a servant of the church which is at Cenchrea; That ye receive her in the Lord, as becometh Saints, and that ye assist her in whatsoever business she hath need of you: for she hath been a succourer of many, and of myself also."*

Romans 16:1–2

*Bathsheba W. Smith,* the fourth general president of the Relief Society and one of the nineteen women present at the organization of the Relief Society, taught that the Prophet Joseph Smith "wanted to make us, as the women were in Paul's day, 'A Kingdom of priestesses.'"[1]

As Latter-day Saints, we know that our modern Church was organized after the Church that Christ established when He was on the earth. As such, we believe that all parts and teachings of that Church have again been restored on the earth, including Christ's organization for women.

 When the Prophet Joseph Smith organized the Relief Society in 1842, he said, "The Church was never perfectly organized until the women were thus organized."[2] Sister Eliza R. Snow, the second president of the Relief Society, repeated this teaching when she said, "Although the name may be of modern date, the institution is of ancient origin. We were told by our martyred prophet that the same organization existed in the church anciently."[3]

While we don't have any direct references in the scriptures to an ancient Relief Society, we do have many bread crumbs of truth scattered throughout the scriptures, especially in the New Testament, that give us insight into how women may have been involved in God's work. We get hints of the type of work this ancient "kingdom of priestesses" would have been engaged in.

Phebe, who is mentioned by Paul in the sixteenth chapter of Romans, gives us an intriguing glimpse into the early Church's organization for women. Even though Paul never personally ministered to the Saints in Rome, he sent them instruction and encouragement in the form of a letter, which was delivered to the Saints by Phebe. At this time, there was no formal mail system. Letters were commonly sent with those who were traveling to certain areas. Apparently Phebe was being sent from Cenchrea to Rome on Church business, and Paul asked her to carry his letter. It is also apparent that

Phebe was unknown to the Saints in Rome and that Paul wanted to make sure she was welcomed with the respect and help she deserved. In his letter, he introduced her to the Saints by saying,

> I commend unto you Phebe our sister, which is a servant of the church which is at Cenchrea; That ye receive her in the Lord, as becometh Saints, and that ye assist her in whatsoever business she hath need of you: for she hath been a succourer of many, and of myself also. (Romans 16:1–2)

The words that Paul used to describe Phebe are especially fascinating. Paul described Phebe as a "servant" of the Church in Cenchrea. In Greek this word is *diakonos*, which means "one who executes the commands of another, especially . . . the servant of a king."[4] *Diakonos* can also be translated as "a deacon, one who, by virtue of the office assigned to him by the church, cares for the poor and has charge of and distributes the money collected for their use."[5] In the King James Version of the Bible, the word *diakonos* is used thirty-one times and is translated twenty times as "minister," eight times as "servant," and three times as "deacon."[6] Whenever it is used, it has always had reference to those who serve and minister in an official office in the Church.

The other word that Paul used to describe Phebe was *succourer*. In Greek the word is *prostatis*. It means "a woman set over others; a female guardian, . . . patroness, caring for the affairs of others and aiding them with her resources"[7] and indicates female leadership. The word prostatis is used

> "*For she hath been a succourer of many.*"

only once in the King James Version of the Bible to refer to Phebe in Romans 16.[8] Scholar Bridget Jack Jeffries wrote, "The Greek verb from which this noun derives . . . literally means "to preside over." The masculine equivalent was well-known for carrying the possible meaning of one's legal guardian. . . . The word has a stronger connotation than that of a meek and submissive helper and is best translated into modern English as "benefactor" or "patron."[9]

Paul's use of these words to describe Phebe indicates that she certainly held some type of leadership and authority position in the early Christian Church. Knowing what we do about an ancient "Relief Society" being organized when Christ was on the earth, it is not hard for Latter-day Saints to envision a woman disciple as a "prostatis," a woman set apart and having authority to preside over and minister to a specific congregation, or perhaps even to the Church as a whole. It actually sounds much like the role of a modern-day Relief Society president or counselor! In that responsibility, she would have embodied Christlike service in caring for the poor, administering to the needy, preaching the gospel, and participating in the councils of the Church.

Even the idea of Phebe being a "deacon" (or more correctly a "deaconess") aligns well with what Latter-day Saints know of the purpose of the Relief Society. As an ancient member (and perhaps leader) of Christ's organization for women, she would have been organized "after the pattern of the priesthood,"[10] and her work would have had a priesthood

> *"The Relief Society is the Lord's oganization for women."*

purpose. In speaking of the role of the modern Relief Society, former Relief Society general president Julie B. Beck stated,

We operate in the manner of the priesthood—which means that we seek, receive, and act on revelation; make decisions in councils; and concern ourselves with caring for individuals one by one. Ours is the priesthood purpose to prepare ourselves for the blessings of eternal life by making and keeping covenants. Therefore, like our brethren who hold the priesthood, ours is a work of salvation, service, and becoming a holy people."[11]

While women in the Relief Society are not divided into quorums of deacons, teachers, priests, and elders like men are, the society's purpose and organization mirrors that of the priesthood quorums. President Beck also stated,

President Spencer W. Kimball taught that "the Relief Society is the Lord's organization for women. It complements the priesthood training given to the brethren." The word society has a meaning nearly identical to that of quorum. It connotes "an enduring and cooperating . . . group" distinguished by its common aims and beliefs.[12]

Relief Society is, in a sense, the female quorum of the Church.[13] Women are full recipients to the power and the blessings of the priesthood and, through their Relief Society sisterhood, share in the responsibilities of administering the work of salvation to all of God's children. This is especially true of Relief Society sisters who have been endowed in the temple. President Joseph Fielding Smith taught that one of the purposes of Relief Society was to help women achieve "exaltation in the kingdom of God and receive authority and power as queens and priestesses."[14]

When we think of the Relief Society as the female quorum of the Church, whose organization and purpose is similar to the priesthood quorum's, then using the term deaconess to describe Phebe is illuminating and not confusing. This word doesn't mean that Phebe was ordained to a priesthood office, but that, perhaps through her work in the Church, she had priesthood authority to administer, serve, teach, and bless those she had stewardship over.[15] As Elder Dallin H. Oaks said,

> We are not accustomed to speaking of women having the authority of the priesthood in their Church callings, but what other authority can it be? When a woman—young or old—is set apart to preach the gospel as a full-time missionary, she is given priesthood authority to perform a priesthood function. The same is true when a woman is set apart to function as an officer or teacher in a Church organization under the direction of one who holds the keys of the priesthood. Whoever functions in an office or calling received from one who holds priesthood keys exercises priesthood authority in performing her or his assigned duties.[16]

Understanding Phebe and her role in the early Church can help illuminate our understanding of what it means to be a member of the Relief Society today. Relief Society is not just a nice class for women to attend on Sunday while the men go to priesthood meetings. It is a vital part of the kingdom of God, a gathering of God's holy women—deaconesses, priestesses, and prophetesses—who are engaged in bringing forth the great priesthood mission of the earth. President Julie B. Beck taught,

> The priesthood is God's power. It is His power to create, to bless, to lead, to serve as He does. The priesthood duty of every righteous man is to qualify for the blessings of holding that priesthood and trust for the Lord so that he can bless his family and those around him. And I will say the priesthood duty of sisters is to create life, to nurture it, to prepare it for covenants of the Lord. Don't confuse the power with the keys and the offices of the priesthood. God's power is limitless and it is shared with those who make and keep covenants. Too much is said and misunderstood about what the brothers have and sisters don't have. This is Satan's way of confusing men and women so neither understands what they really have.[17]

I think that as Latter-day Saint women come to better understand the purpose of Relief Society, and better understand their temple covenants, we will begin to fully grasp and better use power and responsibility the Lord has *already* given us.

As in Paul's day, God has once again organized women as a "kingdom of priestesses" engaged in His work. We are leading, serving, and working alongside men in God's great work of bringing "to pass the immortality and eternal life of man" (Moses 1:39). It is our privilege as modern-day deaconesses, priestesses, and prophetesses to join our ancient sisters in this great and eternal work.

"Join our ancient sisters in this great and eternal work."

# The *Women* of Romans 16

*At the end of Romans 16,* Paul sent a "greeting card" to many of his friends and associates who were then living in Rome. This chapter is remarkable because it gives us a snapshot of what the membership of the early Christian Church would have looked like. It is also interesting because among the twenty-nine people that Paul greeted, ten of them were women. This is one of the largest groups of women that we have in the New Testament and it gives us evidence that women were important and active participants in the early Church. Paul stated that many of these women had "laboured" (verse 12) much for him and for the Church, and that they had been his "helpers" (verse 3) in the sharing the work of the gospel. Paul's remarks about these women are often brief, but the little glimpse he gives us helps us to better understand the type of women who would have been active in the work of the early Church.

> "Ten of them were women."

| Romans 16 | Verse | Description |
|-----------|-------|-------------|
| *Phebe* | 1–2 | She was the woman who carried and delivered Paul's letter to the Romans. (See page 219.) |
| *Priscilla* | 3–5 | She, along with her husband, Aquila, hosted a church in their home. Paul called them his "helpers in Christ Jesus." (See page 199.) |
| *Mary* | 6 | Unlike some of the other women whom Paul mentioned in his epistle who "laboured much in *the Lord*" (verse 12; italics added), Paul wrote that she "bestowed much labour on *us*" (italics added). This statement seems to indicate that she had been involved in ministering to the needs of Paul and his missionary companions. She may have fed, clothed, sheltered, or assisted them in some other way during their journeys. |
| *Junia* | 7 | Paul calls her and Andronicus his "kinsmen" as well as his "fellowprisoners." (See page 233.) |
| *Tryphena* | 12 | To her, Paul wrote, "Salute Tryphena and Tryphosa, who labour in the Lord." His use of present tense suggests that she was currently serving in a missionary or administrative role in the Church. (See page 229.) |
| *Tryphosa* | 12 | Paul said that she did "labour in the Lord," like Tryphena above. (See page 229.) |
| *Persis* | 12 | Paul called her "the beloved Persis," which indicates that not only he but perhaps all of the Roman Saints held her in special regard. He also wrote that she had "laboured much in the Lord." The use of past tense here indicates that she had once been more engaged in missionary or Church work than she currently was, perhaps due to age or other circumstances. |

| Romans 16 | Verse | Description |
|---|---|---|
| The Mother of Rufus | 13 | Paul greeted her, along with her son Rufus, and mentioned that she had been a "mother" to him. We don't know just exactly what this woman did for Paul, but evidently she had a significant influence on him and nurtured him like a mother would her own son. |
| Julia | 15 | Paul mentioned her when he greeted "Philologus, and Julia, Nereus, and his sister, and Olympas, and all the Saints which are with them." Her inclusion among this group may indicate that she was part of a house church in Rome. |
| Sister of Nereus | 15 | We know little about her except that she was related to a man named Nereus. Like Julia mentioned above, we might speculate that she was part of a house church in Rome. |

# Tryphena & Tryphosa

*"Salute Tryphena and Tryphosa, who labour in the Lord."*
Romans 16:12

*At the end of Paul's letter in Romans,* he extended personal greetings to many of his friends and fellow missionaries who were in Rome. Among these greetings are the names of two woman, Tryphena and Tryphosa. In addition to greeting these two women, he also stated that they "labour in the Lord" (Romans 16:12). It is likely that like many of the people on Paul's list, they were working to share and spread the gospel. Paul's use of the present tense tells us that at the time he wrote his letter, Tryphena and Tryphosa were actively engaged in this work.

Even though we don't know much more about Tryphena and Tryphosa than simply their names, those names give us clues to their identity. The names Tryphena and Tryphosa are derived from the same Greek word, which means "dainty, delicate, or luxurious."[1] Christian religious tradition suggests that they came from wealthy families. It impresses me to think that these women may have given up a life of luxury, wealth, and security to follow Jesus Christ. I wonder how hard it may have been for wealthy Romans to lay aside their desire for things of this world and instead focus on working hard to lay up treasures in heaven. Also, considering that Paul mentioned them together and that their names are so similar, I wonder if they might have been sisters, or perhaps even twins.

Regardless of who they were, it is significant that Paul said that they did "labour in the Lord," acknowledging the importance of the work that women did in the early Christian Church. We don't know if women were set apart, or even had formal calls, but there is much evidence in the scriptures that both men and women (and even husband and wife pairs) were active in teaching and sharing the gospel of Jesus Christ throughout the world.[2] I can almost envision Tryphena and Tryphosa being some of the first sister missionaries!

It is also interesting to note that among the people Paul greeted in his epistle to Romans were several with common slave names.[3] This means that Tryphena and Tryphosa, whether or not they were from a wealthy Roman family, may have worked and worshipped alongside men and women who had been, or perhaps still were, slaves. The church Paul describes in Romans 16 appears to be a very diverse group of people.

This diversity among Church members reminds me of an experience I had in college. I was attending a conference in Washington, D. C. around the time Mitt Romney was making his first presidential campaign. The father of one of the girls in our group was serving as a chief of staff to one of President George W. Bush's cabinet members, and so on Sunday, we went the LDS chapel where her parents attended. As we walked toward the church, I became a bit alarmed because the streets got progressively less affluent. I was certain that these weren't neighborhoods I would usually wander around by myself. I was glad my friend knew where we were going.

I was a bit relieved when we finally arrived, and I will never forget the welcome I received when I walked through that church door. A big African man, with the most contagious smile I'd ever seen, grabbed my hand with both of his and said in a booming voice, "Welcome, sister, to the true Church of Jesus Christ. We are so happy to have you here today!" His sincere greeting melted my heart. The Church of Jesus Christ of Latter-day Saints is unique in the fact that members don't get to choose which congregation that they attend. Ward assignments are given based on geographical divisions and members are not (usually) allowed to consistently attend a ward outside of their assigned one. I have lived in several areas where this rule has resulted in economic and ethnic diversity. Yet, while I sat on that Washington, D. C. pew and glanced around me, I marveled at the diversity of the ward.

Next to me were my friend's parents (obviously very wealthy), behind me were several young mothers with their little children (obviously very poor), the bishopric on the stand was composed of three men with three different skin colors, and in front of the sacrament table was the most unusual mix of deacons I had ever seen in my life: white and black, Asian and Latino, poor and wealthy, privileged and impoverished, young and old. That day as I sat in that chapel, surrounded by such an incredible mix of people, I remember thinking, "Wow, if Mitt Romney gets the nomination, he might become president, and this would be his ward."

With that thought came a warm rush of the Spirit that nearly brought me to tears. I not only felt but saw before my eyes what the Apostle Peter understood: "I perceive that God is no respecter of persons" (Acts 10:34). That day I realized one of the most beautiful truths about the gospel of Jesus Christ: all people have equal status and privilege in the eyes of God. He doesn't care if you are a refugee or the President of the United States, your worth in His eyes is the same.

As we look at the early Roman Church that Tryphena and Tryphosa would have belonged to, we see evidence that its members may have been diverse. It impresses me to think that those early Christians, like members today, didn't let cultural or class distinctions keep them from loving and serving all of their brother and sisters. It is a beautiful testament to the truth found in the Book of Mormon: the Lord "denieth none that come unto him, black and white, bond and free, male and female; and he remembereth the heathen; and *all are alike unto God*" (2 Nephi 26:33; italics added).

> *"Your worth in His eyes is the same."*

# Junia

*"Salute Andronicus and Junia, my kinsmen, and my fellowprisoners, who are of note among the apostles, who also were in Christ before me."*

Romans 16:7

*Junia and Andronicus are listed* among those Paul greeted in his epistle to the Romans. He called them "kinsmen" (Romans 16:7), which could be interpreted to mean that they were simply fellow Jews or that they were his actual blood relations. Either way, his greeting indicates that he knew them both well and that they were believers of Christ before he was.

Paul also called them his "fellowprisoners" (verse 7), which lets us know that both Junia and Andonicus had spent time in prison, presumably for teaching the gospel of Jesus Christ. Paul's comment also leads us to believe that they were imprisoned at the same time and place as Paul. I can imagine that being in prison with someone, especially for the same righteous cause, would create a strong bond of friendship between people. It is likely that Paul knew Junia very well.

The other interesting thing that Paul tells us about her is that she and Andronicus were "of note among the Apostles" (verse

7). The wording in this phrase leaves some confusion as to what Junia's role was in the Church. It might be read to mean that she was highly thought of *by* the Apostles, or it could be read to mean that she was *among* the Apostles. While this verse might be interpreted either way, I personally think that it would have been unlikely that Junia was an actual Apostle. We know that when Christ organized His church, He selected only men to be His original Twelve Apostles, and it seems unlikely to me that after His death a woman would have been included.

I think that Andronicus could have been an Apostle and Junia was his wife. Today, even though Apostles' wives are not called to the same priesthood position, they often share in much of their husbands' apostolic work. Often times, they will travel with them on their assignments, speak alongside them to congregations, and bear in the burdens of their work. It seems to me that if Junia and Andronicus were a husband and wife pair who were engaged together in an apostolic mission of sharing the gospel, Paul might refer to them both as "Apostles."

On the other hand, the phrase could simply mean that Junia and Andronicus were very highly regarded by the Apostles for their work in building the Church. Regardless of how we interpret the verse, it is significant that Junia demonstrated the type of faith and courage that compelled Paul to remark that she was "of note," or illustrious, among Christ's followers.

Junia is the only woman who was imprisoned for the gospel whose name we know. Yet, there are several places in the New Testament where we read that many followers of Christ, both men and women, were imprisoned for their faith. Ironically, many of these believers were imprisoned by Paul who, before his conversion, "made havoc of the church, entering into every house, and hailing men and women committed them to

> ⟡
> ## *"They were willing to . . . speak truth with courage."*
> ⟡

prison" (Acts 8:3). Or, in his own words, "I persecuted this way unto the death, binding and delivering into prisons both men and women" (Acts 22:4). Paul had even received permission from the high priest to travel to Damascus and if he found any believers of Christ, "whether they were men or women, he might bring them bound unto Jerusalem" (Acts 9:2). It was on this trip to Damascus that Paul had his miraculous conversion and complete change of heart. Understandably, the Christians in Jerusalem had a hard time accepting him and believing in his conversion. Eventually he proved himself and gained their trust. Still, it is interesting to think that some of the men and women that Paul threw into prison might later have become his friends and associates in the gospel.

As I think of Junia, and the other unnamed women who were imprisoned for their faith, I am impressed by their courage. They were willing to be different, to stand out, and to speak truth with courage, regardless of the consequences. Mostly, they were willing to sacrifice everything—even their freedom—for their testimonies of Jesus Christ. Their examples remind me that sometimes it is not easy to stand up for what is right, but, as Paul wrote, believers are not "ashamed of the gospel of Christ" (Romans 1:16).

# Chloe

*"For it hath been declared unto me of you, my brethren, by them which are of the house of Chloe, that there are contentions among you."*

1 Corinthians 1:11

**The first book of Corinthians** is filled with teachings about women that are confusing and hard to understand. It can be very hard to reconcile these teachings of Paul with what we know of how Christ viewed woman and how women are treated and included in our modern Church today. Yet, as you study the context in which Paul's words were given and open your heart to the guidance of the Holy Ghost, Paul's words can become enlightening and empowering instead of confusing and demeaning. As Camille Fronk Olsen stated,

> The Apostle Paul spoke without 'flattering words,' giving messages that were not always "pleasing [to] men, but [pleasing to] God." We should not be surprised then if we feel our toes stepped on from time to time when we read Paul's epistles. Such a reaction generally means that he has just uncovered a gospel principle that we have not yet fully understood or faithfully followed.[1]

Paul's letter to the Corinthians was written in response to a letter he received from a group of Saints who met in the house of a woman named Chloe. These members were concerned about the divisions occurring among the brethren in Corinth and about how the Church was being run there.[2] One common thread that runs throughout the whole of Paul's epistle to them is their concern about the inclusion and treatment of women. It seems that these early Christians were still trying to figure out women's roles and responsibilities in Christ's Church and in the family. In fact, many of the questions that the Corinthians had are ones that modern members of the Church still wrestle with. It is reassuring to me to know that understanding women's roles and responsibilities has never been easy and that my ancient sisters struggled with many of the same questions that I do today.

## • Marriage •

In chapter 7 of 1 Corinthians, Paul wrote, "It is good for a man not to touch a woman" (verse 1).[3] Paul seems to be demeaning marriage. Yet elsewhere he taught that "marriage is honourable in all, and the bed undefiled" (Hebrews 13:4). What did Paul intend to teach about marriage?

Understanding the context is crucial. The Joseph Smith Translation clarifies that Paul's instructions about not marrying and about abstaining from sexual relations were given to those who "shall be sent forth unto the ministry. Even they who have wives, shall be as though they had none; for ye are called and chosen to do the Lord's work" (Joseph Smith Translation, 1 Corinthians 7:29, in Bible appendix). It appears that the preferred situation was that a missionary should be unmarried. Yet having a wife didn't necessarily exclude one from missionary service. Paul told them, "Art thou bound to a wife? Seek not to be loosed" (1 Corinthians 7:27).

Paul gave instructions about marriage to both male and female missionaries, indicating that women were also engaged in missionary work. In Paul's instructions to the women, he said, "There is difference also between a wife and a virgin. The unmarried woman careth for things of the Lord, that she may be holy both in body and in spirit: but she that is married careth for the things of the world, how she may please her husband" (verse 34).

Paul wasn't discouraging Christians from marrying or encouraging celibacy as a higher aspiration but giving specific instructions to men and women called to serve missions.

## • Submission •

In chapter 11 of 1 Corinthians, Paul taught, "The head of every man is Christ; and the head of the woman is the man; and the head of Christ is God" (verse 3). Similarly, he wrote to the Ephesians, "Wives, submit yourselves unto your own husbands, as unto the Lord. For the husband is the head of the wife, even as Christ is the head of the church: and he is the saviour of the body" (Ephesians 5:22–23). The word *submit* can be hard for modern women to understand. To our ears, it can sound as if Paul were telling women that they were subservient, inferior, or servants to their husbands. Yet in the scriptures, the word *submissive* is often used in a positive way. In fact, Paul wrote that Christ was submissive and that the "head of Christ is God." As Camille Fronk Olsen explained,

> In His unique role, Christ leads us back to God because he is submissive to God. Consequently, we have unsurpassed reverence for the Savior, feeling to thank Him continually for his strength of character, supreme wisdom, devotion to covenant, and selfless love for the Father and each of us. When one uses Christ as the personification of submission, a deeper definition unfolds. True submission requires restraint when one-upmanship is possible; the complete absence of pride when recognition is meted out; strength to stay the Spirit-directed course when letting go may be expected and even rewarded. . . . Recognizing submission in Jesus Christ provides an appropriate definition when the term is applied to His disciples.[4]

Submission does not indicate a place of inferiority or powerlessness; instead, it is a conscious choice to humble oneself and become more like Jesus Christ.

Throughout his epistle to the Corinthians, Paul used the image of the body to illustrate how dependent we are upon God and upon one another. He wrote, "For as the body is one, and hath many members, and all the members of that

> *"Submission . . . is a conscious choice to humble onself and become more like Jesus Christ."*

one body, being many, are one body: so also is Christ. . . . Now ye are the body of Christ" (1 Corinthians 12:12, 27). The head of the body is not only the director of the body, but it also gives the body life. If a body loses any of its appendages—an arm, a leg, a hand, a foot—it will be hurt, but it would still be able to live without it. Yet, if the body loses its head, it will lose the source of its enabling power and it will certainly die. If we think of the Church as being the "body" and as Christ as the "head" of the Church, it is easy to see how the loss of the head—Christ—would result in the death of the Church, because it would no longer have the authority or power to do its sacred work.

In a similar way, we might think of a man as being the "head" of a woman because he, through his priesthood authority, has the power to give spiritual life—rebirth into the kingdom of God—to the woman. In 1 Corinthians 11:8, Paul wrote, "For the man is not of the woman; but the woman of the man." This seems to be backward because we know that it is men who are "of" (created from) women and not the other way around. Paul's words seem to teach that men also give life to women and that women are "of" or born through men, like men are born through women. Or as he would later write, "Neither is the man without the woman, neither the woman without the man, in the Lord. For as the woman is of the man, even so is the man also by the woman" (verses 11–12).

Obviously, this spiritual rebirth offered by men doesn't happen the same way that mortal birth offered by women does. For like Nicodemus asked Jesus, "How can a man be born when he is old? can he enter the second time into his mother's womb, and be born?" (John 3:4). The processes may be different, but they still require the participants to submit. For example, we know that in the premortal life we were noble and great intelligences who, because we desired a mortal body, chose to submit our wills and come to earth as babies—helpless, forgetful, and totally dependent upon others. The process of birth required us to submit ourselves completely to our mothers, trusting them to do for us what we could not do for ourselves—give us life.

Similarly, the ordinances of the priesthood, which are administered by men, allow us to be reborn into the kingdom of God with changed, immortal bodies. Just like the birth process, the rebirth process requires submission to the plan of God. It requires that we submit ourselves to the ordinances of the priesthood and allow ourselves to washed, anointed, and born again into God's presence—something that we cannot do for ourselves but must allow another to do for us. This process requires us to be humble and trust men, just like we trusted our mothers.

A man is not the "head" of a woman because he controls or subdues her, but because through the priesthood ordinances, he makes life—her spiritual life—possible. Christ is the "head" of man because it is only through Christ that a man can receive authority to use the life-giving power of the priesthood, and God is the "head" of Christ because it is from God the Father that Christ receives His power and His glory. This is a beautifully designed plan that does not put women on the bottom, but instead it ennobles and enables women to realize their full spiritual potential and progress on their journey back to God.

## • Veiling •

Paul also addressed the Corinthians' confusion over the "mysteries of God" (1 Corinthians 4:1), or the "hidden wisdom, which God ordained before the world unto our glory" (1 Corinthians 2:7), which may have referred to temple ordinances. It appears that there were divisions between the

> ### "I teach every where in every church."

Christians as to how these teachings were to be taught and administered. These Christians had been taught by various Apostles and missionaries, some saying, "I am of Paul; and I of Apollos; and I of Cephas [Peter]; and I of Christ" (1 Corinthians 1:12). Paul was trying to get the whole Church worshipping in the same way (after the pattern Christ had established) and so he told them that there should not be divisions, but that they should all be imitators of the way he taught. He promised them that he would send Timothy, "who shall bring you into remembrance of my ways which be in Christ, as I teach every where in every church" (1 Corinthians 4:17).

It appears that Chloe's congregation had specific questions about why women were required to veil or cover their heads during worship. In 1 Corinthians 11, Paul again told the Corinthians to follow or to imitate him and to "keep the ordinances, as I delivered them to you" (verse 2). Matthew B. Brown wrote,

> The Apostle Paul in speaking of the "ordinances" that he had delivered unto the Saints, directed that when women prayed and prophesied they were to have their heads covered. The Joseph Smith Translation of this epistle brings verse 10 into line with the rest of the passage by changing power to covering—"For this cause ought woman to have a covering on her head because of the angels." It should be noted that the word translated in verses 5 and 13 as "uncovered" is *akatakaluptos* and means "unveiled" and the word translated in verse 6 as "covered" is *katakalupto* which means to "cover wholly, [or] veil." The word *power* in verse 10 may have also been mistranslated because the fact that in Aramaic the roots of the word *power* and *veil* are spelled the same.[5]

Coverings on the head represent power.[6] Today, many people see a veil as an indicator of oppression and control, but that is because for every righteous symbol, Satan has a counterfeit that he uses to confuse and deceive. Satan has turned the symbol of the veil into a negative one, which can make understanding it difficult. A study of the scriptures will show

that veils are used to cover things that are holy and have great spiritual power—like the veil that covered the entrance into the Holy of Holies. As a spiritual symbol, veils (particularly a veiled face) have three meanings—chastity and virtue, submission and obedience, and divinely recognized authority possessed by the veiled person.[7] As Brown explained,

> Joseph Smith stated that Paul was aware of all the ordinances and blessings of the church, including the privilege of coming into the physical presence of "an innumerable company of angels, hav[ing] communion with [them] and receiv[ing] instructions from them. . . . Paul in his comments, explained that women wore their veil "because of the angels" and this seems to be key to understanding the veil's general symbolism. . . . According to Joseph Smith, all the ordinances of the gospel constitute signs to God and his angels, and unless they are properly carried out in the divinely prescribed manner, mortals cannot receive the blessings that are attached to them. The veil, therefore may have been a sign to unseen angels that a woman honored and maintained the order of creation that was established by God, and she was therefore entitled to heavenly blessings (such as the gift of prophesy).[8]

Perhaps women were to veil or cover during "ordinances" because it was a literal symbol to God of their virtue, power, and authority, and a sign that they were submissive to the ordinances of the priesthood and entitled to speak and participate with power in God's work.

## • Let Women Keep Silent •

In 1 Corinthians 14, Paul taught, "Let your women keep silence in the churches: for it is not permitted unto them to speak; but they are commanded to be under obedience, as also sayeth the law. And if they will learn any thing, let them ask their husbands at home: for it is a shame for women to speak in the church" (verses 34–35). It is important to understand here that Paul was writing about the gift of speaking in tongues. In chapter 12, Paul had taught the Saints about spiritual gifts because they were "zealous of spiritual gifts" (verse 12). In chapter 13, he taught that the best gift of the Spirit was charity and that they should desire spiritual gifts to edify others. Then in chapter 14, he specifically instructed them about the proper way to use the gift of tongues. From his instructions, it sounds like it was a spiritual gift that may have been overused, or was being used inappropriately. Regarding the speaking in tongues, Paul told men that they should "keep silence in the church; and let him speak to himself, and to God" (verse 28) *if* no interpreter of tongues was available.

The instruction to the women seems especially harsh in the King James Version. The word translated as "keep silence" is translated elsewhere in the scriptures as "hold his peace."[9] It is the word used when Peter, James, and John came down from the Mount of Transfiguration and "kept it close" (Luke 9:36) what they had seen and learned. Perhaps Paul's instructions to women to "keep silence" or "hold their peace" was an invitation for them to ponder up in their hearts, or discuss at home with their husbands, the sacred things they had learned or been taught through the Spirit.

The Joseph Smith Translation changes the passage "it is not permitted unto them [women] to speak" to "it is not permitted unto them [women] to rule" (1 Corinthians 14:34, footnote b; from Joseph Smith Translation). Perhaps women in the Corinthian congregations were dominating meetings, perhaps through the too frequent use of the gift of tongues.

Paul's responses to the questions and concerns brought up by Chloe's congregation were doctrinally rich and likely gave them much needed clarity about these challenging topics. As members of Christ's modern Church, we may have questions similar to those asked by Chloe and her congregation. Our questions can motivate us to search for understanding by turning to the prophets and Apostles, by digging deeper into our scriptures, and by filling our hearts with the power of the Holy Ghost. God gave Chloe and her congregation answers and direction and He will give them to you too. Remember what Christ promised to all those who desired more understanding: "Seek, and ye shall find; knock, and it shall be opened unto you" (Matthew 7:7).

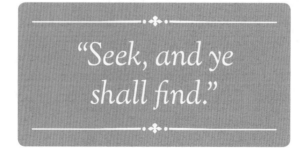

*"Seek, and ye shall find."*

# Euodia & Syntyche

*"I beseech Euodias, and beseech Syntyche, that they be of the same mind in the Lord. And I entreat thee also, true yokefellow, help those women which laboured with me in the gospel, with Clement also, and with other my fellowlabourers, whose names are written in the book of life."*

*Philippians 4:2–3*

*Have you ever had a disagreement* with someone at church? If so, you might be able to relate to Euodia[1] and Syntyche. These two women were members of the early Christian Church who, while strong in their faith, let a disagreement arise between them.

They lived in Philippi, which was the first city in which Paul preached and where he met his first European convert, a woman named Lydia (see page 187), as well as received divine help to escape from prison. The Philippians were one of the most righteous branches of the Church that we have record of and were among the only Saints who remained in constant communication with Paul throughout his travels and while he was in prison at Rome (see Philippians 4:15–18).

In fact, while Paul was imprisoned in Rome, the Philippians sent a man named Epaphroditus to Rome to aid and minister to Paul. Yet, the strain of the work and the city was too much for Epaphroditus and he returned home, carrying with him

> ## "Seek the Lord and His righteousness."

Paul's epistle to the Philippians, which was filled with his love and gratitude for their support. Toward the end of Paul's epistle to the Philippians, he mentioned Euodia and Syntyche. He wrote:

> I beseech Euodias, and beseech Syntyche, that they be of the same mind in the Lord. And I intreat thee also, true yokefellow, help those women which laboured with me in the gospel,

with Clement also, and with other my fellowlabourers, whose names are written in the book of life. (Philippians 4:2–3)

From these verses we learn several things about these two women. First, Paul calls them his "fellowlabourers" (verse 3), which was a term he often used to address those who had been engaged in missionary work. This indicates that Euodia and Syntyche had been active in sharing and administering the gospel. As members in Philippi, they also would have been included among the members of the Church who met in Lydia's home, and perhaps may even have been among the women who were gathered by the river to pray when Paul first met and taught Lydia the gospel.

Second, Paul mentioned that Euodia and Syntyche were among those "whose names are in the book of life" (verse 3). In Revelation 21, the Apostle John speaks about his vision of the celestial kingdom, the New Jerusalem, and wrote, "And there shall in no wise enter into it any thing . . . but they which are written in the Lamb's book of life" (verse 27). Also, in Doctrine and Covenants 76, it states that those "whose names are written in heaven" (verse 68) are those who "received the testimony of Jesus, and believed on his name and were baptized after the manner of his burial" (verse 51); who "receive the Holy Spirit by the laying on of hands of him who is ordained" (verse 52); who "overcome by faith, and are sealed by the Holy Spirit of promise" (verse 53); and who "are

priests and kings [priestesses and queens], who have received of his fulness, and of his glory; and are priests of the Most High, after the order of Melchizedek" (verses 56–57); and "all things are theirs" (verse 59). To have one's name written in the book of life is to have received all the ordinances necessary to return to God and to live a life worthy of celestial glory. It is remarkable that Paul, obviously knowing the character of these women, would declare that their names were written in the book of life. They must have been exceptional women.

Understanding the type of women Euodia and Syntyche were makes the fact that they were having a significant disagreement surprising. These women were obviously among the elite and faithful of their day and strong women of faith. What sort of issue could they have been having that would warrant Paul's public attention and concern? Paul doesn't give us clues as to what it might be, and so we will probably never know. Still, no matter the cause or nature of their argument, their story is an important one for Latter-day Saints.

In a church with members from such diverse social and cultural backgrounds as Latter-day Saints are, disagreements and misunderstandings will arise between members. Even with those differences, we can be united if we follow the counsel Paul gave to Euodia and Syntyche and seek to "be of the same mind in the Lord." This requires that we lay aside what we think, what we feel, and what we want—those self-centered, prideful preoccupations—and instead focus on what the Lord would have us do. As Elder Marion G. Romney said,

> There is but one way that we can be united, and that way is to seek the Lord and His righteousness. Unity comes by following the light from above. It does not come out of the confusions below. . . . The major reason for the world's troubles today is that men are not seeking to know the will of the Lord and then to do it. Rather do they seek to solve their problems in their own wisdom and in their own way.[2]

I think this counsel to be unified is especially relevant to modern women. I know that when I first ventured into the world of motherhood, I was surprised by the "mommy wars": the disagreements among women. I heard arguments about the right way to conceive, the right way to give birth, the right way to feed a baby, the right way to teach your children, and the right way to discipline teenagers. There were arguments about everything! It seemed that everyone, including me, had opinions that they felt passionately about. Right from the start of motherhood, I made choices that were "out of the norm" and often found myself embroiled in heated

## THE TRUE YOKEFELLOW: PAUL'S WIFE?

In Philippians 4:3, Paul entreated a "true yokefellow" to help Euodia and Syntyche reconcile their disagreement. The identity of this "true yokefellow" is not known, though some scholars believe that Paul may have used this term as a reference to his wife. As Brigham Young University Professor Wilfred Griggs explained,

> *Gnésie syzuge*, the words translated "true yokefellow," are here taken as feminine, and [the word used] is a noun that means "wife." Ancient commentators believed that Paul was addressing his wife, and this is the most sensible translation of the Greek in this context. If he were married at the time, one would expect Paul to leave his wife with a faithful group of Saints, where she would least suffer from want and lack of support during his absence. Both her presence in Philippi and the love of the members there for Paul would account for the constant communication with the Apostle, and, if this interpretation is true, it is natural that Paul would ask his wife to assist some of the women who had done so much on his behalf.[5]

Even so, there is still much debate among scholars as to how Paul was using this word and to whom it was addressed. Some scholars think that Paul was addressing a fellow missionary companion, who may have been male or female. This is because even though the word that is translated as "yokefellow" may be translated as "spouse" or "wife," it can also be used in other ways, all of which are centered around the idea of two things being joined together as a pair.[6] It is similar to the modern English word companion, which may be used in a variety of ways depending on to whom someone is speaking.[7]

Still, it is fascinating to think that Paul may have been addressing his wife in his letter to the Philippians and that she may have played an important role in reconciling the disagreement between Euodia and Syntyche.

discussions with people who didn't understand my choices. I found myself becoming increasingly more defensive and passionate, and started to feel estranged from women who didn't think or act like me.

Several years later, I was involved with four other LDS women in writing a remarkable book called *The Gift of Giving Life: Rediscovering the Divine Nature of Pregnancy and Birth*. When I initially joined the project, our goal was to write a book about how to spiritually prepare for giving birth. All of us were passionate advocates for natural birth, so we thought we would be writing about the spiritual experiences women had during unmedicated births. Yet as we worked on the project, we began to receive stories from women whose spiritual birth experiences included C-sections, epidurals, miscarriages, and stillbirths. Our hearts began to change. We began to see things like God did and realized every situation was unique and that what mattered to Lord was that a mother's heart was in the right place and the she was faithfully seeking personal revelation to know God's will for her and her child.

The experience of writing *The Gift of Giving Life* changed my heart. Now I am much less dedicated to my own opinions, no matter how passionate I may feel about them. I have learned that there is a grain of truth in every argument and that usually I am only defensive or critical because I feel that someone else's opinion threatens the validity of my own.

President Henry B. Eyring taught that contention is really an issue of pride:

> Pride is the great enemy of unity. You have seen and felt its terrible effects. . . . Happily I am seeing more and more skillful peacemakers who calm troubled waters before harm is done. . . . One way I have seen it done is to search for anything on which we agree. To be that peacemaker, you need to have the simple faith that as children of God, with all our differences, it is likely that in a strong position we take, there will be elements of truth. The great peacemaker, the restorer of unity, is the one who finds a way to help people see the truth they share. That truth they share is always greater and more important to them than their differences. You can help yourself and others to see that common ground if you ask for help from God and then act.[3]

When we are seeking to know the will of the Lord, our pride and our contention melts away because we know we are following a divine leader. Like musicians in a symphony, we may each play a different instrument and different notes, but it is only when we are each following the direction of the conductor that we will make beautiful music. President Eyring also taught,

> Where people have that Spirit with them, we may expect harmony. The Spirit puts the testimony of truth in our hearts, which unifies those who share that testimony. The Spirit

of God never generates contention. It never generates the feelings of distinctions between people which lead to strife. It leads to personal peace and a feeling of union with others. It unifies souls. A unified family, a unified Church, and a world at peace depend on unified souls.[4]

In the gospel, each one of us will be different, and as the Church becomes more global, those differences will only increase. Yet if we follow Paul's counsel and seek to "be of the same mind as the Lord," we will do beautiful and incredible things to move God's work forward. This is the message Paul was trying to send to Euodia and Syntyche, two stalwart disciples of Christ. We can only hope they listened.

# Apphia

*"And to our beloved Apphia, and Archippus our fellowsoldier, and to the church in thy house: Grace to you, and peace, from God our Father and the Lord Jesus Christ."*

*Philemon 1:2–3*

**Apphia is commonly believed** to be the wife or sister of Philemon. Philemon was a Christian man who owned a slave named Onesimus, who ran away to join Paul on his missionary journey. Paul sent Onesimus back to Philemon with a letter (which is now the book of Philemon) asking that he take back his slave and forgive him for running away. In the introduction of his letter to Philemon, Paul began, "Unto Philemon our dearly beloved, and fellowlabourer, and to our beloved Apphia, and Archippus our fellowsolider, and to the church in thy house" (Philemon 1:1–2). Because this is a personal letter to Philemon, and not a letter to a congregation, it seems likely that Apphia was a member of his household and closely related to him, perhaps being his wife, sister, or daughter. The "beloved" before her name also indicates that Paul was acquainted with her and that he held her in high regard.

It is also interesting that Paul mentioned that Philemon had a church in his house. House churches were common in the early days of the Christian Church. These congregations probably would have consisted of small groups of believers who, because they had no other building, met in the home of a member. Within the home, they would conduct worship services, including the administration of the sacrament and teaching, praying, and fasting together. It is also likely that since they no longer had access to the temple in Jerusalem, early Christians also conducted sacred rituals in these homes as well.[1] Later Christians would build chapels and temples, but in the early days, they had no such luxury and did the best they could.

I imagine these house churches to be much like the type of Church meetings that were held in the early days of the restored Church. The early Latter-day Saints did not have meeting houses and temples, so they met in one another's homes. We even know that the first temple work was received and performed in a public building, the upper room of the Red Brick Store in Nauvoo, which may have been similar to what the Christians in Christ's time did as well.

Even today there are many groups of Latter-day Saints around the world who, for various reasons, still meet and hold church services in homes. My husband's aunt has traveled all over the world with her family and has lived in many different countries, some in which their family were the only members of the Church in that country. She said, "It is not exceptional even today to have our church meetings in homes. It's a big step when the Church buys or leases property for a designated church building; the step before that is usually to hold church meetings in homes. In both Sudan and Bosnia, we held church services in our apartment. We were in Bosnia when the first branch was formed, but we continued to meet in the branch president's apartment for a year, and then after he moved, the branch met for another year in our old apartment, where the senior missionary couple was living. Friends of ours, working in an embassy in another country, took turns hosting church in their homes. Right now, Emma Lucy [her daughter] is serving in a country where missionaries arrived only recently, and they hold their church services in a family's apartment, too."[2] Modern-day Saints who, like my husband's aunt, live in places where the Church is still getting established may be able to relate especially well to what these early Christians would have experienced.

It is also interesting to note that many of the house churches we know about were held in the homes of women. The most notable of these instances was Priscilla and her husband Aquila, who are mentioned twice as having a church in their house, first in Corinth and later in Rome. We also know that in Jerusalem, the home of Mary, the mother of John Mark (see page 177), was where the Saints gathered, and that Chloe hosted a congregation in her home. (See page 237.) It is possible that Lydia also hosted a church in her home in Phillipi. (See page 187.) Some scholars think that the person named "Nymphas" (Colossians 4:15) in the King James Version should really be translated to the feminine "Nyphma" and that the Church in Laodicea, which was "in his house" (verse 15) should really be "in her house."[3]

The church in Philemon's home would have been similar to these other New Testament congregations and it is likely that Apphia, as a member of his household, would have been involved in organizing and hosting the church. When I think of all the different types of work and activities that go on in our modern-day church buildings and temples (worship service, youth activities, lessons, musical performances, missionary discussions, ordinance work, baptism) it makes me appreciate what it must have meant for these early Saints to have hosted the church in their homes.

Their homes were probably always filled with people—gathering, teaching, worshipping, preaching, praying, and visiting. It would have taken a remarkable person to open their home in such a communal way and would have required a lot of work and a lot of patience. Yet, it seems to me that for some of the women in the New Testament, Apphia included, having the church in their home was an influential way for them to minister and build up the kingdom of God. Their love of the gospel and Jesus Christ motivated them to share what they had, and because they did, their homes became sacred places.

# The *Elect Lady*

*"The elder unto the elect lady and her children, whom I love in the truth; and not I only, but also all they that have known the truth. . . . I rejoiced greatly that I found of thy children walking in truth, as we have received a commandment from the Father."*

*2 John 1:1, 4*

*The book of 2 John* gives us another glimpse of what the ancient Relief Society may have looked like. (See "Phebe" on page 219.) John's epistle was addressed to a woman simply known as "the elect lady" (2 John 1:1). The Greek word translated as "elect" is the word *elektos* and means "picked out" or "chosen of God."[1] John's use of this word to describe this unknown lady seems to indicate that she had been chosen or set apart for some specific work in the Church. Furthermore, John stated that "not I only, but also all they that have known the truth" loved her (verse 1). Whoever this "elect lady" was, she was well-known to the whole Church and well-loved.

While John doesn't give us any clues as to who this "elect lady" was, modern-day revelation helps illuminate her role. According to Eliza R. Snow's minutes of the first Relief Society meeting, after Emma Smith was elected and sustained as president of the Relief Society, Joseph Smith stood and read the entire twenty-fifth section of the Doctrine and Covenants (which is a revelation addressed specifically to Emma Smith). He then told the women,

> This revelation was given to me in July of 1830, not long after the church was first organized. Emma was ordained at that time to expound the scriptures to all and to teach the female part of the community. She is not alone in this but others may also obtain to the same blessings.[2]

Joseph then opened the New Testament and read all of 2 John (which is the epistle directed to the elect lady), after which he told the women, "I read this verse to you to show that respect is had to the same thing and that why she was called an elect lady is because she was elected to preside."[3]

He then asked if Elder John Taylor would "set apart the elect lady [referring to Emma] and her counselors."[4]

By reading these scriptures, Joseph Smith compared Emma's role as the leader of the Relief Society to that of the elect lady John addressed in his epistle. This additional insight helps us see that the "elect lady" of 2 John probably held a similar position in the early Christian Church as Emma Smith did in the Restored Church. It is fascinating to think about what type of work this elect lady would have been engaged in and how the ancient sisterhood she was a part of would have been organized.

John closed his epistle to the elect lady by stating, "The children of thy elect sister greet thee" (2 John 1:13). We don't have any idea who this "elect sister" was or why she would have been in company with John. She may have been the elect lady's biological sister, or perhaps simply her sister in the gospel of Christ. Either way, it appears that this sister also held some sort of "elected" or "set apart" position within the Church as well.

These glimpses we have of early Christian women can give us a better understanding of the work and responsibilities that women have in Christ's Church. The elect lady reminds us that women have always held important positions in Christ's kingdom and their contributions are central to the success of God's plan of His children.

# Claudia

*"Do thy diligence to come before winter. Eubulus greeteth thee, and Pudens, and Linus, and Claudia, and all the brethren."*

*2 Timothy 4:21*

*Claudia is listed among the Saints* who were in Rome around the time Paul was imprisoned and awaiting his trial before Nero. While in prison, Paul wrote to Timothy (who was serving as the bishop in Ephesus) telling him how much he loved him, encouraging him to "be not thou therefore ashamed of the testimony of our Lord" (2 Timothy 1:8), and giving him guidance concerning his stewardship over the Saints in Ephesus. Timothy must have been planning on traveling to be with Paul in Rome because Paul asked him to "take Mark, and bring him with thee" (2 Timothy 4:11) as well as to bring "the cloak that I left at Troas . . . and the books, but especially the parchments " (verse 13). Paul also took the time to inquire after several friends in Ephesus and to send greetings to Timothy from several Roman Saints, among whom was Claudia. Paul wrote, "Eubulus greeteth thee, and Pudens, and Linus, and Claudia, and all the brethren" (verse 21). It was not long after this epistle was written that Paul was martyred.

Claudia, and all the early Christian women converts, are inspiring to me because they had the courage to live the gospel in some very difficult circumstances. Claudia was living in Rome at a time when many of the stalwart Saints were falling away from the Church. In 2 Timothy 4:10–11, Paul told Timothy, "Demas hath forsaken me, having loved this present world, and is departed unto Thessalonica; Crescens to Galatia, Titus unto Dalmatia. Only Luke is with me." This was not an easy time to be a Christian, especially not in Rome, and so it is impressive that she stood firm and unmovable in her support of Paul and of the Church.

I think that sometimes the greatest trial of our faith comes when what we believe is not popular and we are perceived as being "old-fashioned" or "radical." It is at those times that we have to search inside ourselves and choose, like Claudia did, to stand firm in our testimony of Christ, no matter what. If we love "the present world" more than we love our testimony of Christ, then it becomes easy to fall away, like the Demas that Paul wrote to Timothy about. I love Claudia's story because it reminds me that the only one who offers true joy and happiness is Jesus Christ and obtaining that joy and happiness means that we must stand firm in our testimonies—even when it means we will be standing alone.

# Appendix

## Women from the New Testament Who Exemplify Young Women Values

*These eight values* are taken from the Young Women's theme[1] and exemplify the type of qualities that are important for women of God to develop. I have listed women from the New Testament who I think are examples, both good and bad, of each value. Several women are listed in multiple categories because their stories exemplify many of the Young Women values. Feel free to add or change this list based on the your own opinions and feelings. I hope that as you study these women's stories, you will be inspired to know how to use their stories to help young women in your life develop these important values.

## Faith

Mary, the Mother of Jesus
Peter's Mother-in-Law
Daughter of Jairus
Woman with an Issue of Blood
Syrophenician Woman and Her Young Daughter
Widow Who Gave Two Mites
Widow of Nain
Martha
Samaritan Woman at the Well
Lydia
Junia
Eunice and Lois

## Divine Nature

Mary, the Mother of Jesus
Mother of Zebedee's Children
Mary Magdalene
Elisabeth
Mary of Bethany
Certain Woman of the Company
Daughters of Jerusalem
Women at the Empty Tomb
Women Gathered in Prayer with the Apostles
Four Daughters of Philip
The Elect Lady
Chloe

## Individual Worth

Daughter of Jairus
Syrophenician Woman and Her Young Daughter
Mother of Zebedee's Children
Mary Magdalene
Anna
Widow of Nain
Woman with a Spirit of Infirmity
Samaritan Woman at the Well
Woman Taken in Adultery
Lydia

## Knowledge

Wife of Pontius Pilate
Anna
Mary of Bethany
Martha
Samaritan Woman at the Well
Eunice and Lois
Damaris
Chloe

## Choice and Accountability

Sapphira
Bernice and Drusilla
Euodia and Syntyche
Mary, the Mother of Jesus
Herodias and Her Daughter
Damsel and Maid at the Door
Widow Who Gave Two Mites
Mary of Bethany
Martha
Woman Taken in Adultery

## Good Works

Tabitha
Elisabeth
Lydia
Priscilla
Phebe
Tryphena and Tryphosa
Apphia
Susanna and the Women Who Followed Christ

## Integrity

Mary Magdalene
Mary, the Mother of James and Joses
Joanna
Susanna and the Women Who Followed Christ
Mother of the Man Born Blind
Mary, the Mother of John Mark
Rhoda
Devout and Honorable Women of the Jews and Greeks
Damaris
Priscilla
Junia
Tryphena and Tryphosa
Claudia

## Virtue

Mary, the Mother of Jesus
Four Daughters of Philip
Woman with the Issue of Blood
Elisabeth
Devout and Honorable Women of the Jews and Greeks

# *Young Women*
## in the New Testament

*These are women who we know* were probably under the age of eighteen.

Mary, the Mother of Jesus

Daughter of Jairus

Herodias's Daughter

Women and Children among the Four and Five
Thousand Fed

Daughter of the Syrophenician Woman

Damsel and Maid at the Door

Rhoda

Damsel Possessed with a Spirit of Divination

Women and Children of Tyre

Four Daughters of Philip

# All the Women in the New Testament

1. Mary, the Mother of Jesus (Matthew 1:16, 18–25; 2:11, 13–14, 20–21; 12:46–50; 13:55; Mark 3:31–35; 6:3; Luke 1:26–56; 2:5–8, 16, 19, 22, 27, 34–35, 43–51; 8:19–20; John 2:1–5, 12; 6:42; 19:25–27; Acts 1:14; Galatians 4:4)
2. Peter's Mother-in-Law (Matthew 8:14–15; Mark 1:30–31; Luke 4:38–39)
3. Daughter of Jairus (Matthew 9:18–19, 23–26; Mark 5:22–24, 35–43; Luke 8:41, 49–56)
4. Wife of Jairus (Mark 5:40–43; Luke 8:51–56)
5. Woman with an Issue of Blood (Matthew 9:20–22; Mark 5:25–34; Luke 8:43–48)
6. Christ's Sisters (Matthew 13:56; Mark 6:3)
7. Herodias (Matthew 14:1–11; Mark 6:17–28; Luke 3:19–20)
8. Herodias's Daughter (Matthew 14:6–11; Mark 6:22–29; Luke 3:19–20)
9. Women and Children among the Five Thousand Fed (Matthew 14:21)
10. Women and Children among the Four Thousand Fed (Matthew 15:38)
11. Syrophenician Woman—also called the Woman of Canaan (Matthew 15:21–28; Mark 7:24–30)
12. Young Daughter of the Syrophenician Woman (Matthew 15:21–28; Mark 7:24–30)
13. Mother of Zebedee's Children (Matthew 20:20–23; 27:56)
14. Woman Who Anoints Jesus (Matthew 26:6–13; Mark 14:3–9; John 12:1–8)
15. Damsel to Whom Peter Denies Christ (Matthew 26:69; Mark 14:66–68; John 18:17)
16. Maid to Whom Peter Denies Christ (Matthew 26:71; Mark 14:69–70; Luke 22:56–57)
17. Wife of Pontius Pilate (Matthew 27:19)
18. Many Women Beholding afar Off (Matthew 27:55–56; Mark 15:40–41)
19. Mary Magdalene (Matthew 27:57, 61; 28:1–10; Mark 15:40–41, 47; 16:1–8, 9–11; Luke 8:2–3; 24:1–11, 22–24; John 19:25; 20:1–3, 11–18)
20. Mary, the Mother of James and Joses (Matthew 27:56; 28:1; Mark 15:40–41, 47; 16:1–8; Luke 24:1–11, 22–24)
21. The Other Mary (Matthew 28:1–10; Matthew 27:61)
22. The Widow Who Gave Two Mites (Mark 12:41–44; Luke 21:1–4)
23. Salome (Mark 15:40–41; Mark 16:1–8)
24. Many Other Women Who Came Up (Mark 15:40–41)
25. Elisabeth (Luke 1:5–80)
26. Anna (Luke 2:36–38)
27. Widow of Nain (Luke 7:11–17)
28. Sinner Who Washed Jesus's Feet with Her Hair (Luke 7:36–50)
29. Certain Women Who Had Been Healed (Luke 8:2–3)
30. Joanna, the Wife of Chuza (Luke 8:2–3; Luke 24:1–11, 22–24)
31. Susanna (Luke 8:2–3)
32. Martha (Luke 10:37–42; John 11:1–6, 17–27, 34–45; 12:2)
33. Mary of Bethany (Luke 10:37–42; John 11:1–5, 17–20, 28–34, 39–45; 12:3–9)
34. Certain Woman of the Company (Luke 11:27–28)

35. Woman with Spirit of Infirmity (Luke 13:11–16)
36. Women Who Bewailed and Lamented (Luke 23:27–29)
37. The Women Who Followed Jesus (Luke 23:49, 55–56)
38. Other Women Who Were at the Empty Tomb (Luke 24:1–11, 22–24)
39. Samaritan Woman at the Well (John 4:7–42)
40. Woman Taken in Adultery (John 8:1–11)
41. Mother of the Man Born Blind (John 9:2–3, 18–23)
42. Mary, the Wife of Cleophas (John 19:25)
43. Jesus's Mother's Sister (John 19:25)
44. Women of Prayer and Supplication (Acts 1:14)
45. Sapphira (Acts 5:1–11)
46. New Women Believers (Acts 5:14)
47. Widows Who Were Neglected (Acts 6:1)
48. Women Committed to Prison by Saul (Acts 8:3; 22:4)
49. Samaritan Women Baptized by Paul (Acts 8:12)
50. Candace, Queen of Ethiopians (Acts 8:27)
51. Women Persecuted and Bound by Saul (Acts 9:2)
52. Tabitha/Dorcus (Acts 9:36–42)
53. Mary, the Mother of John Mark (Acts 12:12; Colossians 4:10)
54. Rhoda (Acts 12:13–15)
55. Devout and Honorable Jewish Women (Acts 13:50)
56. Eunice (2 Timothy 1:15; Acts 16:1)
57. Lois (2 Timothy 1:15)
58. Women at the Place of Prayer in Philippi (Acts 16:13)
59. Lydia (Acts 16:11–15, 40)
60. Damsel with Spirit of Divination (Acts 16:16–19)
61. Chief and Honorable Women of the Greeks (Acts 17:4, 12)
62. Damaris (Acts 17:34)
63. Priscilla (Acts 18:2–3, 18–20, 24–26; Romans 16:3–5; 1 Corinthians 16:19; 2 Timothy 4:19)
64. Wives and Children of Tyre (Acts 21:4–6)
65. Four Daughters of Philip (Acts 21:9)
66. Paul's Sister (Acts 23:16)
67. Drusilla (Acts 24:24)
68. Bernice (Acts 25:13–14, 23; 26:30)
69. Changed Women (Romans 1:26–27)
70. Phebe (Romans 16:1–2)
71. Mary of Rome (Romans 16:6)
72. Junia (Romans 16:7)
73. Tryphena (Romans 16:12)
74. Tryphosa (Romans 16:12)
75. Persis (Romans 16:12)
76. Mother of Rufus (Romans 16:13)
77. Sister of Nereus (Romans 16:15)
78. Julia (Romans 16:15)
79. Chloe (1 Corinthians 1:11)
80. Euodia (Philippians 4:2–3)
81. Syntyche (Philippians 4:2–3)
82. Sister of Barnabas (Colossians 4:10)
83. Claudia (2 Timothy 4:21)
84. Adulteresses (James 4:4)
85. Apphia (Philemon 1:2)
86. The Elect Lady (2 John 1:1–12)
87. The Elect Lady's Sister (2 John 1:13)
88. Nympha (Colossians 4:15)

# Old Testament Women in the New Testament

1. Tamar (Matthew 1:3)
2. Rahab (Matthew 1:5; Hebrews 11:31; James 2:25)
3. Ruth (Matthew 1:5)
4. Bathsheba (Matthew 1:6)
5. Rachel (Matthew 2:18)
6. The Queen of the South (Matthew 12:42; Luke 11:31)
7. Widows in Israel (Luke 4:25)
8. Widow of Zarephath (Luke 4:25–26)
9. Wives Destroyed by the Flood (Luke 17:27)
10. Lot's Wife (Luke 17:32)
11. Sara (Romans 4:19; 9:9; Galatians 4:22–31; Hebrews 11:11; 1 Peter 3:6)
12. Rebecca (Romans 9:10–12)
13. Eve (2 Corinthians 11:3)
14. Hagar (Galatians 4:22–31)
15. Jezebel and Her Children (Revelation 2:20–23)
16. Pharaoh's Daughter (Acts 7:21; Hebrews 11:24–26)
17. Moses's Mother (Hebrews 11:23)
18. Holy Women (1 Peter 3:5)
19. Women Who Received Their Dead (Hebrews 11:35–36)

# Women in Parables

- Woman with Leaven (Matthew 13:33; Luke 13:20–21)
- Wife of the Unjust Servant (Matthew 18:25)
- Ten Virgins (Matthew 25:1–13)
- The Fig Tree (Mark 13:28–29)
- Woman Having Ten Pieces of Silver (Luke 15:8–10)
- Widow and the Unjust Judge (Luke 18:2–5)

# Teachings about Women in the New Testament

1. "Whosoever shall put away his wife, let him give her a writing of divorcement" (Matthew 5:31–32).
2. "Whosoever looketh on a woman to lust after her hath committed adultery with her already in his heart" (Matthew 5:28).
3. "The daughter against her mother, and the daughter in law against her mother in law" (Matthew 10:35; Luke 12:53).
4. "He that loveth father or mother more than me is not worthy of me: and he that loveth son or daughter more than me is not worthy of me" (Matthew 10:37).
5. "Among them that are born of women there hath not risen a greater than John the Baptist" (Matthew 11:11; Luke 7:28).
6. "But wisdom is justified of her children" (Matthew 11:19; Luke 7:35).
7. "Honor thy father and mother" (Matthew 15:4–6; 19:19; Mark 7:10–13; 10:19; Luke 18:20; Ephesians 6:2–3).
8. "The Pharisees also came unto him, tempting him, and saying unto him, Is it lawful for a man to put away his wife for every cause?" (Matthew 19:3–10; Mark 10:2–12).
9. "For there are some eunuchs, which were so born from their mother's womb" (Matthew 19:12).
10. "And every one that hath forsaken houses, or brethren, or sisters, or father, or mother, or wife, or children, or lands, for my name's sake, shall receive an hundredfold, and shall inherit everlasting life" (Matthew 19:29; Mark 10:29–30).
11. "Straightway ye shall find an ass tied, and a colt with her" (Matthew 21:2).
12. "Tell ye the daughter of Sion, Behold, thy King cometh unto thee, meek, and sitting upon an ass, and a colt the foal of an ass" (Matthew 21:5; John 12:15).
13. "That the publicans and the harlots go into the kingdom of God before you" (Matthew 21:31–32).
14. "If a man die, having no children, his brother shall marry his wife, and raise up seed unto his brother" (Matthew 22:23–30; Mark 12:18–25; Luke 20:27–36).
15. "Woe unto you, scribes and Pharisees, hypocrites! for ye devour widows' houses" (Matthew 23:14; Mark 12:40; Luke 20:47).
16. "How often would I have gathered thy children together, even as a hen gathereth her chickens under her wings, and ye would not!" (Matthew 23:37).
17. "And woe unto them that are with child, and to them that give suck in those days!" (Matthew 24:19; Mark 13:17; Luke 21:23).
18. "Two women shall be grinding at the mill; the one shall be taken, and the other left" (Matthew 24:41; Luke 17:35).
19. "For whosoever shall do the will of God, the same is my brother, and my sister, and mother" (Mark 3:34–35).
20. "For the earth bringeth forth fruit of herself; first the blade, then the ear, after that the full corn in the ear" (Mark 4:28).
21. "I have married a wife, and therefore I cannot come" (Luke 14:20).

22. "That servant say in his heart, My lord delayeth his coming; and shall begin to beat the menservants and maidens, and to eat and drink, and to be drunken" (Luke 12:45).

23. "If any man come to me, and hate not his father, and mother, and wife, and children, and brethren, and sisters, yea, and his own life also, he cannot be my disciple" (Luke 14:26).

24. "But as soon as this thy son was come, which hath devoured thy living with harlots, thou hast killed for him the fatted calf" (Luke 15:30).

25. "Whosoever putteth away his wife, and marrieth another, committeth adultery: and whosoever marrieth her that is put away from her husband committeth adultery" (Luke 16:18).

26. "And he said unto them, Verily I say unto you, There is no man that hath left house, or parents, or brethren, or wife, or children, for the kingdom of God's sake" (Luke 18:29–30).

27. "How can a man be born when he is old? can he enter the second time into his mother's womb, and be born?" (John 3:4).

28. "He that hath the bride is the bridegroom" (John 3:29).

29. "A woman when she is in travail hath sorrow, because her hour is come: but as soon as she is delivered of the child, she remembereth no more the anguish, for joy that a man is born into the world" (John 16:21).

30. Man lame from his mother's womb (Acts 3:2).

31. Sons and daughters shall prophesy (Acts 2:17).

32. "And on my servants and on my handmaidens I will pour out in those days of my Spirit; and they shall prophesy" (Acts 2:18).

33. "And there sat a certain man at Lystra, impotent in his feet, being a cripple from his mother's womb, who never had walked" (Acts 14:8).

34. Silver shrines for Diana (Acts 19:24, 27–28, 34–35, 37).

35. "For the woman which hath an husband is bound by the law to her husband so long as he liveth; but if the husband be dead, she is loosed from the law of her husband" (Romans 7:2–3).

36. "I will call them my people, which were not my people; and her beloved, which was not beloved" (Romans 9:25).

37. "It is reported commonly that there is fornication among you, and such fornication as is not so much as named among the Gentiles, that one should have his father's wife" (1 Corinthians 5:1).

38. "Know ye not that your bodies are the members of Christ? shall I then take the members of Christ, and make them the members of an harlot? God forbid" (1 Corinthians 6:15–16).

39. Counsel on marriage for missionaries (1 Corinthians 7).

40. "Have we not power to lead about a sister, a wife, as well as other Apostles, and as the brethren of the Lord, and Cephas?" (1 Corinthians 9:5).

41. Instructions for women prophesying and praying (1 Corinthians 11:2–16).

42. Charity (1 Corinthians 13:5).

43. "Let your women keep silence in the churches: for it is not permitted unto them to speak; but they are commanded to be under obedience, as also saith the law" (1 Corinthians 14:34–35).

44. "And will be a Father unto you, and ye shall be my sons and daughters, saith the Lord Almighty" (2 Corinthians 6:18).

45. "For I am jealous over you with godly jealousy: for I have espoused you to one husband, that I may present you as a chaste virgin to Christ" (2 Corinthians 11:2).

46. Separated from mother's womb (Galatians 1:15).

47. "There is neither Jew nor Greek, there is neither bond nor free, there is neither male nor female: for ye are all one in Christ

Jesus" (Galatians 3:28).

48. "Wives, submit yourselves unto your own husbands, as unto the Lord" (Ephesians 5:22–25).

49. "Husbands, love your wives, and be not bitter against them" (Colossians 3:18–19).

50. "But we were gentle among you, even as a nurse cherisheth her children" (1 Thessalonians 2:7).

51. "For when they shall say, Peace and safety; then sudden destruction cometh upon them, as travail upon a woman with child; and they shall not escape" (1 Thessalonians 5:3).

52. "Knowing this, that the law is not made for a righteous man, but for the lawless and disobedient, for the ungodly and for sinners, for unholy and profane, for murderers of fathers and murderers of mothers, for manslayers" (1 Timothy 1:9).

53. "In like manner also, that women adorn themselves in modest apparel, with shamefacedness and sobriety; not with broided hair, or gold, or pearls, or costly array" (1 Timothy 2:9–15).

54. "A bishop then must be blameless, the husband of one wife, vigilant, sober, of good behaviour, given to hospitality, apt to teach" (1 Timothy 3:2).

55. "Even so must their wives be grave, not slanderers, sober, faithful in all things" (1 Timothy 3:11–12).

56. "But refuse profane and old wives' fables, and exercise thyself rather unto godliness" (1 Timothy 4:7).

57. "The elder women as mothers; the younger as sisters, with all purity" (1 Timothy 5:2).

58. "Honour widows that are widows indeed" (1 Timothy 5:3–16).

59. "For of this sort are they which creep into houses, and lead captive silly women laden with sins, led away with divers lusts" (2 Timothy 3:6).

60. "If any be blameless, the husband of one wife, having faithful children not accused of riot or unruly" (Titus 1:6).

61. "The aged women likewise, that they be in behaviour as becometh holiness, not false accusers, not given to much wine, teachers of good things" (Titus 2:3–5).

62. "Without father, without mother, without descent, having neither beginning of days, nor end of life; but made like unto the Son of God; abideth a priest continually" (Hebrews 7:3).

63. "But let patience have her perfect work, that ye may be perfect and entire, wanting nothing" (James 1:4).

64. "Pure religion and undefiled before God and the Father is this, To visit the fatherless and widows in their affliction, and to keep himself unspotted from the world" (James 1:27).

65. "If a brother or sister be naked, and destitute of daily food" (James 2:15–16).

66. "And he prayed again, and the heaven gave rain, and the earth brought forth her fruit" (James 5:18).

67. "Likewise, ye wives, be in subjection to your own husbands; that, if any obey not the word, they also may without the word be won by the conversation of the wives" (1 Peter 3:1–7).

68. "But it is happened unto them according to the true proverb, The dog is turned to his own vomit again; and the sow that was washed to her wallowing in the mire" (2 Peter 2:22).

69. "And they had hair as the hair of women, and their teeth were as the teeth of lions" (Revelation 9:8).

70. "And there appeared a great wonder in heaven; a woman clothed with the sun, and the moon under her feet, and upon her head a crown of twelve stars" (Revelation 12:1–2, 4–6, 13–17).

71. "These are they which were not defiled with women; for they are virgins. These are they which follow the Lamb whithersoever

he goeth. These were redeemed from among men, being the firstfruits unto God and to the Lamb" (Revelation 14:4).

72. Babylon (Revelation 14:8; 18:3–11, 15, 18–20, 24).

73. "And another angel came out from the altar, which had power over fire; and cried with a loud cry to him that had the sharp sickle, saying, Thrust in thy sharp sickle, and gather the clusters of the vine of the earth; for her grapes are fully ripe" (Revelation 14:18).

74. The great whore (Revelation 11:1–7, 9, 15–18; 19:2–3).

75. The bride of the Lamb (Revelation 18:23; 19:7–8; 21:9; 22:17).

76. "And I John saw the holy city, new Jerusalem, coming down from God out of heaven, prepared as a bride adorned for her husband" (Revelation 21:2, 11).

77. "In the midst of the street of it, and on either side of the river, was there the tree of life, which bare twelve manner of fruits, and yielded her fruit every month: and the leaves of the tree were for the healing of the nations" (Revelations 22:2).

# Endnotes

## INTRODUCTION

1. James E. Talmage, *Jesus the Christ: A Study of the Messiah and His Mission According to the Holy Scriptures Both Ancient and Modern*, 3rd ed. (Salt Lake City: Deseret Book, 1915), 442.
2. H. Shirt, "Women in the Image of the Son: Being Female and Being Like Christ," in *LDS Women's Treasury: Insights and Inspiration for Today's Woman* (Salt Lake City: Deseret Book, 1997), 57.

## LEARNING TO SEE WOMEN

1. See Heather Farrell, "How Many Women Would You Guess Are in the Scriptures," *Women in the Scriptures*, last modified March 9, 2011, http://www.womeninthescriptures.com/2011/03/setting-record-straight-there-really.html.
2. See "Teachings about Women in the New Testament" in the appendix on page 267.
3. Zina D. H. Young, "How I Gained My Testimony of the Truth," *Young Woman's Journal*, April 1893, 319. The word *scriptures* replaces "own hearts" from the original quote.
4. Gordon B Hinckley, "Words of the Prophet: The Book of Mormon: Read All about It," *New Era*, September 2003.
5. Shirt, "Women in the Image of the Son," *LDS Women's Treasury*, 55, 60.
6. Julie B. Beck BYU Women's Conference 2011. Access at https://www.lds.org/callings/relief-society/messages-from-leaders/messages-from-leaders/womens-conference-2011?lang=eng.

7. Boyd K. Packer, "The Witness," *Ensign*, May 2014.

## CHRIST'S LINEAGE

1. For a list see "Old Testament Women in the New Testament" in the appendix on page 265.
2. Talmage, *Jesus the Christ*, 81.
3. Jeni Broberg Holzapfel and Richard Neitzel Holzapfel, *Sisters at the Well: Women and the Life and Teachings of Jesus* (Salt Lake City: Bookcraft, 1993), 21.
4. See Leviticus 2:13.
5. Mary Hendren, "Birth and Salt," *Women from the Book Blog: A Journey of Discovery*, posted October 6, 2013, http://womenfromthebook.com/2013/10/06/birth-and-salt/.

## ELISABETH

1. Bonnie L. Oscarson, "Oh, How We Need Each Other," *Ensign*, May 2014.
2. Heather Farrell, "Elisabeth: Go before the Face of the Lord," in *The Gift of Giving Life: Rediscovering the Divine Nature of Pregnancy and Birth*, Felice Austin, Lani Axman, Heather Farrell, Robyn Allgood, Sheridan Ripley, Lynn Callister (Madison and West, 2012), 506–7.
3. The only other place in the New Testament where the word *kataluma* is found is in Mark 14:14 to refer to the "upper room" where Jesus held His last Passover.

4. See Leviticus 12.

## THE SEVEN SORROWS AND JOYS OF MARY

1. Bruce R. McConkie, *The Mortal Messiah: From Bethlehem to Calvary*, 4 vols. (Salt Lake City: Deseret Book, 1979), 1:326–7.
2. The traditional Seven Sorrows are: 1. The Prophecy of Simeon (Luke 2:34–35); 2. The Flight into Egypt (Matthew 2:13); 3. The Loss of Jesus in the Temple (Luke 2:43–45); 4. Mary Meets Jesus on the Way to Calvary; 5. Jesus Dies on the Cross (John 19:25); 6.The Piercing of the Side of Jesus, and Mary's Receiving the Body of Jesus in Her Arms (Matthew 27:57–59); and 7. The Body of Jesus Is Placed in the Tomb (John 19:40–42).
3. Elaine S. Dalton, "Remember Who You Are!" *Ensign*, May 2010.
4. These scriptures are part of Mary's Psalm found in Luke 1:46–55. It is also interesting to compare Mary's Psalm to the Psalm of Hannah, the mother of Samuel, found in 1 Samuel 2:1–10.
5. Doug Batchelor, "Why Did Jesus Call Mary 'Woman' Instead of Mother," *Amazing Facts*, accessed July 15, 2014, http://www.amazingfacts.org/media-library/media/e/1172/t/why-did-jesus-call-mary-woman-instead-of-mother.aspx
6. Talmage, *Jesus the Christ*, 620. In Chapter 35, "Death and Burial," Talmage states,

The strong, loud utterance, immediately following which He bowed His head and "gave up the ghost," when considered in connection with other recorded details, points to a physical rupture of the heart as the direct cause of death. If the soldier's spear was thrust into the left side of the Lord's body and actually penetrated the heart, the outrush of "blood and water" observed by John is further evidence of a cardiac rupture; for it is known that in the rare instances of death resulting from a breaking of any part of the wall of the heart, blood accumulates within the pericardium, and there undergoes a change by which the corpuscles separate as a partially clotted mass from the almost colorless, watery serum. . . . The present writer believes that the Lord Jesus died of a broken heart. The psalmist sang in dolorous measure according to his inspired prevision of the Lord's passion: "Reproach hath broken my heart; and I am full of heaviness: and I looked for some to take pity, but there was none; and for comforters, but I found none. They gave me also gall for my meat; and in my thirst they gave me vinegar to drink." Psalms 69:20, 21; see also 22:14.

7. Fred H. Wight, "Marriage Customs: The Apparel of Bride and Groom," *Manners and Customs of Bible Lands* (1953). Found online by the Moody Bible Institute of Chicago at http://www.baptistbiblebelievers.com/OTStudies/Mannersand CustomsInBibleLands1953.aspx.
8. It is interesting to note in Revelation 21:9–11 that when the angel shows John "the bride, the Lamb's wife," he shows him Jerusalem whose "light was like unto a stone most precious." This is an indication that precious stones were an important part of a bride's wedding attire.

## ANNA

1. Jeffrey R. Holland, "Lord, I Believe," *Ensign*, May 2013.

## SAMARITAN WOMAN AT THE WELL

1. This was the well that Jacob, the father of the twelve tribes, had erected. It was known as a constant and reliable source of water.
2. Samaritans believed that the Messiah would be a restorer, or one

who would restore true worship of God and elevate Samaritans to their rightful place in the house of Israel. Camille Fronk, "Give Me This Water, That I Thirst Not: The Woman at the Well," BYU Women's Conference, 2000.

3. Dieter F. Uchtdorf, "The Reflection in the Water" (CES Devotional, Brigham Young University, Provo, Utah, November 1, 2009). Access at https://www.lds.org/broadcasts/archive/ces-devotionals/2009/01?lang=eng.

4. Holzapfel and Holzapfel, *Sisters at the Well*, 9.

## WIDOW OF NAIN

1. Richard Neitzel Holzapfel, Jeffrey R. Chadwick, Frank F. Judd Jr., and Thomas A. Wayment, "Jesus and the Ossuaries: First-Century Jewish Burial Practices and the Lost Tomb of Jesus," *Behold the Lamb of God: An Easter Celebration* (Provo, UT: Brigham Young University Religious Studies Center, 2008) 1–16.

2. See Matthew 14:14; 9:36; Mark 1:41; 6:34.

3. See D&C 101:9 and 3 Nephi 17:6.

## DAUGHTER OF JAIRUS

1. For example, in Luke 5 we read how some men brought to Christ a man who was stricken with palsy. When they could not bring him through the door because of the crowd, they put him on his bed and lowered him through the roof. Christ, upon seeing their faith, looked on the man with compassion and said, "Man, thy sins are forgiven thee" (verse 20). When the scribes and the Pharisees heard this, they began to complain, claiming that Christ spoke blasphemy because only God had power to forgive sins. Christ perceived their thoughts and answered them by saying, "But that ye may know that the Son of man hath power upon earth to forgive sins, (he said unto the sick of the palsy,) I say unto thee, Arise, and take up thy couch, and go into thine house" (verse 24). Immediately the man rose up, took his bed, and walked to his house, glorying God.

2. Orson F. Whitney, in Conference Report, April 1929, 110. Taken from "Hope for Parents of Wayward Children," *Ensign*, September 2002.

3. Daniel Rona, *Israel revealed: Discovering Mormon and Jewish insights in the Holy Land* (English Foundation, 2001), audiobook.

## MENSTRUATION

1. Shraga Simmons, "Tazria: Spiritually Pure," last modified April 1, 2000, http://www.aish.com/tp/b/sw/48962456.html.

2. Ibid.

3. Ibid.

## WOMAN WITH AN ISSUE OF BLOOD

1. The guidelines for a man who had an issue of blood or who was unclean were actually more strict than they were for women. For comparison, see Leviticus 15:1–30.

## HERODIAS AND HER DAUGHTER

1. See Acts 12:1–24.

2. Flavius Josephus, "The Banishment of Archelaus to the Departure of the Jews from Babylon," *The Antiquities of the Jews*, trans. William Whiston (1737). Book 18:136.

3. We can conclude this because we know that Herodias left her husband shortly after Salome's birth and Herodias and Herod had been together for about ten years.

4. M. Russell Ballard, "Mothers and Daughters," *Ensign*, May 2010.

## SYROPHENICIAN WOMAN AND HER YOUNG DAUGHTER

1. Throughout the scriptures, we learn that the Jews, who were the first to hear the gospel, will be among the last of God's children to accept it in the last days.
2. See Ether 3:6–19.
3. Michelle Linford, "On Mormon Women and the Priesthood: God Does Not Give Crumbs," *Mormon Women*, last modified September 27, 2013, http://mormonwoman.org/2013/09/27/on-mormon-women-and-the-priesthood-god-does-not-give-crumbs/comment-page-1/#sthash.pDwgKZtu.dpuf.

## MARY MAGDALENE

1. Mary Ross D'Angelo, "Mary 3," in *Women in Scripture: A Dictionary of Named and Unnamed Women in the Hebrew Bible, the Apocryphal/Deuterocanonical Books, and the New Testament*, ed. Carol Meyers, Toni Craven, and Ross S. Kraemer (Grand Rapids, MI: William B. Eerdmans Publishing, 2000), 120–21. Also see "New Testament Greek Lexicon—King James Version," Bible Study Tools, s.v. "magdala," http://www.biblestudytools.com/lexicons/greek/nas/magdala.html.
2. Historically, Mary Magdalene has been unfairly portrayed as a harlot and a sinner. Nowhere in the scriptures do we have evidence of that. This belief probably originated with people assuming that the woman mentioned in Luke 7:37–50, who is called a sinner, was the same person as Mary Magdalene, who is mentioned only two verses afterward. The assumption is that she had devils because she was a sinner, but that is likely not true. Mary of Bethany has also been linked to the sinful woman in Luke 7 (see page 117), but there is no reason to link her to the story either.

3. Jeffrey R. Holland, "Like a Broken Vessel," *Ensign*, November 2013.
4. Lani Axman, "Antepartum Depression," in *The Gift of Giving Life*, Austin, Axman, Farrell, Allgood, and Riply, 334–35.
5. Holland, "Like a Broken Vessel."

## THE MARYS IN THE NEW TESTAMENT

1. Ann N. Madsen, "Cameos: The Women of the New Testament," *Ensign*, September 1975.
2. Blair G. Van Dyke and Ray L. Huntington, "Sorting Out the Seven Marys in the New Testament," *The Religious Educator* 5, no. 3 (2004): 58. For more see "The Seven Sorrows and Joys of Mary" on page 21.

## JOANNA

1. Richard I. Pervo, "Joanna," in *Women in Scripture*, ed. Meyers, Craven, and Kraemer, 103.
2. Holzapfel and Hozapfel, *Sisters at the Well*, 129.
3. Dallin H. Oaks, "Desire," *Ensign*, May 2011.
4. Holzapfel and Hozapfel, *Sisters at the Well*.

## MARTHA

1. Julie B. Beck, BYU Women's Conference, 2011. Access at https://www.lds.org/callings/relief-society/messages-from-leaders/messages-from-leaders/womens-conference-2011?lang=eng.
2. Ibid.
3. *Daughters in My Kingdom: The History and Work of Relief Society* (Salt Lake City: The Church of Jesus Christ of Latter-day Saints, 2011), 12.
4. Ibid, 7.

5. Beck, BYU Women's Conference.

## A CERTAIN WOMAN IN THE COMPANY

1. These scriptures are taken from the Joseph Smith Translation of the Bible (also called Joseph Smith's Inspired Translation of the Bible), but it cannot be found in the footnotes of the LDS scriptures. Many of Joseph Smith's translations are in our modern day scriptures and can be found in the footnotes or in the appendix of the LDS version of the Bible. But there are many translations which were not included. I am not sure why some were included and others were not, but it may have had something to do with the fact that for many years the LDS Church did not have access to Joseph Smith's original manuscript and therefore were not sure which translations were correct and which weren't.

Yet, in the last decade, the Community of Christ has allowed LDS scholars to view the original manuscripts. They found the that the versions of Joseph Smith's Inspired Translation of the Bible, which had already been published, Joseph Smith's original corrections. The Community of Christ also allowed a group of BYU scholars to view the original manuscript and make their own side-by-side comparison of it to the KJV. Studying this complete translation of the Bible made by Joseph Smith can be a powerful scripture study tool and greatly enhance your spiritual insights.

If you are interested in learning more about Joseph's Smiths Inspired Translation of the Bible, there is an article entitled "Joseph Smith's Inspired Translation of the Bible" in the December 1972 *Ensign* by Robert Matthews, a BYU scholar who studied the JST extensively, which does a good job of explaining how this manuscript relates to Latter-day Saints. You can find it at https://www.lds.org/ensign/1972/12/joseph-smiths-inspired-translation-of-the-bible?lang=eng.

2. See John 19: 20–22.
3. Shirt, "Women in the Image of the Son," in *LDS Women's Treasury*, 57–58.
4. Holzapfel and Holzapfel, *Sisters at the Well*, 81.

## WOMAN TAKEN IN ADULTERY

1. Jesus probably taught them in the "Court of the Women." This was the place where rabbis traditionally taught in the temple and where Christ usually taught when He was in the temple.
2. Holzapfel and Holzapfel, *Sisters at the Well*, 91.
3. Ibid, 91–92.
4. The absence of the adulterous woman's partner in this narrative illustrates the unfair double standard of the day toward sexual sin. There was no similar process or test for a man who had been caught in adultery, and we can assume that her sexual partner faced no threat of death or punishment.
5. James L. Ferrell, *The Peacegiver: How Christ Offers to Heal Our Hearts and Homes* (Salt Lake: Deseret Book, 2004), 96–97.
6. Holzapfel and Holzapfel, *Sisters at the Well*, 78.

## THE MOTHER OF ZEBEDEE'S CHILDREN

1. Also see Mark 10:35–40. The stories are almost identical except for one major difference: Mark doesn't mention the mother

of Zebedee's children. In Mark's account only James and John approached the Lord. This is interesting because some Bible scholars believe that Matthew used the Gospel of Mark as one of his sources for his gospel, thus the reason many of the stories in the two books are similar. From what we know of Bible authors, it makes more sense to me that a woman would be omitted from story rather than added in, making me suspect that perhaps she was originally included in the Mark's account and was later removed or forgotten. Such a possibility seems much more likely to me than a woman actually being added in to the story at a later date. This woman is also sometimes identified as Salome (see page 145).

## JESUS WEPT FOR WOMEN

1. Linda S. Reeves, "The Lord Has Not Forgotten You," *Ensign*, November 2012.
2. Jeremiah 9:17–18 reads, "Call for the mourning women, that they may come; . . . and let them make haste, and take up a wailing for us." Amos 5:16 also refers to calling those "such as are skilful of lamentation to wailing."
3. Luke 23:48 says that when Christ died, people "smote their breasts" as a sign of grief.
4. Holzapfel, Chadwick, Judd, and Wayment, "Jesus and the Ossuaries," *Behold the Lamb of God*, 1–16.

## MARY OF BETHANY

1. The similar accounts given are in Matthew 26:1–13 and Mark 14:1–9. It is also interesting to note that Matthew and Mark both say this event took place two days before Passover, while John stated it took place six days before.

2. Holzapfel and Holzapfel, *Sister at the Well*, 136.
3. Ibid, 135–136.
4. Matthew B. Brown, *The Gate of Heaven: Insights on the Doctrines and Symbols of the Temple* (American Fork, UT: Covenant Communications, 1999), 127.
5. See Leviticus 8:12; Exodus 29:7; and Psalm 133:2.
6. Acts 10:38 tells us that "God anointed Jesus of Nazareth with the Holy Ghost and with power," but there is no other account of Christ being physically anointed with oil.

## DAUGHTERS OF JERUSALEM

1. Holzapfel and Holzapfel, *Sisters at the Well*, 121.

## WIDOW WHO GAVE TWO MITES

1. This would have been the area of the temple where Jesus overturned the tables when He cleansed the temple.
2. The first box was for the temple tax for that year; the second one for the temple tax for the last year; the third box was specifically for women's offerings of doves, related to their purification rite after childbirth. Women were required to give two doves and, perhaps for privacy's sake, instead of presenting their offerings individually, women put their money in this box. At the end of the day the priests would count up how many offerings were made and perform them all together. This is the box into which Mary would have placed her offering when she presented Jesus at the temple. The fourth box was for money for pigeon offerings; the fifth for contributions for wood for the temple; the sixth for contributions toward incense; the seventh for contributions toward the golden vessels used in the temple. Boxes eight through thirteen were used for various different

offerings including offerings related to Nazrite vows and the cleansings of lepers as well as tithes used for helping the poor and freewill offerings.

3. Neal A. Maxwell, "Swallowed Up in the Will of the Father," *Ensign*, November 1995.
4. Ibid.

## DAMSEL AND MAID AT THE DOOR
1. In the account given in John, the gender of the person to whom Peter denies Christ the second time is not given (John 18:25). The account in Luke says that the second denial was given to a man (Luke 22:58). Yet the accounts in both Matthew and Mark state that "a maid" was the person to whom Peter denied Christ the second time (Matthew 26:71; Mark 14:69). It is possible that the second denial might have been given to a man. The scriptures are unclear on this.
2. Spencer W. Kimball, "Peter, My Brother," in *Speeches of the Year*, 1971.

## WIFE OF PONTIUS PILATE
1. Felice Austin, "What Does Personal Revelation Feel Like?" *Progressive Prophetess*, last modified September 28, 2012, http://progressiveprophetess.blogspot.com/2012/09/what-does-personal-reveleation-feel-like.html.
2. Julie B. Beck, "And upon the Handmaids in Those Days Will I Pour Out My Spirit," *Ensign*, May 2010.

## MARY, THE MOTHER OF JAMES AND JOSES
1. See Matthew 27:56; Mark 15:40.

## MARY, THE WIFE OF CLEOPHAS
1. Van Dyke and Huntington, "Sorting Out the Seven Marys in the New Testament," 58.

## SALOME
1. Elizabeth Struthers Malbon, "Salome 1," *Women in the Scripture*, 148.
2. The other female ruler was Athaliah (see 2 Kings 8:18, 26; 2 Kings 11:1–3, 13–16; 2 Chronicles 21:6; 22:2–4, 10–12; 23:12–15, 21; 24:7). It is also to be noted that Salome Alexandra is the only woman mentioned in the Dead Sea Scrolls.
3. Kenneth Atkinson, *Queen Salome: Jerusalem's Warrior Monarch of the First Century B.C.E.* (Jefferson, NC: Mcfarland, 2012), 22.

## WOMEN AT THE EMPTY TOMB
1. Robyn Allgood, "Birth in Remembrance of Him," in *The Gift of Giving Life*, 348–49.
2. John 20:6–7 says, "Then cometh Simon Peter following him, and went into the sepulchre, and seeth the linen clothes lie, and the napkin, that was about his head, not lying with the linen clothes, but wrapped together in place by itself" (italics added). When Christ was resurrected, He took nothing with Him, not even His clothes. The women who came to anoint His body found the empty clothes lying in the empty tomb, bearing testimony to the truth of what Job said in Job 1:21, "Naked came I came out of my mother's womb, and naked shall I return thither."
3. Holzapfel, Chadwick, Judd, and Wayment, "Jesus and the Ossuaries," 1–16.

## WOMEN GATHERED WITH THE APOSTLES TO PRAY

1. Acts 1:13 lists Peter, James, John, Andrew, Philip, Thomas, Bartholomew, Matthew, James the son of Alphaeus, Simon Zelotes, and Judas the brother of James. Of course, the one missing was Judas Iscariot, who killed himself after Jesus's death.

2. It is interesting to me that in Nauvoo, before the temple was completed, the "upper room" of Joseph's red brick store was used as an ordinance room and was the place where the first full endowments were given. It seems to me that this "upper room" where the Apostles and women met could have had a similar function and purpose for the early Church.

3. Pentecost also coincided with the Jewish festival of Shavuot or the Festival of the Weeks. In Leviticus 23:16 the Lord instructed the people to count seven weeks or fifty days from the end of the Passover before celebrating the next holiday. Shavuot was celebrated to remember the giving of the law to Moses on Mount Sinai as well as the time of harvest.

## SAPPHIRA

1. Gordon B. Hinckley, "An Honest Man—God's Noblest Work," *New Era*, October 1976.

2. Linda K. Burton, "The Power, Joy, and Love of Covenant Keeping," *Ensign*, November 2013.

3. Linda S. Reeves, "Claim the Blessings of Your Covenants," *Ensign*, November 2013.

## WIDOWS WHO WERE NEGLECTED

1. Jared W. Ludlow, "The Book of Acts: A Pattern for Modern Church Growth," in *Shedding Light on the New Testament*, ed. Ray L. Huntington, Frank F. Judd, Jr., and David M. Whitchurch (Provo, UT: Religious Studies Center, Brigham Young University, 2009), 1–29.

2. This is the same Philip whose four daughters prophesy (see page 205).

3. Stephen G. Dempster, "Widow," *Baker's Evangelical Dictionary of Biblical Theology*, ed. Walter A. Elwell (Grand Rapids: Baker Book House, 1996. Access at http://www.biblestudytools.com/dictionaries/bakers-evangelical-dictionary/widow.html. The scriptures that use each term as referenced by this dictionary are as follows:

Weeping: Job 27:15; Psalm 78:64.

Mourning: 2 Samuel 14:2.

Desolation: Lamentations 1:1.

Poverty: Ruth 1:21; 1 Kings 17:7–12; Job 22:9.

Indebtedness: 2 Kings 4:1.

Orphan and landless immigrant: Exodus 22:21–22; Deuteronomy 24:17, 19–21.

Poorest of the poor: Job 24:4; 29:12; 31:16; Isaiah 10:2.

## SAMARITAN WOMEN BAPTIZED BY PHILIP

1. Taylor Halverson, "Who Were the Samaritans?" *Interpreter: A Journal of Mormon Scripture*, last modified August 17, 2013, http://www.mormoninterpreter.com/who-were-the-samaritans/.

2. Ross S. Kraemer, "Samaritan Women (and Men) Baptized by Philip," *Women in Scripture*, 460.

3. The relationship between the Jews and the Samaritans reminds me of the Jewish and Arab conflicts that are going on in our modern day Israel and Palestine. This conflict can also be traced back to a time when Jews, returning to their homeland, came in conflict with the people who were already living there.

Today the Palestinians, who once owned all of Israel, have been relegated to several small pockets of land throughout the region. Interactions between Israelis and Arabs are often not friendly, and generally both groups tend to try to stay away from the other group's territory. This modern-day situation may be, in some ways, similar to the situation between the Jews and the Samaritans in Christ's day.

4. Talmage, *Jesus the Christ*, 172.
5. Ibid, 173.
6. Ibid, 161.

## CANDACE, QUEEN OF THE ETHIOPIANS

1. See 1 Kings 10:1.
2. Carolyn Fluehr-Lobban, "Nubian Queens in the Nile Valley and Afro-Asiatic Cultural History" (presentation, Ninth International Conference for Nubian Studies, Boston, Museum of Fine Arts, August 20–26, 1998).

## TABITHA

1. Holzapfel, Chadwick, Judd, and Wayment, "Jesus and the Ossuaries," 1–16.

## RHODA

1. See Mark 5:42.
2. Rhoda is called a "damsel," which in Greek is the word *paidiske* and means a "young girl," specifically a servant girl. The word paidiske is also used throughout the New Testament to refer to a servant girl who had charge of keeping the door. Comparatively, the daughter of Jairus is also called a "damsel," but the word used for her is *paidion*, which means a "young child." Both *paidiske*

and *paidion* are diminutives of the word *pais*, which means "child." The only difference is that *paidiske* refers to a child who is a servant. This tells us that Rhoda, while similar in age to the daughter of Jairus, would have been a slave or a servant in the household of Mary, the mother of John Mark. Knowing this helps explain why, out of everyone in the household, she would have answered Peter's knocks.

3. Steven C. Walker, "Between Scriptural Lines," *Ensign*, March 1978.

## MARY, THE MOTHER OF JOHN MARK

1. John Mark would later die as a martyr for the Church.
2. See Acts 12:25; 15:36–40; 2 Timothy 4:11.
3. Her home appears to be the place where the members of the Church in Jerusalem met. We might speculate that it was also her home where the Saints were gathered on the day of Pentecost when the Holy Ghost filled the house like a mighty wind.

If this is true, then it might also be likely that her house had the "upper room" where Christ held His last Passover and where the Apostles met after Christ's ascensions.

## DEVOUT AND HONORABLE WOMEN OF THE JEWS AND GREEKS

1. D. Todd Christofferson, "The Moral Force of Women," *Ensign*, November 2013.
2. Ibid.
3. Bruce C. Hafen, "Motherhood and the Moral Influence of Women" (speech, World Congress of Families II, Plenary Session IV, Geneva, November 16, 1999).

4. Christofferson, "The Moral Force of Women."

## EUNICE AND LOIS

1. In Deuteronomy 7:3–4, the Lord commands, "Neither shalt thou make marriages with them; thy daughter thou shalt not give unto his son, nor his daughter shalt thou take unto thy son. For they will turn away thy son from following me, that they may serve other gods."

In Orthodox Judaism, people who intermarried (a Jew marrying a Gentile) were considered dead to their families. If a Jew chose to intermarry, they may have been totally cut off from their family, having no interaction with them and even having their name taken off the family record. The greatest fear behind intermarriage was that a couple's children would not be raised Jewish. This can be seen with Timothy, who was not circumcised, which may be evidence that he was not raised in a Jewish home.

2. We know that Timothy's father was not a Jew, but that he may have converted to Christianity with Lois and Eunice. While that is a possibility, the scriptures seem to indicate the he and Eunice had different religious practices and backgrounds. One of the strongest evidences of this is the fact that Timothy was not circumcised. Acts 16:3 says, "Him [Timothy] would Paul have to go forth with him; and took and circumcised him because of the Jews which were in those quarters: for they knew all that his father was a Greek." His mother being a Jew would have made Timothy of Jewish heritage, as one is considered Jewish if their mother is a Jewess. Yet it appears that it was well known among the Jews that his father was not a believer and before he could teach them and enter into the synagogue, he needed to evidence to them that he was really Jewish. I think these circumstances surrounding Timothy's circumcision are strong indicators that Eunice and her husband did not share the same religious beliefs or practices.

3. We don't know if Lois was Timothy's maternal grandmother or paternal grandmother. If she was his paternal grandmother, she was likely Greek. If she was his maternal grandmother, she was probably Jewish. Either way, we know that she converted to Christianity around the same time Eunice did and that she was influential in shaping and teaching Timothy's faith.

4. Julie B. Beck, "Mothers Who Know," *Ensign*, November 2007.

## LYDIA

1. See 1 Kings 17:7–24; 2 Kings 4:8–17.
2. Richard G. Scott, "For Peace at Home," *Ensign*, May 2013.
3. David Jacoby, "Silk Economics and Cross-Cultural Artistic Interaction: Byzantium, the Muslim World, and the Christian West," *Dumbarton Oaks Papers*, vol. 58 (2004): 210.
4. *Theopompus, Athenaeu: the Deipnosophists*, trans. C. D. Yonge (1854), 12:526.
5. Lloyd B. Jensen, "Royal Purple of Tyre," *Journal of Near Eastern Studies* 22, no. 2 (1963): 113, http://www.jstor.org/stable/543305.
6. Ibid, 144.
7. E. J. Banks, "Thyatira," *International Standard Bible Encyclopedia*, ed. James Orr (Grand Rapids, MI: William B. Eerdmans Publishing, 1939), http://www.internationalstandardbible.com/T/thyatira.html.
8. Madsen, "Cameos: The Women of the New Testament."

## DAMSEL POSSESSED WITH A SPIRIT OF DIVINATION
1. Bible Dictionary, "Soothsayer."

## DAMARIS
1. Jeff W. Childers, "A Reluctant Bride: Finding a Life for Damaris of Athens (Acts 17:34)," in *Renewing Tradition: Studies in Texts and Contexts*, ed. Mark W. Hamilton, Thomas H. Olbricht, and Jeffrey Peterson (Princeton Theological Monograph Series; Eugene, OR: Pickwick, 2007), 212.
2. Ibid.
3. Ibid.
4. Ibid.
5. Adrián Ochoa, "Look Up," *Ensign*, November 2013.

## PRISCILLA
1. Jouette M. Bassler, "Prisca/Priscilla," *Women in Scripture*, 136.
2. See "Apphia" on page 251 for more on house churches.
3. Bassler, "Pricsa/Priscilla," *Women in Scripture*, 137.
4. It is interesting to note that Priscilla and Aquila's names are always listed together, indicating that they were a strong and unified team. Also, in four of the six instances where they are named, Priscilla is listed before her husband. This structure is unusual in the New Testament and gives us an idea of how respected and influential Priscilla may have been in the early Church.

## FOUR DAUGHTERS OF PHILIP
1. Bible Dictionary, "Evangelist."
2. See Judges 4:4; Exodus 15:20; 2 Chronicles 34:32; 2 Kings 22:14. Noadiah (Nehemiah 6:4) and Jezebel (Revelations 2:20) are also called prophetesses, but of the false type.

3. See Isaiah 8:3 and Luke 2:36.
4. Dallin H. Oaks, "Spiritual Gifts," *Ensign*, September 1986. This was a talk delivered at a Brigham Young University women's conference held March 28, 1986.
5. James E. Talmage, *Articles of Faith*, 12th ed. (Salt Lake City: Deseret Book, 1984), 228–229.
6. Bruce R. McConkie, "Our Sisters from the Beginning," *Ensign*, January 1979. This address was delivered at the dedication of the Nauvoo Monument to Women on June 29, 1978.

## PAUL'S SISTER
1. Information for this chart came from the entries "Sadducee" and "Pharisee" in the Bible Dictionary, as well as from "Major Jewish Groups in the New Testament" by Victor L. Ludlow, accessed at http://maxwellinstitute.byu.edu/publications/transcripts/I001 04-Major_Jewish_Groups_in_the_New_Testament.html.
2. These numbers come from estimates made by the Jewish historian Josephus. Flavius Josephus, *The Antiquities of the Jews*, trans. William Whiston (1737), Book 17, ch. 2.4.

## DRUSILLA AND BERNICE
1. Drusilla was only six years old when her father, Herod Agrippa, died. Before he died, he betrothed her to Epiphanes, heir of Commagene (a city on the Euphrates River), on the condition that he embrace and be circumcised. This marriage did not take place because the groom wouldn't consent to circumcision. When she was about fourteen or fifteen, Drusilla married Azizus, the king of Emessa, who did agree to be circumcised. According to the Jewish historian Josephus, not long after Drusilla's marriage, Felix, the Roman governor of Judea, saw Drusilla. He

was attracted by her incredible beauty and convinced her to leave her husband for him. Josephus wrote:

> While Felix was procurator of Judea, he saw this Drusilla, and fell in love with her; for she did indeed exceed all other women in beauty; and he sent to her a person whose name was Simon one of his friends; a Jew he was, and by birth a Cypriot, and one who pretended to be a magician, and endeavored to persuade her to forsake her present husband, and marry him; and promised, that if she would not refuse him, he would make her a happy woman. Accordingly she acted ill, and because she desired to avoid her sister Bernice's envy, for she was very ill treated by her on account of her beauty, was prevailed upon to transgress the laws of her forefathers, and to marry Felix. (Flavius Josephus, *The Antiquities of the Jews*, trans. William Whiston (1737),Book 20, 7.2)

2. Ross S. Kraemer, "Ber(e)nice," *Women in Scripture*, 69.
3. Dallin H. Oaks, "The Challenge to Become," *Ensign*, November 2000.
4. Josephus, *The Antiquities of the Jews*, 20:7.2.

PHEBE
1. Jill Mulvay Derr and Carol Cornwall Madsen, " 'Something Better' for the Sisters: Joseph Smith and the Female Relief Society of Nauvoo," in *Joseph Smith and the Doctrinal Restoration* (Provo: Brigham Young University Religious Studies Center, 2005), 123–43. Originally taken from "Relief Society Reports," Women's Exponent, July and August 1905, 14.
2. *Teaching of Presidents of the Church: Joseph Smith* (Salt Lake City: The Church of Jesus Christ of Latter-day Saints, 2007), 451.
3. Eliza R. Snow, "Female Relief Society," *Deseret News*, April 22,

1868, 1; punctuation standardized.
4. "New Testament Greek Lexicon—King James Version," *Bible Study Tools*, s.v. "diakonos," http://www.biblestudytools.com/lexicons/greek/kjv/diakonos.html.
5. Ibid.
6. Ibid.
7. Ibid, s.v. "prostatis," http://www.biblestudytools.com/lexicons/greek/kjv/prostatis.html.
8. Ibid.
9. Bridget Jack Jeffries, "Romans 16," *LDS & Evangelical Conversations: A Discussion of Differences and Similarities Between Mormonism and Evangelical Christianity*, last modified November 22, 2010, http://ldstalk.wordpress.com/2010/11/22/romans-16/.
10. Sarah Granger Kimball, "Auto-biography," *Woman's Exponent*, September 1883, 51.
11. Julie B. Beck, "Relief Society: A Sacred Work," *Ensign*, November 2009.
12. Julie B. Beck, "Why We Are Organized into Quorums and Relief Societies," in *Brigham Young University Speeches*, January 17, 2012.
13. Ibid.
14. Joseph Fielding Smith, "Relief Society—an Aid to the Priesthood," *Relief Society Magazine*, January 1959, 5–6.
15. The term deaconess is similar to the term prophetess or priestess. As explained earlier, one can be a prophetess, and use the gift of prophecy, without being ordained to the priesthood or being the prophet. In a similar manner, one can be a priestess and be endowed with power without being ordained to a priesthood office. A deaconess would be a woman who, by virtue of her calling in the Church, cares for the poor and distributes the money collected for their use.

16. Dallin H. Oaks, "The Keys and Authority of the Priesthood," *Ensign*, May 2014.
17. Julie B. Beck, speech given at BYU Women's Conference, 2011.

## TRYPHENA AND TRYPHOSA

1. Herbert Lockyre, "All the Women of the Bible," in Tryphena and Tryphosa, 164–65. Access at http://goo.gl/WHnuvQ.
2. Throughout the New Testament, we see evidence that missionary work in the early Church was performed by male-male missionary pairs, like Paul and Timothy, female-female missionary pairs, perhaps like Tyrphena and Tryphosa, and husband-wife missionary pairs, like Priscilla and Aquila. This is the same pattern used for latter-day missionaries and is another example to me of how the Church of Jesus Christ of Latter-day Saints is patterned after the Church that Christ established when He was on the earth.
3. For example, Persis (a common female slave name), Ampliatus and Hermes (common male slave names), and Herodion ( a common male name for a slave belonging to the house of Herod) were listed among the saints in Romans 16. They may or may not have been slaves, but it is possible that they could have been.

## CHLOE

1. Camille Fronk, "Submit Yourselves . . . as unto the Lord," in *Go Ye into All the World: Messages of the New Testament Apostles*, 31st Annual Sidney B. Sperry Symposium (Salt Lake City: Deseret Book, 2002), 98–113.
2. Some of the things they wrote to Paul about were: questions about how the "mysteries of God" (1 Corinthians 4:1), which may have been temple ordinances, were being administered; questions about marriage among those who were called on missions; concerns about a member who had committed fornication and not been excommunicated; the nature of the body and sexuality; concerns about people offering to idols; questions about the use of spiritual gifts (specifically the gift of tongues), tithes, and offerings; and questions about the resurrection and baptism for the dead.
3. The Joseph Smith Translation for this verse adds the word saying, indicating that Paul was repeating what he had been written.
4. Fronk, "Submit Yourselves . . . as unto the Lord."
5. Matthew B. Brown, *The Gate of Heaven: Insights into the Doctrines and Symbols of the Temple* (American Fork, UT: Covenant Communications, 1999), 158.
6. A good example of this is crowns. A crown, whether worn by a man or a woman, represents the power that they have been endowed with to rule and command.
7. Alonzo Gaskill, *The Lost Language of Symbolism: An Essential Guide for Recognizing and Interpreting Symbols of the Gospel* (Salt Lake City: Deseret Book, 2012).
8. Brown, *The Gate of Heaven*, 158.
9. 1 Corinthians 14:30 uses the phrase "hold his peace," which is the same word used in verses 28 and 34.

## EUODIA AND SYNTYCHE

1. In the King James Version, the name is Euodias, which is a male name. Yet, some scholars now feel that a better translation of the name is "Euodia," the female version. This distinction is important because if the name is male, then this is a story about an argument between a man and a woman—perhaps even a husband and wife; whereas if the name is female, then this story

is about an argument between two women. I have chosen to portray this story based off the modern translation of the name as "Euodia."

2. Marion G. Romney, "Unity," *Ensign*, May 1983.
3. Henry B. Eyring, "Our Hearts Knit as One," *Ensign*, November 2008.
4. Henry B Eyring, "That We May Be One," *Ensign*, May 1998.
5. C. Wilfred Griggs, "I Have A Question," *Ensign*, February 1976.
6. Thomas A. Wayment and John Gee, "Did Paul Address His Wife in Philippi?" *Studies in the Bible and Antiquity* 4 (2012).
7. Ibid.

## APPHIA

1. Brown, *The Gate of Heaven*, 178–181.
2. Personal e-mail correspondence with Annette Pimentel, April 8, 2014.
3. Some scholars feel that "Nympha" would be the best translation of this name because the name Nymphas is an usual name and has not been found on any Roman transcription from this time period. On the other hand, Nympha was a common name and has been found more than sixty times on Roman documents, mostly referring to slaves and freed women. (See Meyers, Craven, and Kraemer, "Nympha," in *Women in Scripture*, 133.

## THE ELECT LADY

1. "New Testament Greek Lexicon—King James Version," *Bible Study Tools*, s.v. "elektos," http://www.biblestudytools.com/lexicons/greek/kjv/elektos.html.
2. Eliza R. Snow, *Nauvoo Relief Society Minute Book*, accessed http://josephsmithpapers.org/paperDetails/nauvoo-relief-society-minute-book. Before the Relief Society notes were online, I went to the Church History Museum and transcribed the digitized Relief Society minutes notebook, word for word. It took me almost a whole day, but then I wrote a reenactment script of the first Relief Society meeting for our Relief Society. These quotes were taken from the notes I made.
4. Ibid.
5. Ibid.

WOMEN IN THE NEW TESTAMENT WHO EXEMPLIFY
YOUNG WOMEN VALUES

1. Young Women Theme:

We are daughters of our Heavenly Father, who loves us, and we love Him. We will "stand as witnesses of God at all times and in all things, and in all places" as we strive to live the Young Women values, which are:

Faith
Divine Nature
Individual Worth
Knowledge
Choice and Accountability
Good Works
Integrity
and Virtue

We believe as we come to accept and act upon these values, we will be prepared to strengthen home and family, make and keep sacred covenants, receive the ordinances of the temple, and enjoy the blessings of exaltation.

# Artwork

# Heather Farrell

*Her love for the scriptures* began young, when at the age of eleven she hid a flashlight under her pillow so she could read the Old Testament late at night. Her love for the women in scriptures began when her oldest son was born around Christmastime and she felt a kinship with Mary, the mother of Jesus. As she began to research Mary, she realized that there were hundreds of women in the scriptures, but very little had been written about them. Excited by all the women she discovered, she began sharing what she learned on her popular blog, Women in the Scriptures (womeninthescriptures.com). Primarily self-taught in the scriptures, Heather is a testament to the truth that becoming a scholar of the gospel is not beyond anyone's reach; it just takes a inquisitive mind and the companionship of the Holy Ghost. Heather grew up in Idaho but currently lives in Boone, Iowa, with her husband, four children, two sheep, a goat, and a flock of chickens.

# Mandy Jane Williams

*grew up in the little town of* Darlington, Idaho. She has always had a love for beauty and art, which her parents encouraged. Mandy met her husband, Bryan Williams, in 2005, and they were married in the Idaho Falls Temple. Although Mandy has taken classes in art and photography, becoming a mother has played the biggest role in her finding herself as an artist. Beauty, joy, passion—all are intensified when you open your heart to loving others. Little things stand out to you in daily life, and you are able to notice and be grateful to them with artistic eyes. From the way the rising sun catches the eyelashes of a sleeping baby, or the look on a child's face when Daddy comes home—all of these are an inspiration and a blessing. Mandy currently lives in Grace, Idaho, with her husband, Bryan, and her four greatest works of art—Kate, Case, Holland, and Alice.

For more of Mandy's art: www.mandyjanewilliams.com